Statistical Development Volume IV

The Communist countries

S.S. ZARKOVICH
Federal Statistical Office, Belgrade

Avebury

Aldershot · Brookfield USA · Hong Kong · Singapore · Sydney

Published by:
Avebury
Gower Publishing Company Limited
Gower House
Croft Road
Aldershot
Hants GU11 3HR
England

Gower Publishing Company
Old Post Road
Brookfield
Vermont 05036
USA

ISBN 1 85628 118 3
Set ISBN 1 85628 093 4

Printed in Great Britain by
Athenaeum Press Ltd, Newcastle upon Tyne.

Contents

Preface

Some years before the last war statistics entered a period of big changes. New ideas invaded the collection of data. Rules were developed to put data collection on a scientific basis. Theory was developed to study samples and make inferences about population. Data collection has thus become possible even in countries where guessing was the only available tool in the past.

During this period all countries rushed to absorb the fruits of the new statistics. In order to speed up this process, the United Nations took the lead in the promotion of statistical development. Its action was particularly intensive in the less developed countries (LDC). As a result, in a relatively short time substantial progress in statistics was achieved in the whole world.

Yugoslavia participated in this effort. As early as 1949, sample surveys were introduced on a regular basis. Soon after that the measurement of accuracy was introduced. In the 1953 Census of Population, sampling methods were used for a variety of purposes. Parallel to that, various attempts were made to modernize the curricula of statistical education. Besides, in 1951 an official programme of exams was published that was obligatory for all government employees who wanted a career in statistics. The requirements of that programme included much more material than was customary at that time in other countries. The progress of new statistics was thus quite fast.

This was a stream of statistical development that was conceived and implemented by statisticians on the basis of the progress achieved in the world. At the same time, Yugoslavia had a politics-based stream of statistical development. Being a part of politics, this stream was much stronger than science. It acted in the name of political power and used the power as its tool. Both streams pretended expansion. As a result, they collided in the early days of postwar Yugoslavia. The conflict had far-reaching negative consequences on the subsequent statistical development of the country.

This book is an account of the conflict.

The origin of the politics-based view of statistics is in the political achievements of the Yugoslav Communist Party (YCP). After the last war, the YCP succeeded in taking over political power. Immediately after the seizure of power, the YCP started with the implementation of its programme. In fact, all the communist parties that managed to take power in their respective countries, had on their action programme the establishment of the model of society that was developed in the USSR. However, in building a communist society, the YCP had the ambition of being second only to the USSR. The YCP did not recognize any obstacle in its way. The YCP had in mind to achieve, in a few years, more than the USSR did between the two wars. The YCP practiced a very militant brand of communism. Yugoslav communism was an embodiment of dogmatism, i.e. a domination of ideology over the realities of life. No matter what happens and what difficulties arise, the ideology is always right. Communist ideology is infallible; it is based on a "scientific" theory of the society. Besides, Yugoslav communism had another feature. It was a fanaticism of an extreme type. The YCP was proud of its achievements during the war and it believed in its special role in the building of a communist society. Its striking force and its determination exceeded comparable characteristics of other communist parties.

The ideology that the YCP took over from the USSR included very definite views of statistics. The most important activity of the communist society is social and economic planning. Statistics is a tool of planning in the sense that it provides data for both the formulation of plans and the measurement of the fulfillment of plans as well. For that purpose record keeping (or recording) is established in each unit of work. The resulting data facilitate the management. Through an appropriate summarization the same data become available at the level of various administrative units, by branches of work, etc.

Recording consists of simple operations of counting or physical measurements. To get data there is no need for any theory. In fact, a view was imposed that the theory of statistics was established in Western countries as a tool of the capitalist class. Its purpose is to secure the domination of privileged positions. Mathematical statistics is a game with abstract numbers and formulas. It is built to detract the attention of people from social problems. In a communist society there is no place for mathematical statistics.

The fanaticism of the YCP pushed this theory to its absurd consequences. An interest in modern statistics (that is using mathematics) is a "treason" of socialism. In a communist society there can be no place for this statistics. As a bourgeois weapon, statistical theory should not be allowed to have any impact on young generations in a communist society. A mathematical statistician cannot be a member of the YCP. In fact, faithful members of the YCP have to do their best to oppose new statistics in order to protect the socialist society. The supporters of the theory of statistics are a continuous source of danger for the society. Therefore, a person with sympathy for statistical theory cannot be appointed to any position of influence. Interest in theory implies low-level jobs, lower salaries, and no chance of influencing developments in the profession.

This is how the fanaticism introduced passions into statistics. Those who practice the new theory of statistics have become "enemies", "reactionaries", "anti-marxists", and, in general, remnants of capitalist society. On the other side are the good ones, "cadres of revolution", "cadres of socialism", progressive elements of the society, etc. The good ones fight for the new society under the guidance of the YCP. In this capacity, they belong to the avant-garde of the society. They keep all the leading positions in data collection services; they direct the work; the work is just what they do.

As was customary in all communist countries, various occasions were designed for self-praising of the achievements of the avant-garde. In data collection such an occasion falls on "Statistics Day", December 14 of each year. On that day the achievements of the past year are officially praised and awards are distributed. Such a self-praising attitude is particularly expressed in documents that are expected to have a longer life. An illustration is the book *Thirty Years of Statistics in FSR Yugoslavia (Trideset Godina Statistike SFR Jugoslavije)*, Federal Institute of Statistics, Belgrade, 1974.

This book is an official review of statistical events in the first thirty years of postwar Yugoslavia. The book is a chronological presentation of events with an emphasis on legislation, changes of names, organization of various sectors of work, changes in the organization that took place in the course of time, etc. Briefly, the book is a history of statistics as seen from a formal point of view.

In fact, *Thirty Years of Statistics in Yugoslavia* takes readers away from real problems. In the postwar period, statistics passed through a complete overhaul. After the first tides of big changes were over, the history of statistics could not avoid such questions as: what has Yugoslav statistics done to absorb the benefits of the new statistics, what arrangements have been made to transfer to Yugoslavia the rapidly growing know-how in the world, what changes have been made in Yugoslav statistical education, in what way have new developments in statistical methodology been introduced in data collection, what has Yugoslavia done to secure the benefits of the use of statistics in specific fields of work, etc.

These are just some questions that had to be considered in an official document of history. However, none of these questions was touched upon either in *Thirty Years of Statistics* or in any other official account of national statistical development.

In this book I am raising my voice against this type of bias in history. I joined Yugoslav statistics immediately after the last war. I participated in all the attempts at its modernization up to recent years. I am also the last living person who is able to talk about the events on the basis of first-hand experience. Therefore, I felt I had to say what problems and policy issues Yugoslav statistics has been facing since the last war, what were the contributions to statistical development of the country that were never mentioned in the official history, and what Yugoslav statistics failed to do to be in line with developments in the world. Calling attention to these issues was a contribution to recent efforts to eliminate distortions in the presentation of events of our history.

However, in the compilation of my account great difficulties have appeared. Regarding a number of points my recollection of events needed further detail and/or confirmation. I went to see various office holders to consult them about their memories. However, they refused to enter into the matter by saying: "I do not remember". Obviously, they were afraid of being accomplices in an interpretation of events that could be different than the party line as interpreted by those who keep the power. The need for obedience is absolute. So is the need to protect the party line and see to it that it is never questioned or subject to doubt.

After that failure, I requested permission to study the archives and take therefrom the documents that I wanted to have. However, various requests failed one after the other. I realized that my wish went beyond the limits of acceptable behavior. Obviously, the facts at my disposal might be used to criticize the approaches followed. My interest in facts was a serious mistake.

In the course of my efforts to use the archives, I learned that past directors of statistical services, upon the termination of their mandate, took with them or destroyed the files about policy matters that arose while they were in charge. I asked some of them to give me, for study purposes, some documents kept under personal custody. However, nothing has come out of it. My work was not part of a project approved by the party. Nor would the results of my study be submitted to the party for approval or correction. I thus learned that history was party property. Only the party is allowed to talk about what happened.

It has therefore become clear that my recollection is the limit of what I can do. My account of statistics under communism has taken the form of memoirs.

Such a presentation of events has a number of shortcomings. However, in some situations it provides the only possible alternative to the "official" view or the course of history as approved by the power. It thus becomes an essential road to truth.

The compilation of this account involved a need to touch upon some unpleasant matters. Namely, in order to secure the domination of politics, measures were applied from time to time that cast serious doubt on the ethical principles of their respective authors. The action against the influence of the new theory of statistics was not carried out with the help of scientific arguments. Instead, cries and appeals were made against "ably masked" "agents of imperialism" who wanted to restore capitalism. This is the equivalent of keeping the doors of a jail open as a warning to those who insist on the promotion of the new theory of statistics. One of the best Yugoslav statisticians of the epoch was put in a jail and never came out. In order to please their supervisors in the party and/or the government and thus establish the basis for their own career advancement, some people used different occasions to demonstrate their "patriotism" and come down on "enemies" with unusual brutality and recklessness.

Should one write about these tragic events?

After many hesitations, the attitude was taken in favor of the truth. It was done after long consideration of the issue. Some of the acts committed are incredible. It is difficult to believe that human beings were able to fall in the mud of amorality up to their necks and demonstrate examples of shocking behavior. Keeping quiet about these tragic acts would help the protagonists to enjoy the benefits of their action as if nobody was aware of the methods they used in climbing up to their privileged positions. Besides, keeping quiet about the past would certainly not be fair to the victims of immorality. Eventually, it is hoped that awareness by the population of the cruelty, madness, and dishonesty of the regime that ruled the country in the name of communism, should provide a barrier against the repetition of similar events in the future. Therefore, the tragedy should be known in as many of its details as possible.

Eventually, a general remark about communism. The characteristics of communism as discussed in this book refer to what used to be understood under this term in the political philosophy of countries where communist parties were at power. Should in some country at any time a different type of communism appear, the discourse in this book would not be applicable.

A word will also be appropriate about the subtitle of this volume. As a result of this subtitle readers might expect that a separate review of the position of statistics was given for each country with a communist regime. In fact, the book essentially deals with the events in Yugoslavia. A broader subtitle is used because the course of statistical development was very similar in all the communist countries. Guiding principles have come from the same source. In this sense the title used is adequate.

It is also pointed out that this book was written before the fall of communism on a world scale in December 1989. Its original purpose was to call the attention of public opinion to the intellectual and moral bankruptcy of the Yugoslav brand of communism and provide as many indications as possible about the road that should help Yugoslavia recapture what was lost during the orgies of political madness. However, the events were faster than the publication of this book. December 1989 brought the odor of freedom. Many people have used the new circumstances to build ample evidence of the tragedy that the country was passing through. It will be a pleasure should this book remain in the future just a picture of statistical events in a period of a remote past.

Many names in the text do not correspond to names actually used in Yugoslavia. This was done because of frequent changes of names. Had these changes been followed, cases would occur that some institutions or organizations would be called in different ways at different parts of the book. It would of course confuse the readers. In that situation a solution was adopted to keep in most cases one name all the way through. The choice of names to use was made by taking into account the usual terminology in other countries.

S.S.Z.

1 The dreamers

In 1947 I went for vacation to the Southern part of the Yugoslav seacoast. At the same place there was a colony of children of USSR embassy officers and the USSR army personnel stationed in Yugoslavia. The children were guarded by a group of ladies brought for the purpose from the USSR. As my wife was a teacher of Russian language, she established contact with one of these ladies hoping that it would give her a chance to practice her Russian and ascertain the differences between the language used by Tolstoy, Dostoyevsky, Gogol, Turghenev and others and the language spoken in the streets of the modern USSR cities.

During their chats at the beach the Russian teacher asked my wife: "What does your husband do"?

My wife said: "Nothing. I mean nothing important. He is a statistician".

The Russian lady jumped up. Her face was full of joy. She said smilingly: "Good, very good. Good for you. I am so glad".

At that moment my wife jumped up. She said: "What is good about the dull work of adding up figures"?

The Russian answered: "If he were a director of something important, such as a factory or some great agency in the army, he would be killed sooner or later. None of the important people has a chance to survive. As a director of statistics he will live. Nobody cares about statistics. You don't know, Danica, how lucky you are".

"What director of statistics are you talking about"?, said my wife. "My husband is not any director of statistics".

The Russian apologized: "I am sorry. I went too far. Of course your husband is director of statistics. Otherwise you would not go for vacations to the seacoast. However, I should not have mentioned that. Don't worry. I will not talk about it any more".

"Our vacation", said my wife, "has nothing to do with the work that my husband is doing. I am telling you that my husband is nobody in statistics. Just nobody. He is

1

on the bottom of the payroll. Nobody else in statistics has a lower salary than my husband".

"Wonderful, wonderful", said the Russian. "You don't know how lucky you are. Good for you, Danica. I am so glad".

While the Russian teacher was genuinely happy, my wife was unable to understand the statement. She inquired:

"What is good about the lowest salary? I do not understand what makes you excited".

The Russian said: "Of course I am excited. It is so nice to see a couple of people who will grow old next to each other. Nothing will happen to your husband. Who cares for a statistician"?

My wife did not answer. She probably fell into contemplations about the possibility of being killed because of the work that one does. She heard that a person might do the work bad or well. However, she never heard that somebody might be killed because of the work. This was a new and confusing aspect of life. She seemed shocked. She kept quiet. She was probably trying to make sense of what she had heard. She needed time.

A part of her confusion was also due to the idea of getting killed in statistics. According to popular views at that time, statistics was a job without any prestige. People looking for job would knock at doors of statistics only after they had failed in all other attempts. This is why my wife asked me frequently:

"What is wrong with you? I am unable to understand that you gave up so easily and agreed to work in statistics. If a political appointee takes the job of director of statistics - that is not difficult to understand. Although not very high, the director of statistics is still some position in the government hierarchy. However, if a young person goes into statistics as a result of his own choice and stays at the job without ever getting out of the category of "nobody" - that is more difficult to understand".

Well, this is my case. Even today, so many years after I entered statistics, I keep in my mind the above event. When I knocked at the door of statistics I did not think of either prestige and security or physical survival. I was not aware of these issues. Nor did I tie my life to statistics because of the salary. In fact, my employment in statistics was a matter of chance while my interest in statistics had developed much earlier, at an age when people do not think about income and related matters.

During the last two years of my high school[1], I frequently raised with myself the issue of what course of life I would wish for myself. I thought I should be aware of my inclinations so that I could put my life in line with my interests. However, these attempts hardly ever ended in a clear answer as I would usually come to the conclusion that I was interested in a large variety of topics, such as psychology, mathematics, physics, engineering, literature, geography, explorations of far out areas of the globe, etc.

---

1   At the age between 16 and 18 years.

Depending upon the variations in my readings, I would get excited about any one of these topics. I frequently had the impression that my preferences had become clear. However, later on I would get excited equally strongly about something else.

When the time came to go to the university, my choice was mechanical engineering. It was a compromise between my own interest and the wishes of my parents. We did not have anybody with that profession in our family. It was felt that this choice would provide me with an interesting job and an income that should be sufficient for a relatively high level of living. For my parents mechanical engineering was thus the right field of studies for their own son. As far as I was concerned, I accepted these suggestions. In a sense, I was happy to see that my wishes were so near to my parents' views. I had a mystical respect for machines. Any machine was an attraction for my curiosity. On so many occasions I looked through the windows of the local electricity power station at a Diesel engine and the electric generator. These machines were, in my mind, the most respectable products of man's genius. The choice of mechanical engineering as the topic of my studies was for me an opportunity to familiarize myself with these products, master the built-in know-how, and engage, if the chance arose, in my own search for new ideas. I was thus happy with my choice. As a result, in September 1931 I enrolled at the Department of Mechanical Engineering of the University of Belgrade.

However, events at the university took the course of my life in a direction that was quite different than my expectations. This was the year of students' unrest. In the course of the academic year, the university was closed on several occasions for long periods. Regular studies were made physically impossible. Even if somebody wanted to stay at home and study, it was difficult to do so because of the excitement among the students. The excitement was due to conflicts with the police, the brutality of the regime, arrests, riots around university buildings and in the main streets, etc. In these fights some students were beaten up, others were wounded or chased by the police if seen in the streets even in small groups of two or three persons.

It was difficult to assess the impact of the unrest. Some students were unhappy with the elements of vandalism that appeared on several occasions in the form of the destruction of university furniture, libraries, and the equipment for practicals in the various laboratories. Others, including myself, were inclined to put the primary emphasis on the political situation in the country. Yugoslavia at that time was a very difficult country to govern. When freedom was abolished, everything became worse. Rather than being a matter of public discussions, the problems were pushed under the surface of the society. There they generated passions, hatred, and similar qualities that made impossible any rational approach to the political issues. A lesson seemed obvious to me. Namely, there is a price to pay for the lack of freedom.

Needless to say, the average student did not go into the collection of facts related to the social, economic, and political situation of the country and an appraisal of their impact. Such an attitude would require a degree of maturity and experience that cannot be expected from an excited student body. This does not mean, however, that the students had no political orientation. In fact, the majority of students were ready to support a simple political programme, such as opposition to the monarchy, political freedom as a way to re-examine the position of the different regions within Yugoslavia, some participation of the regions in the political life, the formulation of rights and responsibilities of the regions, etc. Students were thus open to a dialogue. However, the dialogue meant political freedom and the freedom of press in particular. As this was barred by the regime, the outcome consisted of conflicts with the police and a transformation of unsolved problems into passions, violence and brutality.

In that tense atmosphere, the communist ideology probably did more to attract students than any other political party of the opposition movement in that period. I say "communist ideology" rather than "communist party". The Communist party had a negligible membership and was unable to influence the feelings of major segments of the population in different parts of the country. The impact of the Communist party did not go beyond sporadic and small-scale protests at a limited number of points in the country. In addition, the Communist party was intellectually weak for the complex activity of keeping an eye on particular aspects of national life and reacting to current events with adequate projects and programmes.

Quite different was the impact of communist ideology that started spreading with the help of a vast body of literature from all parts of the world. It included philosophy, social sciences, economics, politics, etc. It gave the impression of an all embracing and well elaborated theory of politics that was easily adaptable to any situation. For a person familiar with that ideology it was not difficult to outline the way out in any situation. The communist theory pretended applicability to any society and any type of issue. This is why it was particularly attractive to young people who preferred broad philosophical sketches of changes in the human society to a boring and tedious study of facts, possibilities, limitations, and restrictions in the value of various political programmes.

As compared to the impact of communist ideology, other political parties of the opposition were almost unable to influence the youth. These parties were relatively young and primarily oriented toward power as a means of achieving their respective programmes. This is why none of them was ready to launch a programme for the orientation of students at the moment of awakening of their interest in political issues. The exceptions were, to some extent, the political parties based on nationality, religion, or something similar. Croatian youth primarily followed the attitudes of the existing Croatian political parties. Apart from that there were no differences among the political parties of the country with respect to their ability to guide students on the basis of an elaborate political programme. Communism thus seemed superior to its alternatives. In addition, there was a moral point in its favor. While other political parties were power-oriented, communism insisted on fights, sacrifices, the abolition of the power of money, etc. It was thus able to make an appeal to students.

Together with a number of colleagues in my group, I was attracted by moral aspects of the communist ideology.

In this connection, an interesting point was the sudden orientation of many students toward communism. In fact, in a relatively short period of time, such as a couple of months, strong sympathies for communism developed on the part of the politically neutral or uncommitted students.

This transformation had certainly nothing to do with knowledge of the facts or studies of actual possibilities of the country at the moment. Any serious study takes a great deal of time. On the contrary, the transformation that I am talking about was made

4

in a very short time. In addition, continued studies normally build a selective mind, viz. a person who is not able to accept with enthusiasm the political programmes in blocks and follow them blindly. The broader the knowledge is of the complexity of social life and of the variety of experiences with certain measures and programmes in politics, the more obvious becomes the need for the assignment of a relative value to any man's effort. A knowledgeable person is aware of the impact of a large number of facts on political movements and their achievements. Thus, one could say: the less one knows the more one is convinced of the value of particular prescriptions.

The matter of sudden changes in political attitudes or in the intensity of people's involvement in politics is certainly an attractive issue for political scientists. Before it is abandoned to those who specialize in these matters, let me mention that this phenomenon seems to be connected in Yugoslavia with the issue of freedom. In a democratic society, social issues are kept under constant consideration. In the course of this process, issues are raised and solutions to problems are proposed. In this way the problems are kept on a rational basis. The communication channels are open. At any moment new ideas and contributions can be presented. There is no need for violence. Sudden shifts in the mood of the population are not likely.

In the societies without freedom, the issues are not threshed out and there are no alternatives. Without democracy it frequently happens that facts lose the meaning of arguments. The value of rational approaches to problems is suppressed. In fact, the issues are transferred to an emotional basis where their course is governed by the dynamics of emotions and is resistent to standard logic.

This is what happened in our situation. Had the regime opened the doors of the university buildings and arranged for discussions of problems with students by some authorities in science or public life who are known for their liberal attitude, the events would have taken a course toward reasoning and discussion. The impact of emotions would have been reduced if not eliminated altogether and the student body would have accepted a dialogue. Instead, the police entered the university buildings and spoiled the situation entirely with the result that its action was the best contribution to the rise of communist influences.

As far as I am concerned, my sympathies for the communist movement were based on what I considered at that time as the superiority of the communist students with respect to others.

In this period the students used to devote an unusual proportion of their time to contacts and grouping. The purpose was to get news about developments from different parts of the university, ascertain the reactions of their colleagues to the events, get comments of colleagues about the expected developments, etc. In contacts of that kind I normally kept quiet. I was a young and rather timid student. I thought that I should essentially listen to the words of more senior students. In this way, viz. by keeping quiet, I collected, in a very short time, a great deal of information about my colleagues, their ideas, and their political reasoning.

These impressions told me that communist students were superior to the others. In fact, other students essentially behaved as a mass without shape. They were unable to provide an explanation of surrounding developments. They were particularly unable

5

to insert the events at the university into a broader picture of national and international political and social developments. These students primarily kept quiet and looked around for ideas and guidance.

On the other hand, the communist students demonstrated a remarkable tranquility. None of them felt lost. They were not only able to insert the university developments into a broader process of social and political changes. They also had a design of the future. Their ideology made it possible for them to talk about what would be the next stages of the political crisis of the country, about the intensification of social conflicts, their impact on politics, the growth of socialist tendencies in the society, etc. They impressed the students of my type with a kind of political maturity that we appreciated as we did not possess anything similar.

Communist students showed an equal superiority from a purely human point of view. As a rule, they were modest. Even when they came from rich families, they did not care for qualities based on money, such as expensive clothes, famous restaurants, luxury vacations, etc. They tended to depend upon the facilities accessible to average students. Communists were also friendly to younger students. In fact, they treated younger students as their equals. They abolished the separation of student body by seniority. They also talked frequently about books, new novels, literary achievements, theater, etc. In this respect they were quite above other students. Even if their knowledge was superficial, it was still above the level of other students. It was thus a pleasure to have communist students as friends.

With all these sympathies and feelings I became ready to accept further communist influences. Thus, I accepted with pleasure the books that I got from colleagues. In fact, I plunged into that reading with a great fever as I felt ashamed of my ignorance and my inability to use the terminology currently used by communist students. I interpreted my inability to use their terminology as a defect in my education. I thought that my level was below the level of a decent student. My reading was to me a matter of personal prestige. In this way, I thought I would reduce the humiliating distance between my education and the knowledge of those whom I considered high above me.

The situation at the university gave me a lot of time for my reading. I went with interest through most books that were given to me by my colleagues as "good" literature. These books related to all sorts of topics, such as novels, history, philosophy, popular science, etc. In this way I picked up a great deal of material from different fields. I was not able to assess the impact of my reading on my education. However, the terminology and the discussions of communist students did not seem impressive any more. I followed them without difficulty. Moreover, I found that I was able to use the same language. I was very happy about that. I some times thought that I made good progress.

There was another aspect to my reading. Namely, before I started it I had already developed a deep respect for the knowledge that I wanted to acquire. My reading was not a process of collection of facts that I would subsequently use in my own thinking and my own construction of views and opinions. My attitude was biased. I accepted beforehand the interpretations, the views, and the philosophy contained in the material that I was about to read. Therefore, my reading had the purpose of providing me with illustrations. It helped me in the presentation of views that I had already accepted. I accepted the conclusions before the reading.

In doing so, I did the same thing that millions of people have done in politics before me and after me. Political orientations are accepted on some basis that is independent of the awareness of the related facts. Most people remain at that point forever. Some go further and add to this essential orientation an intellectual structure that makes the basic orientations nicer, richer, and suitable to a person with a higher degree of education. That is what I was doing in the course of my reading.

The reading and the discussions that I was involved in at that time had a considerable influence on my future. For one thing, my interest was taken away from mechanical engineering to social sciences and philosophical issues in general. At that time, discussions were quite frequent among students in my group about issues, such as the philosophical meaning of modern physics, determinism and indeterminism in the light of new theories in physics, social sciences versus natural sciences, theory of knowledge in relation to achievements of different sciences, etc. Needless to say, our competence for talking about these issues was not very high. However, the interest was there. Some of these issues were extremely exciting to me. An illustration is the relationship between social sciences and natural sciences and the relationships of both of them to mathematics. Whenever I got something to read about these issues, I would forget about other commitments and proceed passionately with my reading. That reading was obviously far from a systematic study. I was not guided by any expert hand. My main source of supply of the reading material was a student of forestry whose knowledge I appreciated greatly. He himself was probably not very knowledgeable. He never finished the school and later on became an insignificant employee in the municipal administration.

The progress of my involvement in political thinking and reading was followed by a change in my social contacts. My company consisted of two colleagues from high school who also came to Belgrade University. In fact, we came together. We were intimate friends and were also living in the same room. I accepted their company as normal. We used to spend our leisure time together.

After I developed an interest in politics our friendship started waning. They did not care for my reading nor had they any interest in politics. When they saw me reading they frequently laughed at me. They never hesitated to make fun of me. This is why I started taking their friendship with reservation. When they wanted to go out, I used to tell them that I was busy. I also found other excuses for doing my own shopping and eating alone. In other words, my friends were a burden to me. *Vice versa* was probably also true. After the semester vacation, I left them.

In fact, I had a desire to live with students of my own orientation. I soon realized my wish. My new roommate was a student of biology who, as myself, was devoting all his time to activities resulting from his political interest. He was doing a lot of reading. In addition, he was going to theaters, movies, concerts, etc. He had many friends who were coming frequently to see him. Sometimes our room was full of young folks and smoke from our cigarettes.

The most frequent subject of our discussions was the society of tomorrow. We went over all aspects of it. We were sure that it would be a society of justice and equality. In that society the people would be honest. The power of money would be abolished. Therefore, there would be no reason for corruption or any other activity oriented toward money making. Everybody would be able to get the necessary resources

7

for a decent living. Therefore, there would be no protectionism or appointments to important posts of persons who did not deserve it. There would be no secret forces behind the screen. All public matters would be done at public places with open access to everybody.

Our discussions would continue over days and nights. I was happy to see that so many young people detested the vices of our existing society and were anxiously waiting for the dawn of new history. Whatever we said about the superiority of the new society was accepted by all of us. Nobody had doubts. It was for us a strong proof that we were rapidly approaching the beginning of a new era.

I appreciated my new company. It seemed to me that everybody else did so. We were all made of the same flesh and bones. We had identical hopes and we were always unanimous in our judgement. We were a separate world. In fact, we lived in a world of dreams that was magnificent as there was nothing in it that would not be supreme.

II Struggling for life

This is how my first academic year ended. There was no achievement whatsoever along the line of mechanical engineering. I did not prepare any exam and I even do not know whether it was possible to do better than I did. The school was closed for long periods and teachers did not have time to deliver their lectures and get in touch with students.

My parents were worried about my disappointing achievement. They had no money for my education. My studies far away from my own house obliged them to tighten the family budget and reduce all other expenditures to an unavoidable minimum. In this sacrifice the only bright point for them was the hope that I would do a good job at the university. I spoiled their hopes. Later on, when I became aware of how miserable were the resources of my parents, I felt guilty about my poor performance. That feeling was a great burden on my conscience.

In that situation my parents decided to send me to continue studies at the University of Zagreb. In that way they thought they would give me another chance at a place that seemed to be more quiet. They were afraid that in the next year the situation at Belgrade University might easily become as bad as it was a year ago.

I accepted their arguments as adequate and went to Zagreb in September 1932.

In my new school I did a bit more work than the previous year. I had to start from scratch. I passed some exams. However, I was not able to recuperate what was lost. My achievement was definitely below the level that could be expected from a person who had many reasons to be more responsible with respect to his own duties.

The change of university did not affect my political interest. I found new friends and discussions continued of the same type as a year ago in Belgrade. This time, however, a new element was added to my political involvement. I somehow adopted the view that an interest in the leftist philosophy and the reading of publications coming from the left was the normal first step. The next step should be to participate in the daily activities of the organizations aiming at a realization of the respective political programmes. I accepted the attitude that adoption of the communist ideology without subsequent involvement in the work of communist organizations would mean the lack

9

of consistency, a kind of defect in the structure of personality. The crux of the orientation toward the left is in the acceptance of the role of a soldier in the militant communist organizations. The victory of the left will not come by itself. The victory requires many fights and great sacrifices by masses of the proletariat and the educated people who have understood the dynamics of the modern society and are willing to serve as means of the progress.

This was approximately the language used. I accepted its main arguments. As a result, I became a member of the organization of communist youth at the school of engineering.

Our cell would meet from time to time with a rather constant agenda. We would review the events at the school, the university, and in the country as well. We also reviewed the names of potential candidates for membership in our organization and the steps that we could take to speed up their recruitment. We also discussed "action" projects, such as reproduction of leaflets, distribution of illegal publications of the communist party at places considered important, participation at students' demonstrations, participation at public appearances organized by the left, such as lectures, theater performances, excursions, etc.

Now when I look at our political activities during that period, they give me an impression of being very naive and of little impact, if any at all. The foolishness of the then government was needed to attribute any importance to leaflets distributed by students or to their shouting of slogans. The police badly needed communist students to keep themselves busy while the communist organizations badly needed the police to be able to develop the feeling of their own importance. That political activity was certainly not connected with the capture of power by the communist party after the last war.

The organizations of the communist party were not so childish to believe that students' protests here and there are able to hurt the bourgeois class. However, they were obliged to organize as many "action" projects as possible to keep the rank and file busy and in the necessary state of excitement. After people accepted the theory of the necessity of bitter conflicts between progressive elements and the bourgeoisie in which the avant-garde is to be ready for bloodshed, you possibly could not let these people stay idle. If so, they would get disappointed and would abandon the party. On the other hand, the organization of conflicts with the police and similar "actions" make them trust the theory and believe in the arrival of the new society.

The state of excitement was sustained in a number of ways. Before a conflict with the police, one kept thinking of what was going to happen, who would be beaten up, who would finish in jail, be wounded, etc. After the "action" was over, you felt the need to stay with your friends, refresh the memories, discuss experiences, draw conclusions and lessons in favor of the next "action", etc. The same was true of other activities, such as strikes, production and distribution of leaflets, writing of slogans over walls or in streets etc.

The excitement was the state of mind that is incompatible with any work that requires concentration. A very large fraction of communist students of that period never finished studies nor did they achieve anything else. It was not the lack of time for studies that prevented them from working. With a properly organized day the busiest revolutionnaries did not have more to do than what could be done in a few hours. It was the state of their mind that kept them far from work and the usual duties and commitments in the society. They excluded themselves from the society they lived in hoping that the day would come when the new society would need them as they were.

In this respect the YCP was very lucky. When the young generation of devoted members grew up and reached the point of the need to solve the problem of living, the party took power and the old students who had never finished their studies or learned any useful skill, became ministers, generals, ambassadors, etc. Otherwise they would have become a burden to the party and the society as well.

This question of the future, the place in the society, and the resources of living bothered me more and more as the time was passing. In the first year of my studies in Zagreb, I did not think of it intensively. I passed some exams and I thought that I would make it. Later on, in 1933 and 1934 I engaged in time consuming illegal printing of leaflets and other documents that could be produced with the help of simple means. This work and the distribution of products took me quite a lot of time. My studies did not progress and I was becoming aware that I would never make it.

I was unhappy with myself. I thought that my political activity was alright and worth any sacrifice. However, it seemed to me that I was not able to sufficiently master my time and properly organize my day. A few hours a day were sufficient to be successful at the university. Alas, I was not strong enough to impose on myself that much of discipline.

At moments I had some justification for my life. My theory told me that I was a revolutionary living at the expense of my parents who were, in this way, included in the service of the revolution. I thought that a duty of a good revolutionary was to use all the available means of the capitalist society for strengthening of revolutionary activities. I considered the goals of revolution so noble that they justified many unpleasant matters, such as living at the expense of somebody else, imposing sacrifices on others, creating problems and trouble to the family, etc.

However, the moments were more and more frequent when I was not happy with myself. I had strong doubts as to my moral principles. It did not seem to me honest to require freedom for oneself and engage in political activities while living, at the same time, at the expense of somebody else. The principle thus imposed itself on my mind that economic independence was a condition for a person to be free in the choice of the own political activity. Any politics at the expense of somebody else's pocket seemed to me sheer parasitism. And I saw myself falling steadily into parasitism.

In 1934 I realized that I had to make some decisions regarding my future. My studies of mechanical engineering were at a standstill for quite some time. I, therefore, decided to abandon engineering for good and take philosophy and mathematics. I was putting my time in studying of these fields anyway. If I continued that work within a university programme it would give me both the satisfaction of studying problems that I was interested in and a chance to graduate and thus establish foundation for some career in the future. My decision was firm. I enrolled at the Department of Philosophy of the University of Zagreb.

11

In 1935 another important event took place that had a bearing on my subsequent life. This was the end of my political involvement in the communist youth. In that year the police had arrested many young communists. My turn also came. Two agents came to the house of my parents very early in the morning while we were in bed. They took me away. I do not know how they got the information about me nor have I ever managed to know it. During the investigation it became clear that the police wanted to uncover two of my contacts. They knew details and they wanted names. Somebody told them before what information should be obtained from me. It might have also happened that those who were arrested before me put the responsibility for the activities of the organization on those who were not caught. This was a usual device to minimize one's own responsibility and protect the organization from new arrests. Those who were not arrested may escape into hiding or abroad or anything else.

Whenever I was thinking before about a likely end in jail, I expected that I would not open my mouth to the police nor would I make any statement that could be useful to the police. However, this time I did not behave up to this standard. I was upset by the number of friends in jail and the amount of information known to the police. I disclosed additional details about my contacts that probably helped the police to arrest other persons. In this way I contributed my share to the number of people arrested.

Later on communist organizations blamed me for the arrests carried out at that time. In fact, I had nothing to do with them. When I was arrested the police already had information about the main channels of our network. However, the membership of the organization was put on guard against me. I was presented as an "agent of the police" who entered the organization to sell to the police information about the rank and file.

After that incident I turned to my studies on a full-time basis. I was not an exceptional student. I kept my involvement within the limits of what was necessary to get a degree. The rest of the time I used for reading whatever I was interested in. The subject of my primary interest was the methodology of sciences with an emphasis on social sciences. In this period I established a rather strong contact with statistics. Statistics was to me an important source of data about social phenomena. As such, it was an indispensable tool of social sciences. In addition, it was a way toward generalizations. Somehow I was convinced that statistics was a key to many puzzles and I decided to know more about that key.

In 1938 I finished my studies and went off to complete my military service. At the same time I applied for a fellowship from the French government to go to Paris and continue studies of the methodology of social sciences. The fellowship was granted and I went to Paris as soon as I did my military service.

In Paris I had a very active period. It meant concentrated studies from the morning till late at night with occasional interruptions to attend lectures and visit teachers.

In Paris I worked under Morrice Halbwachs, Albert Bayet, and partly Morrice Frechet. This gave me a chance to familiarize myself with a group of scientists belonging to Emil Durkheim's school and with their numerous achievements. I was also greatly impressed by Halbwach's *"Les niveaux de vie de la classe ouvriere"*. Halbwach advised me to devote a good part of my time to studies of statistics as the methodology of the collection of data and to statistical publications that provide sources of information for social scientists. At Halbwach's advice I took a statistics course with Frechet and thus started studies of statistics under a very competent person.

In this period I prepared a number of accounts of problems of the French sociological school. Two articles, viz. "Topic of sociology" and "Sociology of religion" were published in Yugoslavia before the war in periodicals of that period.

I left Paris when German troops were approaching the city. After many movements in different directions, I came to Yugoslavia and took a teaching assignment at a private religious school in Visoko, where I taught courses of languages, mathematics and anything else if the need appeared. I was a kind of Jack of all trades. I never refused additional jobs and this is why the director of the school treated me with great sympathy. It might be that in this way I managed to survive the atrocities of war.

In Visoko I continued my studies. My stay there was not long. However, it was filled with hard work. In the spring of 1941 I was mobilized by the army. I left Visoko and was in the short war that Yugoslavia had with Germany. However, in Belgrade's surroundings I was made a prisoner of war and taken to various camps in Germany.

There was nothing glorious in the way I was captured. My unit was on the run all the time and particularly during the night. At some point we stopped and I fell asleep. Somebody woke me up. I opened my eyes and saw a German soldier pushing me with his gun. When I looked around I realized that I was a drop of water in a sea of soldiers of a defeated army.

This is how I started the life as a prisoner of war. We were kept in a camp near Belgrade. Then we walked to a camp near Temisoara in Rumania. There we stayed in the open air, on a large meadow. We were a large group of several tens of thousands. We had no shelter. It was very cold. The rain and the snow were falling intermitently. We were wet and frozen. We had no food nor did anybody arrive at the idea to give us something warm to drink. This is how we lived for about two weeks. Even today I don't understand how we survived.

Next followed our trip to Germany. We went by train, in open coaches, and we were wet. When the train started moving we were all shivering from cold. I was young and able to stand any hardship. However, many older officers were crying loudly and begging German soldiers to kill them.

In Germany my main problem was the hunger. I was terribly hungry all the time. I had nothing on my mind but food. I saw our barracks made of bread while the roof consisted of steaks instead of tiles. I would sit on the roof with a knife in my hands and I would eat and eat without stopping. After some time the content of my conscience was reduced to food and nothing else.

After some time I broadened my concern. In addition to food, I also developed a health problem. While I was lying in my bed I felt all right. However, as soon as I stood up and wanted to move, I felt I would faint. I was losing the ability to walk straight. When I was standing I needed some support such as a wall or something else. I went to see the camp physician. When I explained my problem he started laughing like crazy. I got angry with him. He realized that and added: "My dear friend, there is nothing

13

wrong with you. If you had a steak a day for your lunch and a good dinner you would be able to walk straight".

After that I decided to reduce my energy expenditure to a minimum. Most of the time I was lying down in my bed. However, the starvation continued. I found another prisoner who was not so badly hungry. He was probably sick. Maybe he had contacts to get some food. He proposed to me to have an hour of conversations with him in French and he would pay me, at the end of each lesson, a honorarium of a potato. This was the cheapest work I ever did in my life. However, I accepted it with enthusiasm.

The group of prisoners to whom I belonged was frequently moved from one camp to another. I did not know the reasons. In course of one of these trips, we stopped at the railroad station in Kassel. I looked out of the window and saw on the platforms several containers full of hot potato soup. This was arranged along the train for distribution to prisoners. At that moment, the sirens started blowing all around to announce the danger of allied bombardments. The order came for all the prisoners to line up to go to a refuge. At that moment the idea came to me that it would be foolish to leave behind the hot soup. I kept my plate in my hands and could not resist the temptation to eat. At that moment I suddenly decided to put myself under a coach and wait for a chance to eat alone as much as I wanted. I was sure that the railroad station would be emptied and so I would be able to realize my dream of eating. I did so. It worked. One of the containers was near to me. I finished five platefuls of potato soup. After two hours the prisoners came back. The soup was warmed up for us and the distribution started. I entered the queue to get another plate of soup as part of regular supply.

After several months of this type of life, the opportunity came to go home. I was born on the territory that was part of the "Independent State of Croatia", viz. one of the states established by the Germans after the defeat of Yugoslavia. This is how I entered the group of prisoners from Croatia. The group was sent home. However, when the train approached the Croatian territory it stopped and the Serbs from the group were separated into another group. The Serbian group continued the trip under a special guard. Upon arrival in Zagreb we were all taken to a jail.

At that time jail was the place where all the inmates were candidates for extermination. It was so easy to kill a person. There was little interest in "trivialities" and "formalities", such as investigation, proofs, courts, sentences, etc. I sent a message to a relative of mine. He knew the new chief of police in Zagreb. In fact, in the prewar period my relative was the boss of the future chief of police. The chief agreed to release me.

In Zagreb I had many friends and I thought that it should be easy for me to get in touch with some of them and stay at their houses as long as needed. However, it was not so. Everybody was afraid of having anything to do with Serbs or Jews. In despair, I knocked at the door of a French family whom I had never met before. I told them what my problem was. I did not wait to witness the splendor of generosity and solidarity. They told me they themselves had to report to the police each morning. Thus, they did not know how long they would enjoy freedom and be able to treat me. However, they invited me to stay in their house as long as they were there. My host gave me two suits, some shirts and everything else that I needed. He also gave me an amount of money that was quite considerable so that I had reserves.

14

I stayed with that family for some time. I do not know their name nor have I been able to trace them. This has been a burden for my heart. I kept thinking of this case. To express my thanks to the unknown French family, I decided to help people whenever I can in situations when there would be no chance for them to get in touch with me and know who I was.

After that I continued depending on generosity. From Zagreb I wrote to the director of my school in Visoko and told him what had happened to me. In fact, the school belonged to Franciscan priests. Most teachers were priests. I told him that I wanted to leave Zagreb if it were possible. But, for each trip it was necessary to have an authorization from the police. Being a Serb in hiding and without documents I could not hope to get an authorization for the trip. As a result, a priest came from Visoko. We took the train for Visoko without authorization. He assumed that the company of a priest in his Franciscan dress would be sufficient. It was so. We arrived safely to Visoko. In fact, a police patrol passed by us twice. However, at that moment we talked to each other to make it clear that we were together. The police did not pay any attention to us.

Upon our arrival at Visoko my guardian told me: "Let us go now to our school". I thought it would be for a cup of coffee. In fact, he took me to the monastery that was adjacent to the school. It housed priests and students. The manager of the monastery expressed his welcome to me and told me that he would be happy to provide me with full board in the monastery's premises. I accepted the offer and stayed there.

The news about my arrival spread around quite fast. Some people came to see me although it was not a part of "decent behavior". One of these visits was not pleasant. Two policemen came to the monastery to take me away. The headmaster told them: "You can get hold of him only if you walk over my dead body". They left.

My host then realized that I was not safe. The priests discussed the matter and decided that the best thing for me to do would be to go to Serbia. It was another state established by the Germans after Yugoslavia was dismembered. As documents were needed again and I could not get them, they decided that another priest in his full dress would travel with me and protect me.

The trip was rather boring. We did not see anything that we could interpret as a sign of any organized maneuver to get hold of Serbs on the train and take them away. When we came to Vardiste, I told my guardian to leave the train and go back. He did it at my insistence, although he did not seem to be convinced that he was doing the right thing. About five minutes after he left a unit of "ustashi" encircled the train and started the identification process. They collected about thirty male Serbs. We were taken out of the train and kept for some time in a courtyard.

After about two hours of waiting, we were escorted out of the town, in the direction of a forest. The escort advised us to throw away our luguage as we would shortly not need anything any more. They told us that this march was our last effort. They also made many other hints that we interpreted as messages saying that shortly everything should be settled finally.

15

I do not have any idea how long we marched. At one point we left the main road and came in front of a rather small house. They arranged all of us in a line facing the front of the house and one of the guardians entered the house. After some minutes he came out and told us: "You have no luck. The commander is wounded. He will certainly be very tough with you".

After some time three people came out of the house. One of them had a better uniform than the others and more of those signs and gadgets that show the rank. His head was in a bandage. Only the eyes and the mouth were free. He started his inspection and went from one to the next, looking at our faces as if he were anxious to find some acquaintances. When he was facing me, he said:

"What are you doing here, my professor"?

I could not answer as I did not recognize him. He realized that and said:

"You certainly do not recognize me. You were my teacher in Visoko. My name is... I was not a good student and you helped me greatly to find my way".

"Ah, yes", I said.

"How did you come to this group"?, he said.

"I was in the train on my way to Serbia and your people took me off".

"Have they taken anything away from you"?, he said.

At this moment the idea came to my mind that he might set me free. His talking to me was in a very conciliatory mood. Therefore, I thought that I should do my best to speed up the matter. In order to do it I said:

"No, nothing".

Then he said:

"Professor, I give you one of my soldiers to take you to Serbia".

Then he called a soldier and gave him some instructions that I did not understand. After the soldier was ready to go, he told me:

"Now you go, professor. Have a good trip. I hope you agree that we had a good time in the school".

I left with the soldier. The next day I was in Serbia.

As the train was moving toward Belgrade I felt very bad. Maybe I had a fever. I don't know. I was trembling. I put my hands on the bench and sat on them. I did not want questions about my health. The people in the compartment would certainly realize that something was wrong with a person who was unable to sit without moving his hands around. Apart from these efforts to control my body and look like other passengers on the train, my mind was with the group of people whom I left on the other side of the border.

"What happened to them"?

"Have they been killed"?

I did not know the people in that group. Nor did I hear any of their names. Nor did I ever receive any information later on regarding their destiny. It was time of easy killing. It might be that nobody paid attention to such a small group. Known tragedies of bigger groups were accompanied so frequently by indifference. In that slow moving and overcrowded train this aspect of human nature came to my mind.

After a long and fatiguing trip, I arrived in Belgrade. Through contacts with my friends, I learned that most members of my family were in Belgrade as refugees. Parts of families of my close relatives were also there. We examined our position and found out that it was extremely grave. The big crowd of persons consisting primarily of old people, females, and youngsters were there to live somehow. The members with sufficient working capacity were killed, put in various camps and jails or disappeared in some other way. Many eyes were looking to me. I interpreted my duties accordingly.

The unpleasant thing was that we were all refugees. We all lost our homes. We lost everything we had. However, we had stomachs that needed food and we had bodies that needed clothing, washing, beds, etc.

We had no solution whatsoever. However, when there is no solution visible, generosity will intervene and provide a solution. We were all placed in different homes with an invitation to stay as long as we wanted. All those who have a guest for a single night and are not able to sleep because of disturbed privacy - they should think about these cases. The faces of our hosts were friendly and full of sympathy for us even after months of "disturbed privacy".

After some months we managed to find a flat. We entered our flat without suitcases. Neighbors never had a chance to see our furniture. And when the people in the area realized that we were living in a flat without a single chair to sit in, let alone beds, they started knocking at our door and bringing gifts, i.e. cushions, chairs, blankets, beds, pots, plates, etc. After some time we got along somehow.

Soon after that, the supply of money that I got from my French protectors in Zagreb was exhausted. I thought it would last till the end of the war so that I did not need to work. I expected a "Blitzkrieg" and I was wrong. I realized I needed a job. It was not only to get some income. It was equally needed as a source of protection. The job gave the right to get an identity card. The Germans would pick up people in the streets without identity cards and would take them away to work in the mines. A friend of mine helped me to get a job in an agency for metallic goods.

My job was boring. However, it gave me the protection that I needed. In addition, my office was heated. This was special luck. Whenever I was free from running around in search of food, I would go there to continue my studies.

At that time I planned to get a teaching job where I could give a course on methodology. I thought I should start preparing my lecture notes. I was doing that work during the whole duration of the war. I concluded the work in November 1944.

The book that I was writing was an account of methodological views of social scientists who made important contributions to methodology. It included two chapters under the title "Statistics and Social Sciences". The purpose was to illustrate the contributions of statistics to social sciences and thus orientate students toward the collection of facts and use of factual material in the analysis of social phenomena. In the prewar tradition social sciences in Yugoslavia were primarily a branch of philosophy. My concern was the state of social sciences in more developed countries.

However, subsequent developments prevented me of making direct use of that work. It was never published.

III The ghost of totalitarianism

Political developments in the last war took a course in favor of the Yugoslav Communist Party (YCP).[2] It may be that the communist wing of the anti-hitlerian alliance was particularly able to make political gains wherever possible. The Soviet Union advised the YCP on attitudes and actions to take in order to fit the agreements between the allies. The Soviet Union has also protected the interests of the communist movement all over the world and in Europe in particular. This protection has created a very favorable climate for the YCP. The YCP captured absolute power. Wherever German troops abandoned a region under pressure of the Soviet army, the units established and controlled by the YCP filled the vacuum and organized power immediately.

When the YCP controlled units entered Belgrade that way, one of the measures taken was the mobilization of the prewar reserve officers. I was one of them. In fact, an order was issued to all of us to report on a particular day to a particular place. I went there at the time indicated and saw a crowd of about four hundred persons. We were told to wait. After some time several high ranking officers came and we saw, in front of us, a man wearing a nice uniform. We were told that he was a general. He took the position of speaker. He gave us a speech that I shall never forget. He addressed us as "traitors", "cowards", etc. and continued: "I could take a machine gun and kill all of you. This is what you deserve. While we were fighting for the liberation of people in our country and had to go through incredible sufferings, you enjoyed yourselves in warm beds, under soft blankets, and in luxury houses under the protection of German fascists..." He continued in this style.

Even now, after so many years, I keep asking myself what happened in the past of that man. What kind of youth did he have? The hatred that he carried in his heart had greatly affected his reasoning.

We were all mobilized and assigned to different units. I was sent to the School of Artillery Officers. My job was to teach mathematics. I had a workload of about eight lectures a day of 50 minutes each. In May 1945 the crash courses were discontinued and

---

2 Although this name was changed later on, it will be retained throughout this book.

I was demobilized.

As a civilian I thought that the time had come for me to go back to my professional work. One of the ideas was to arrange for publication of some of my manuscripts. However, it was obvious that there would be difficulties. The newly established publishers were strictly controlled by the party[3] and their primary aim was to promote party views and engage in political propaganda. Along that line they obviously had more important problems to worry about than to consider my manuscripts.

In the beginning I thought that some publisher might be willing to consider my material. It seemed to me that it had nothing to do with politics. However, after some inquiries and contacts with various colleagues, I realized that I was wrong. There was an official theory of social sciences. That was marxism. Anything else was a bourgeois theory that had "nothing to do with science". A more orthodox party mind would go as far as to say: "Bourgeois theories were produced with a view to confuse people and prevent them from understanding the society". At that time the only possible way of talking about "bourgeois theories" was to start with marxism as the only "scientific" theory of social sciences and continue afterwards with a presentation of "wrong" bourgeois theories as illustrations of mistaken views. In the end, a conclusion was also needed to express surprise at the blindness of authors of bourgeois theories and their inability to understand social processes as analyzed in marxism.

From this point of view my manuscripts belonged to the class of political literature. They were accounts of contributions of French sociology. However, they did not express any surprise at mistakes committed by the respective authors. Nor did they warn readers against the political dangers of French sociology that was putting emphasis on different issues than marxist theory. My account also omitted an appeal to readers to take French sociology as an additional reason to stick to science, viz. marxism. My manuscripts did not include any recommendations. They did not mention marxism at all. In that respect they were dangerous. They could generate the idea in the mind of some readers that marxism is just one of the many products of science. The danger thus arises that some readers might take away from Marxism the aureole of "absolute truth".

It was difficult for me to understand the new orientation. Politics was pushed to the forefront of any activity. All the events were viewed in the light of their potential political implications. Politics was a balance. Whatever was likely to contribute to the party political programme was to be supported as valuable. Similarly, everything that did not strengthen that programme was to be erased as negative. All the events were either "white" or "black". There was nothing in between, there was nothing "neutral". "Neutral" meant a refusal to be "white".

It took time to understand such a polarization of everything. It eliminates the beauty of life's colors. It transformed human beings into "good" ones and "bad" ones. It creates an adoration for everything labelled "good" and a hatred for everything "bad". An emotional ground was thus established for an all-embracing discrimination process. Party interest made things nice, beautiful, useful, progressive, revolutionary and *vice*

---

3   In this book "Party" means the YCP. No other party was allowed. If the term is applied in some other
     meaning that meaning is explained.

versa.

Consequences and generalizations followed. "Good" was to be promoted and "bad" was to be suppressed. People who lived before the war in nice houses were forced out in order to create space for the class of "good" ones. As this action had to be legalized, the courts were used to pass the corresponding sentences. Property was confiscated of a gentleman and he was sentenced to two years in jail because of collaboration with the Germans during the war. In fact, he had left before the war and lived in England all the time of the war. It was so easy to manufacture certain sins. As a result, the "bad" ones were sentenced and put in labor camps. One of their duties was to repair, clean, and maintain the houses of the "good" ones.

The power of the communist party was thus taking shape. However, that power was a new phenomenon in the national experience. The events were taking a clear course toward totalitarianism.

Communist parties are power-obsessed. Power is the aim of all political parties. However, communist parties devote more attention than any other political party to the conquest of power and its control once it has been captured.

Obsession with power is a part of its ideology. Namely, the exploitation of masses in the capitalist society and the continuation of the privileged position of the minority is defended by all means involving police, army, legislation, the system of education, etc. The only way to establish the rule of justice is to overthrow the capitalist order by means of a revolution. In this fight of the masses for a new society, communist parties assume the leading role. Their ranks include the most conscious elements of the proletariat. The communists are aware of the course of history; they have the necessary determination to pursue the goal of revolution; they will utilize all the means available to break the capitalist power, impose their own rule, and keep the captured power in order to establish a new social order. Power is the key to success. Power is above all. Power penetrates all the thinking and all the doing. Power is the condition for the fulfillment of the programme. Power is the door to a new society.

However, the conquest of power is not the end of the fight. In fact, power is to be kept. Many people will not understand the new society and the difficulties to be overcome on the way. Therefore, success depends upon the determination of the communist party to persist till the end. Mild supporters of socialism will get discouraged by the difficulties of the fight. Many of them will withdraw. Also, the defeated capitalism will not give up easily. Capitalism will use all the opportunities to hurt the growing socialism and establish its rule again. However, the communist party is aware of the enemy's intentions. Therefore, it will take all the precautionary measures to keep power and crush the enemy's action. Power is thus more than a means on the way to destroy the capitalist society. Power is the duty. The ability to keep power is a fundamental characteristic of a successful communist party. Without power there is no socialism. The party that is unable to keep power has failed in the pursuit of its revolutionary ideals.

The first part of the task of YCP, viz. the seizure of power was achieved with what could be called the dance of terror. The old state machinery was broken into pieces. It had to be clear to everybody that the communist party was determined to eradicate all the traces of capitalist society. The only way to achieve this aim was to seed fear. This is what all the communist parties in power have done, although none of them wants to talk about. In fact, the rule of fear is the beginning of the communist power. All the communist parties begin with measures intended to spread fear and make it clear to the population that any deviation from the prescribed order will expose the deviants to persecution, jail, torture, extermination, all sorts of sufferings, inconveience on the job, low salary, difficulties for the members of the family, etc. The beginning is thus the rule of lawlessness.

In the course of the dance of terror, many people were killed. Many of them may have committed acts that deserved punishment. However, the executions were carried out on the spot by young people who did not know anything about law nor did they care for investigation. My uncle was killed although he was honesty and modesty at its best. A couple of young people sat together for a few minutes and the sentence was passed. The execution followed. At the same time goods were taken away from those who had them, houses and flats were confiscated, cars were taken away by the authorities, the property was lost, etc. Very soon the feeling of helplessness would spread around and make the people very cooperative. All the decisions of the power were accepted and carried out without any trace of resistance.

In this way the first task was over. Capitalism was crushed. Full power was captured. However, it was to be kept to build socialism.

For that purpose communists have a more elaborate theory of power than other political parties. The essential point of that theory is the view of power as a result of a large number of different factors that all have some bearing. Power is very weak if reduced for its survival to physical repression. Bourgeois parties tend to depend upon police and the armed forces. In fact, power is very weak if made dependent upon force. Communists have well understood that components of power include almost everything, viz. the ideology of power, the impact of that ideology over the territory, the relationships between the top officers and the ruling ideology, the reliability of the government machinery, staff selection and promotion procedure, the attitude of communication media, etc. Power is thus everything. The one who wants to remain in power has to keep an eye on all aspects of the society and interfere with all of them in a way that is suitable for the maintenance of power. Power is an outcome of the totality of social life.

An important component of the power protection programme is the battle for souls. This means propaganda to an extent that history has never seen before.

There is an amount of sincerity behind the propagandist campaign. Namely, communists are convinced that they keep in their hands a "scientific" theory of history. The theory says that capitalism has to disappear from the historic scene as it does not make possible further progress. The fall of capitalism is a necessity as in phenomena governed by natural laws. The transition to socialism will thus be made easy if the population is aware of the theory and the inevitability of socialism. In this case there will be no need for drastic measures. The proletarian dictatorship will be mild.

For the purpose of spreading around communist ideology, propagandist machinery is established that does not leave any chance to escape. People are taken in crowds to places where political leaders give them explanations of what is going on. Radio, television, newspapers, movies and all other communication media are essentially used for propaganda. Walls in schools, places of work, factories, and even the street pavements are full of slogans. Collective reading of newspapers is also organized wherever large numbers of people live or work together. Work as such loses its meaning. Propaganda is everything. Processions are organized almost each day to take people from places of work to places of commemorations. On the way slogans are distributed to the people which they are supposed to shout to express their enthusiasm and happiness about the beginning of the new society.

A particularly important means for strengthening control of power is a large-scale glorification of that power. Although this practice is alien to socialism, the USSR adopted it as part of the inherited tsarist tradition and developed it to an incredible degree. Glorification of the power became a permanent theme of all the communication means. The power is endowed with a maximum of superb qualities, such as wisdom, intelligence, love, infatiguable service to the people and the like. Everything coming from the power is superb. The best thing that citizens can do is to offer absolute obedience. Any doubt regarding the power is an act of opposition. However, obedience is not sufficient. An expression is also needed of the happiness about decisions and arrangements made by power. This is why celebrations of the power and expressions of enthusiasm of the population are features of public life.

Whoever had a chance to listen to any of the Yugoslav radio stations or see the television programme must have been surprised at the amount of celebrations. Celebrations were carried out all over the country and all the year around. Celebrations referred to anything from the history of the communist party no matter how minor the events might be, such as meetings of an infinite number of party bodies, the places where committees used to be located, the battles that party units had on the way to power, etc., etc.

Communists are sincere about these celebrations. In their opinion, the history of mankind is divided into two parts. The first part includes everything up to the communist seizure of power. The rest is part two. In the first part, the exploitation and sufferings of the poor dominated. People were slaves of difficulties and limitations. In the second part, people are liberated from all the evils. The period of injustice is over. Equality will be established for everybody and a period of final and eternal freedom for mankind will start. That historic achievement in favor of mankind was made by the present generation of the communist party, viz. the present leadership. They arranged for the cutoff point between history as slavery and history as freedom. That is why the intensity of celebrations did not show any sign of relaxation.

In this complex of ideology, glorification, and celebrations apologetics is in the center. Everything that the power was doing was the right way. Each act of the power was to be praised with the help of all possible means. For that purpose an unmatched orchestration of life was maintained. All the communication media talked about the same issues and in the same way. No deviations were allowed, nor anything personal. A huge orchestration machinery organized the flow of information from all possible directions with a view to imposing the adherence to instructions and searching for enemies. The enemy was anybody who dared to express views different from the official ones. Any personal view caused large-scale alarm and a real hysteric reaction.

23

In its consolidation of power, the party also made ample use of the human underground. The underground refers to qualities, such as hatred, love, envy, servility, flattery, sycophancy, position hunting, power hunting, money hunting, etc. If the power wants to hurt somebody, it is very useful to find another person who is not on good terms with the first one. The second person will provide a great deal of useful information against the suspected person. The second person will also agree to keep an eye on the first one and gladly report the collected results.

No ocean is as wide as the human underground. There is no limit to how far one can go in its exploitation. Communist power is aware of these possibilities in the same way as any other power. Yugoslavia made an ample use of these possibilities. All the means should be used in the realization of great ideals. In order to save their children, mothers accepted to serve as points of observation against people, wives accepted to work as police informants in order to release their husbands from jail, children of bourgeois families accepted to spy for the police and thus obtain pardons for their parents, etc.

Another important means of the protection of power was to establish a faithful machinery in the government agencies and in all other types of work. This was achieved through a large-scale discriminatory selection of staff. Young people who were looking for a job had to fill in a questionnaire that contained a question: "Are you a member of the YCP". Members of the party were preferred even when they were significantly below the level of other candidates. Members of the party could not be unemployed. As a result, sufficiently early in their careers young people started attending political meetings and asking for the floor hoping to being noticed by the party leadership. They also participated in other youth events. Eventually they were offered membership in the party. They were qualified to answer "Yes" to that important question. On their way to the "Yes" answer, they might also be able to pick up some other benefits as well, such as fellowships for participation on organized trips, membership in the youth exchange programme with foreign countries, free courses to study foreign languages, etc.

Those who failed to join became part of a mass without dimensions. Their destiny was governed by rules.

Once the "Yes" people got a job, their subsequent career depended upon what they added to the original "Yes". A recipe for success was simple: attend party meetings, accept an office in party activities, show interest in these activities through proposals and discussions, etc. In doing so, one was not likely to wait long to get a promotion, an increase in salary or become a boss.

The recruitment of personnel for all kinds of jobs all over the country was carried out with a clear preference for party members or those who were likely to support the power. The higher the job the more the party's confidence was needed. The whole labor force machinery was strictly controlled by the party. It became clear to everybody that the party kept in its hands the future of people, their career, their recognition, their happiness, their comfort, and the happiness of their children and their beloved ones. And it worked. A large majority bowed their heads.

The measures taken were successful. A strong control of everything was achieved. However, in similar situations power normally hits back. Namely, with such a strong power a decline of moral standards is unavoidable. The people realize that hard work, drive, and ability are neglected or, in the best case, become secondary qualities. Leading roles, recognition, high positions, impact on work, high salaries, promotions, development chances, etc. are beyond the reach of work. Discrimination in favor of power supporters becomes a pattern of public life. The louder a person is in the expression of enthusiasm about the power, the more one is entitled to hope for. Those who are unable to accept life as service to power have to disappear in the anonymous mass that makes up the bottom of society. On the other hand, the committed ones are classified according to their contribution to power. Those who do not persist in the role of means of power will fall off. The unconditional and steady supporters move toward all the blessings that power is able to grant.

However, among the power supporters there is no difference between sincerity and profiteering. Both talk the same language. This is how paradise is established for the activation of underground feelings. The career makers, flatterers, liars of all kinds, and other forms of dishonest people get their chance. The same is true of people without abilities and those who failed in creative work. In this group are also business-minded people who have chosen to involve themselves in public support of the power in exchange for the hope to get favors, such as promotion, higher salary, fellowships, mission abroad, a "society owned" car, house, etc. As the motives of human acts cannot be identified, the power accepts everybody. In this way the battle for moral standards is lost. Rather than being a society of high moral principles, the communist countries took the course toward a negative selection.

Many people were concerned observers of these developments. The country got a first serious chance in our history to move toward socialism. However, the events diverged from expectations. In the views of people with inclinations toward the left, socialism had to mean, above all, the highest possible respect for freedom as the foundation of a modern society. Therefore, we were puzzled as to the meaning of what was going on.

Pending further developments, I decided to stick to my own programme. It seemed appropriate to see to it that some of my manuscripts be published. In this respect it was clear that any deal with the newly established publishers would be a waste of time. Therefore, I decided to go on my own, without any publisher. At that time it was still possible to publish modest size manuscripts by using small printers whose shops were not yet "nationalized". Some of them still existed. It was difficult to find anything against them and justify confiscation of property.

In some of these small printing houses I published two booklets, viz. *The Primitive Mind* and *An Introduction Into Sociology of Religion*. Both of them were accounts of the respective areas of French sociology. Both booklets appeared in Belgrade in 1945.

While involved in printing, I did not think of distribution. I thought that I could give a good commission to bookshops and they would make the sale for me. I went to Prosveta which was the largest "government-owned" bookseller. They took 150 copies for sale through their network. Other bookshops were suspicious. They expected trouble and refused to have any contact with publications issued privately. However, I found a bookseller whose shop was still in private hands. He agreed to be the distributor of my booklets.

25

The sale went quite well. However, a man who was at that time Assistant Minister of Public Education, by the name Kosta Grubachich, publicly made vehement attack on my booklets and called on the authorities and other organizations to take measures to destroy this type of "poison of our youth who are anxious to study". I was not a state employee at the time of the attack and it looked to me as a pleasant illustration of what kind of man can be put at the ministerial level. However, my wife was dead afraid. She almost had a nervous breakdown. She was aware of how far the consequences might go. The first and simplest step might be to put somebody to live with us. This was equivalent to living in hell. As I lived in a single and very humid room, there was no danger of this kind. However, the programme of possibilities was much broader. For example, the police practiced the step of taking away residence authorization. In other words, the police were able to move people to some other place, obliging them to live without a job and home. In practice, this was equivalent to a death sentence. Those who had a job might also be penalized with a low salary, a humiliating position at the place of work, no facilities for any progress in the career, etc.

As is usual in this kind of situation, the attack by the Assistant Minister on my booklets had the opposite effect of what was planned. Interest in my booklets increased sharply. The distributor took the *Sociology of Religion* to a market and sold several hundred copies to peasants in a couple of hours. At the market, he advertized the booklet by shouting loudly: "New book about religion". Of course, religion was a hot political issue. Nothing about religion was available in printed form except the repetitions of standard formulae that religion was a means of the bourgeois class to extend ignorance of the population. As my booklet was on sale at the market, viz. outside the officially established channels for circulation of printed material, the buyers expected to find in it stories written in a way different from the communist propaganda. Those who opened the booklet later on must have been terribly disappointed. However, this was the position of intellectuals under the totalitarian polarization. We are not welcomed either by "white ones" or "black ones".

After I fell short of additional copies of my booklet, I went to Prosveta to inquire if some copies were left over. I realized that something was wrong as nobody wanted to talk to me. An employee told me to go to their headquarters. I went there and I got a reply from an employee: "That book is not on sale any more. However, we shall pay you for all the copies that you left with us". I got the money and went to see a relative of mine who worked at Prosveta. He told me that my *Sociology of Religion* was removed from sale. Next to him was another employee whom I had never seen before. He told me: "Your books, together with some other undesirable books, were burned. Influential people requested that they be destroyed".

I took the latter information as an authentic interpretation of what happened. Subsequent events were in line with it.

Needless to say, it was a great honor to me to be on the list of authors whose books were burned. I remember the books that were destroyed in Hitler's Germany. I admired these books. Now I felt very proud of being in that company.

Let me also add that my booklets were available in many public libraries. Later on they disappeared. In the course of the implementation of totalitarian principles, all the books in all the public libraries were checked with a view to destroying everything that did not belong to the category of "good titles". My books were destroyed at that time and nobody has ever made an effort to arrange for their rebirth. Moreover, once your name is painted in black, the same color is put over everything else that is associated with it. In the National Library in Belgrade, that is the largest library in the city, almost everything with my name was removed from the catalogues. "Titles" were also removed that dealt with graphs, numbers, mathematical formulae, etc. Everything was bad.

Poor Orwell. He invented the rewriting of pieces of the text published in the past with a view to securing the conformity of printed material with the present views. Here a more efficient method was offered. All traces of work of those who ever dared to say something different than the official views were erased by fire, searching catalogues, "cleaning" shelves, etc. In this way the respective authors became "nobody" for ever. They lost the authority and impact. They had committed suicide. In this way, there was no need for rewriting. Those who said something "bad" had no proof that they ever said anything. The right to exist was restricted to "good" literature.

An interesting aspect of totalitarianism is its intransigence, its inability to tolerate anything outside its reach and its control. Totalitarianism implies absolute control of everything. The text that was published was of secondary importance. The matter of primary importance was the publisher. If the party had full control over a publisher's programme, this publisher would not be excessively bothered in the choice of material to publish. If he was independent of the party he would be persecuted even for the publication of the *Communist Manifesto*. After all the blame was put on me because of French sociology, various party controlled publishers published books by authors belonging to French sociology and they were not blamed.

I am sure that those who were involved in eradication of my booklets have never read a single page of my text. Had they done so and applied some reasoning after the reading, they would have easily come to the conclusion that my text had many points in common with the philosophy in whose name they militate. In sociology, religion is a complex aspect of human society, the degree of its development, and so many other factors. In sociology, religion is put on the desk for analysis as in a laboratory. The aim is to examine each form of religion in relation to its natural and social environment, identify its changes in time, etc. This is what science does. However, totalitarianism does not care for science nor its motivation is guided by logic of facts.

Needless to say, incidents of this type that push the party into unpleasant interventions are possible only at the beginning of a totalitarian regime, before it becomes a full-fledged system with all its wheels working smoothly. The period when my booklets appeared belonged to such a beginning. Later on, after all the bookshops and printing facilities became the property of the "society" or, in other words, after the party had established its full control over all management channels, no publication and no circulation was possible of anything that did not fall in the class of "good" reading. From that moment onwards, there were no more incidents. Everything moved quietly and smoothly. The existing literature was "good" literature.

The development of a full-fledged totalitarian publication system takes time. The following steps are usually applied. A draft of the publication programme of each publisher is prepared by the senior staff of publishing houses. This implies an initial screening process by persons who are appointed to their respective positions because of their demonstrated adherence to the party line. The Belgrade newspaper *Politika* of June 30, 1985 carried a vacancy announcement (page 28) for an editor of marketing publications. The condition imposed on candidates was ideological and political involvement in the politics of socialism based on self-management, equality of Yugoslav nationalities, and the foreign policy of independence and non-alignment of Yugoslavia. In other words, the candidate must be known for his faithfulness to the regime. It is easy to realize what the conditions are like for editors of publications dealing with social and political issues.

Needless to say, this condition makes the censorship tighter and more rigid than any other version of control of freedom of press by special offices established for censorship purposes.

Should, however, any of the editors appointed in this way fail to behave accordingly in the course of his duty, he will be transferred at once to another job. In addition, should there be somebody who is not sufficiently strict in the observance of party instructions, he will be corrected by the others. All the senior staff work as a team with a kind of collective responsibility. Thus, they keep an eye on each other and compete for the respect of the party line.

However, this is a small part of the controls introduced. For each item of each publication programme there are two reviewers, viz. two external persons who have a specific responsibility for a line by line examination of the proposed text. Upon the review of the text they have to present a signed report of the "suitability" of the text. The "suitability" refers to technical matters, editorial issues, and, of course, to political implications should there be any. This is why a technician can be used to review a technical manuscript. However, for books dealing with issues that are not far from politics, the reviewers are always selected from among recognized supporters of the party line. Should the case arise, the reviewer's report might change the previous decision to publish a text.

Another means of controlling the communication channels is censorship as "patriotic duty" or an "expression of party loyalty". After identity is established between the party politics on one hand and the "nation", the "national interest" or the "requirements of our people" on the other hand, the publication of any text that is in any sense different than the official party line is against the "national interest" or against the "socialist society". In other words, an "unsuitable" text is a crime against the society. A "conscious" citizen will never fail to report that sort of case. The newspapers, television, all sorts of committees and assemblies keep talking about such crimes as soon as somebody has pointed out a case of concern. The hunting for "crimes" is done with an extreme fervor. Many people want to be "patriots". This is very useful. It represents a better contribution to one's own career than any work. "Patriots" become university professors without qualifications, members of academies of sciences, ambassadors, etc. A long chain of privileges follows. The "enemy" is removed from his job to spend the rest of his life at an insignificant post in bookkeeping or in a village. The senior staff at the agencies where the "crime" takes place are demoted without a chance left to recover. They demonstrated the inability for leadership. All those who were lucky to stay out will remember the lesson for ever.

From time to time scenes of hysteria arise about "abuses of freedom" as a result of some paragraphs or sentences discovered in articles or books previously examined and accepted for publication. Vehement speeches are made against the culprits and the agencies that are associated with it. Parliaments, government agencies, and various party committees compete with each other in the sharpness of their reactions.

IV New statistics

When I realized that the controls of everything and everybody were getting tighter and tighter each day, I thought that I should find a job and live as everybody else.

In that respect, the idea came to my mind that I should inquire if I could continue my involvement in methodological studies within the Department of Philosophy of Belgrade University. I went to see Prof. Dushan Nedeljkovich, who was appointed the new head of that department. Nedeljkovich was, at that time, the strongest man in the party in all matters related to philosophy in a broad sense. I told him what I had studied so far and what I had published. He told me that he would not be able to support my association with his department in any form. He said: "You studied in France and you will never be able to get rid of Durkheim and his ideas. It might be that we could have done something about you had you never published anything. Your publications represent a commitment. Your mind is blocked by what you did".

He then advised me to go to the State Statistical Office (SSO). He thought that my study of statistics would be useful at the SSO while my "bourgeois" education would not have a chance to interfere with the production of statistical data. He went so far as to call Dolfe Vogelnik, the director of SSO. He recommended me for a job. He also added to Vogelnik: "You might be able to use a man who knows foreign languages". It seems that Vogelnik agreed to appoint me. I was asked to report to the SSO.

The next day I went to the "Personnel" of SSO. This was my first contact with the institution of "Personnel". At that time I had no idea of what it was. Later on I realized that it was a cell in the huge network of points of observation of the behavior of people and a source of information about all the employees.

At that time some people considered the office of personnel as an outposted police cell. In fact, this was only partly true. The personnel offices of that period had a duty to help secure good staff, assist in the improvement of their skills, and keep an eye on their behavior. The personnel offices systematically collected information about everybody including work performances, private life, use of leisure time, social contacts, etc. One of the most important pieces of information was political attitudes. The personnel office was thus the best informed place about the staff concerned. When somebody, including the police, needed information about a person, the first step was to check with the corresponding personnel office.

Because of this amount of information available in "Personnel", no decision could be made about a person without consultation with "Personnel". This is why the employment in "Personnel" was restricted to people with recognized loyalty, such as wives of high ranking party bosses, their children, retired police officers and their families, etc.

I was received in the "Personnel" of SSO by a young lady whose face was like a statue, without any motion, cold, in fact frightening. She asked me for my name, address, schools attended, etc. She told me to come in three days. After these three days were over, I called again. She told me that I could start work as of the next day. "You will work in the office headed by comrade...", she told me.

At the time of my next visit, she was even colder than the first time I saw her. In the previous three days, she had probably contacted persons of confidence in the house where I was living. The information obtained was certainly not favorable. Adding to the fact that I had a clear defect in my education and an expressed interest in wrong theories, it was easy to decide about my salary. The payroll list of the staff at the SSO was arranged in descending order of salary. I was given the honor to occupy the last row, viz. the position below the youngest clerk.

My employment at the SSO had far-reaching consequences for me. I had a job that was much better than I was able to appreciate at that time. My involvement in statistics took me away from the sensitive issues of social sciences. At that time any attempt at a discussion of methodology of social sciences would take me straight into trouble. In the ruling party ideology, the methodology of social sciences meant historic materialism. Any alternative attitude would lead to a conflict with the official ideology and a variety of grave consequences. On the other hand, a public repetition of the known principles of historic materialism would mean a disgusting servility. I was possibly not able to do that. No matter to what extent one would be willing to recognize the importance of the basic ideas of historic materialism, the methodology of social sciences was obviously a broader issue. One cannot close his eyes in the face of the essential importance of statistics in social sciences. It is no less important for students to be familiar with the contributions of different sociological schools and their methodological approaches. As I could not do anything that would be different than my views on the subject, it is easy to understand how lucky I was by getting the job in statistics. Prof. Nedeljkovich was probably aware of the situation. It seems that his refusal to support my association with Department of Philosophy was based on the expectation that, sooner or later, he might need to rebuke me for the expression of my views.

As far as I am concerned, I did not expect at that time that my job in statistics would be more than a temporary arrangement. From the point of view of my own interest, I realized that my employment was likely to add an important component to my education. I knew something about statistics. However, this was knowledge from books. The involvement in statistical production was, therefore, a chance to provide me with an experience that was not available to those who have never participated in data collection. It was also clear that it would lead me to problems that I was not aware of at that time. This is why I accepted my job with pleasure and curiosity.

In the beginning my work did not offer much along the line of my expectations.

31

The SSO was established in 1944. Of necessity, it had very modest tasks. One of them was the staffing. The other aim was the reconstruction of the prewar statistical data according to newly established political divisions of national territory. In other words, the aim was to provide a statistical picture of the newly established republics and autonomous provinces on the basis of data collected before the war. In this way, a basis would be built for the formulation of programmes of social and economic development. Also, bench marks would be obtained for the measurement of socialist achievements.

Both of these tasks were carried out within the limitations imposed by circumstances. As to staffing, the party had quite many people available to talk about politics. However, there were only a few persons who knew some statistics. This is why the doors of SSO were open to commoners, viz. the people who did not belong to the party ranks. This was the only solution available and the best one at the same time. The best available statistical staff in Yugoslavia joined SSO and did the work that left a long-lasting effect. I was in the same office with Dr Joze Lavrich, who was on expert in agricultural statistics. He belonged to a "family of enemies". However, he was a precious stone in the office. Other people of great value were Ivo Lah, and D.Tasich. A long list of other senior staff without any interest in politics included Pavichevich, the chief of foreign trade statistics, Dr. Musulin, D.Popovich, etc.

The second task, viz. the reconstruction of prewar data was carried out in a way that was not very satisfactory. Wherever possible, data by the new division of the country were obtained by reshuffling the lowest units according to new borders and summing up the related totals. Difficulties in the procedure arose because in many cases the lowest units were cut into two or more pieces. In such a situation guesses were made of proportions included in separate pieces. The totals for the units concerned were split accordingly.

More sophisticated approaches in carrying out this task were not possible as the interest was switched to quite new problems. Yugoslavia accepted the Soviet model of the organization of both the national economy and all other aspects of life in general. The YCP decided to strictly follow the approaches used in the USSR. The implementation of that programme started immediately after the war. We were in the midst of "socialization" and "nationalization" of all the property and of the means of production in particular. The package of new steps included the introduction of economic and social planning. It was thus clear that there was not much point in an effort to carry out a satisfactory restoration of prewar data. New changes in the organization of the economy would make the value of such an effort very relative.

The statistical implications of the new measures were obvious. After the abolishment of private property and the related type of management, the responsibility for decisions regarding the economy and social life in general was transferred to various governing bodies starting from the elementary units of work up to the federal government. In order to be able to perform their duties, these bodies needed current information about all the relevent activities under their competence. This is how the need arose for an unprecedented large-scale data collection. Data collection or recording on the spot was in view everywhere, viz. wherever people do something. I read in a document that more than two million persons worked at some point of time in the recording process of the Soviet industry. Of course, I do not know how accurate the information is.

32

However, it shows the extent of the operation.

Data that follow from this elaborate system were work-related. They provided a basis for decision making. In other words, data became a part of the work itself, an indispensable component of any management. The management requirements implied the collection of data in each unit of work, such as factories, agricultural cooperatives, retail stores, restaurants, etc. Decisions are made in all these units. The need for data is universal. These needs also climb along a hierachy scale. For that purpose, data for lowest level units are aggregated in any way appropriate for a specific hierarchy. Data for individual factories can be aggregated at the level of different administrative units, within the same branch of industry, etc.

As for social and economic planning, data represent an attempt at a direction of social and economic activities toward the established targets either in terms of production of goods or services. The national targets are broken down geographically, administratively, by branches of industry, etc. At the end, each individual unit of work has its plan or its share in the total effort.

Planning generated the same need for data as the current management. It assumed a detailed knowledge of resources, capacities, potentialities, needs, etc. Rational formulation of targets is not possible otherwise. It equally assumes a measurement of the output in order to follow the fulfillment of individual targets. Needless to say, data needed for planning purposes have to be available by the smallest units of work, such as individual factories, villages, agricultural cooperatives, etc. Each of these units has its plan that is to be fulfilled or followed.

Data collection for the purpose of planning and current management of the socialist society was thus our essential aim. This was a great shifft in both the role and the meaning of statistics. While the users of data were unspecified before, now they are known. They consist of the hierarchy of managers and planners starting with those in each work unit. They start their day with a study of the related statistical data. Statistics tells them what decisions are needed. Statistics is in the foundation of the society.

After the introduction of the Soviet model, the work of our statistics moved along two different lines. One of them was statistics in the usual sense. It continued the production of data for general purposes. It consisted of censuses and surveys. This part was conceived essentially in the same way as before. The other line was related to recording of the results of various operations, such as counting (the number of pieces produced, number of workers present, hours of work done, etc.) or measuring the weight, volume, area or something else.

The relationship between these two lines of work was the subject matter of many discussions.[4]

The same organization of statistics was used in other countries that fell after the last war under Soviet influence. The resulting data were used for intercountry compar-

---

4 Soviet literature on this subject is available in Vogelnik, D.: Recording and statistics (O evidenciji i statistici), *Statistička Revija (Statistical Review)*, Vol.I, 1951.

isons and as a basis for the preparation of various cooperative arrangements. The system was thus unavoidable within the Soviet orbit.

The introduction of the Soviet model of statistics in Yugoslavia was not carried out by a group of Soviet advisors although we had some of them. This was done by ourselves while Soviet advisors were primarily instrumental in making available the respective reading material.

The literature that was coming to us from the USSR dealt essentially with problems of recording. I do not remember that I ever saw anything about methodology of censuses or surveys. The books that were available dealt with recording in different areas of work. In fact, these books were primarily written to serve as instructions to people working in the respective areas. They spoke about characteristics to be included, concepts and definitions used, the organization of work, the presentation of data, etc. They did not contain any theory or references to open problems, the issues to be studied, the experiences collected, etc. Even the general textbooks of statistics were not different. The highest level of theory touched upon was normally a chapter dealing with averages. In fact, the only "theory" included referred to two points presented as Lenin's contributions to statistics. One of them dealt with the classification of data and the other with extreme values of distributions.

In his studies of the agricultural problems of tzarist Russia, Lenin was bothered by the classification of farms into two classes only. In that way, it was not possible to see the size and the characteristics of poor segments of the agricultural population. In that situation, Lenin concluded that it was done deliberately by tzarist statisticians in order to hide from the public the position of the poor. The practice was qualified as an abuse of statistics with a view to achieving political purposes. The classification of data without prejudice had to be based on a sufficient number of classes so that clear insight is obtained in the structure of the related population.

Needless to say, Lenin was not a statistician and it was not surprising that he saw a problem where there was no problem. The number of classes and the specification of limits of various classes is primarily the problem of users of data and the related international agreements. Quite a different issue is the realization of the agreements made. At present, with computers available, there is not much of a problem in the use of a detailed classification. However, tzarist Russia used manual processing. In that case the difference between two or more classes was quite considerable. Needless to say, we do not know whether the resources available in tzarist Russia permitted a better classification than the one used.

The other problem is also connected with classification. If the number of classes is large, it might happen that the classes covering the tails of distributions do not contain more than a few units. Hence the recommendation to reduce the number of classes. However, Lenin pointed out that in this case the information would be lost about individual cases. That information is sometimes very valuable. If a classification presents the output of coal miners and a class contains one single miner with an exceptionally high output, a study of this case could be very indicative as it would show under what conditions good results were achieved. Other miners might wish to follow the example and thus substantially increase production.

Obviously, large-scale data processing has nothing to do with the search for individual examples. Statistics cannot use data for individual units. That would be suicide. Means other than statistics are available to study individual cases.

The same type of statistics that we found in Soviet books was presented to the senior staff of SSO in a special course that was expected to equip the staff for their leading role in statistical matters. The course was obligatory. We all had to know what Lenin said about classification and the use of statistics for study of individual cases. Our course ended with a chapter on averages. We were not told anything beyond averages, nor were we requested to do any study on our own of matters that come in the theory after averages.

The same spirit invaded statistical education.

The first change that took place with respect to the state of prewar statistical education was the expansion of educational facilities. After the last war, statistics was introduced in almost all the schools at all the levels. In this way statistics was given considerable prominence. Most graduate students had to go through course of statistics.

As to the related curriculum, it was statistics of the type presented above. The university teaching disregarded the theory in the same way as the books about courses for practitioners of government offices. The difference between statistical programmes at the school of medicine and the school of commerce was in the illustrations and operational matters. Medical students had to be familiar with reports by hospitals, public health stations, ambulances, etc. and the presentation of data contained in these reports. The commerce student had to study the reporting system in banks, retail stores, etc. and the related concepts and definitions, the presentation, uses of data, etc.

It will now be useful to provide more details about our new statistical education as it reveals an insight into the state, problems, and shortcomings of our "new statistics".

Generally speaking, the university curricula consisted of two parts, the general statistics or the theory of statistics and separate branches of statistics viz. the specific fields of data collection, such as population statistics, agricultural statistics, foreign trade statistics, internal trade statistics, health statistics, etc. Each curriculum consisted of these two parts and they were both obligatory for all students.

As to general statistics, a widely used text was Kreynin, R.S.: *Course of Statistics* that appeared in the USSR before the last war. We had a translation of the 1946 edition by Gosplanizdat in Moscow. It was a booklet of about 130 pages. It included the following chapters: topic of statistics, data collection, grouping and statistical tables, distributions, averages, index numbers, associations, time series, method of sampling, and graphic presentation. It was a verbal presentation of basic ideas of each chapter with numerical illustrations from different fields of data collection and no formulas. The text was a kind of popular reading material for purposes of general education. The reader obtained from the text some idea of statistics although many parts can hardly be understood without more information and, at least, some elementary algebraic treatment. For instance, without elements of descriptive statistics it is difficult to understand the concept of sampling distributions, estimation, precision of estimates, etc.

However, Kreynin's textbook was a relatively high level compendium of theory. Other books went into a more reduced material. At the Department of Economics of the University of Belgrade the teaching of statistics was more elaborate than at other schools. The professor of general statistics was N.Popovich who prepared for students the textbook *Statistics*, (Belgrade 1947). The text included a general introduction to statistics and its topics by Popovich. Then followed translations of Russian authors: Nemchinov (Basic elements of statistics and its history), Yezhov (Grouping), Strumilin (Tasks and problems of Soviet statistics), Pisarev (Methodological issues of Soviet statistics) and Volin (Statistics in the service of politics in the works of V.I. Lenin). This was a small size textbook of 215 pages and was obligatory for students of economics.

There were some other textbooks by our authors. They were of the same type. For that reason it was customary to have, within a single small size volume, an introductory chapter of general statistics and, in the continuation, a presentation of specific fields of statistics.

These specialized fields of statistics referred to basic concepts of the field concerned, information about what data are useful in this field, and what the existing system of data collection is doing. For illustration, a widely used text was Scholz, S.V.: *Course of Agricultural Statistics* that was translated from Russian and published in Zagreb in 1948. It included the following chapters: basic issues of agricultural statistics (aims, units, grouping of data, averages), land use, statistics of plant production, livestock statistics, statistics of agricultural production, labor statistics and productivity of work, cost of production, mechanization, and statistical reporting at kolkhoses. In each chapter the related concepts are presented. Thus, livestock statistics includes livestock numbers, livestock production, indicators of livestock production, varieties of livestock, average number of livestock, organization of livestock statistics at kolkhoses, improvement of varieties of livestock, turnover of livestock, components of livestock production, etc. The same approach is used in other chapters.

Similarly, statistics of culture and arts is divided into the following chapters: culture and arts, public education, publishing, and self-management. In the area of science, data are collected about scientific institutes, academies of sciences, academic councils, lexicographic institutions, patent bureaux, institutions for the protection of antiquities, scientific and professional associations, and the education of scientific personnel. Within each of these topics characteristics are presented that need to be used in data collection together with the related concepts and definitions, periodicity of data collection, etc.

An equivalent approach is used in chapters about culture and arts, public education, etc.

A similar approach is used in the most common manuals for students. Known illustrations of such manuals are: *Material for Studies of Statistics*, published by Scientific books for students of economics, Belgrade, 1949 and *Manual of Statistics*, published by Federal Planning Commission, Belgrade, 1948. The latter included the following chapters: basic tasks and methods, industrial statistics, agricultural statistics, statistics of investments, automobile transport, statistics of communal economy (city areas, housing, housing conditions of the population, communal enterprises, etc.), retail trade, financial statistics, labor force statistics, population and health statistics, and educational statistics.

36

It is thus seen that characteristics of the new statistical education were:

i) very reduced presentation of basic concepts of the theory. The material covered is essentially insufficient to make any use of statistical methodology. In addition, the theory is separated from specialized statistics. No use is made of courses of general statistics in the subsequent specialized statistics;

ii) specialized statistics is heavily oriented toward the subject matter of the related fields. It covers the material that is greatly a part of subject matter studies. For persons familiar with subject matter there is very little in this statistics that adds to the already acquired knowledge.

As a result of the orientation to this type of topics, statistical courricula of the various university departments were mostly very short. There was not much to talk about. The programmes of the majority of schools did not go beyond one semester courses. An exception was the department of economics, where short courses were given on several topics, such as statistics of prices, national income, agricultural statistics, statistics of transport, demography, etc. This is why the department of economics was declared the central school of statistics and statistical education. It has kept this designation till today.

Another result of this orientation is the equalization of programmes of statistics at different levels within the same subject matter. The school of medicine (leading to M.D. degree) and a school of medical assistants would provide the same course of statistics. After the theory was dropped out and the interest abolished in problems and research, not more than purely conceptual and operational matters remain. They are the same at any level of presentation.

Needless to say, these approaches have contributed to the elimination of the statistical profession. Behind each profession there is particular knowledge and specific skills that the members of the profession have to possess to qualify for membership. If you want to be a shoemaker, a mason or a tailor, you have to know something that other people do not know.

This was not so in statistics. A couple of hours of reading of essential instructions related to a particular field together with some participation in operational matters were sufficient to acquire all the know-how needed. Even that much was not always needed. In these early years, I was sent to Montenegro to help establish the statistical office of that republic. As there were no staff available, I had to visit the head of the office responsible for the allocation of veterans to different agencies. As he was not in, I arranged with his assistant to get five persons of whom X was recommended for a higher position. Afterwards we went to report the deal to the head. When I mentioned X, he said: "Why do you want to put X in statistics? You have to be careful in dealing with people. X is an intelligent guy".

This was a widely spread opinion about statistics. My wife was a school teacher. On one occasion her colleague asked: "What does your husband do"? She answered: "He works for a ministry". Another colleague, who knew me, said: "Why don't you say statistician"? My wife added simply: "I would be ashamed of having a statistician as my husband. This is usually a job for people who are good for nothing else".

Developments in statistical education contributed to this attitude. Before the war, the main institution for statistical education in Yugoslavia was the school of law. Teaching was in the hands of lawyers who were responsible for other topics and were given the course of statistics as a secondary job.

After the war, lawyers continued to dominate the teaching of statistics. However, they encountered more and more difficulties. They started dropping out. Lawyers did not feel comfortable in medical matters or in the face of agricultural problems. This is why the corps of teachers substantially expanded to include economists, engineers, agronomists, surgeons, etc. In this way an understanding of the subject matter on the part of teachers was secured. As there was no theory of statistics, the knowledge of which would serve as a prerequisite, the door of teaching opened wide to people from any profession. However, the practice prevailed that each school preferred a teacher of statistics from its own profession. Medical schools want physicians, schools of agronomy want agronomists, the department of economy an economist, etc. These teachers of statistics contributed substantially to the poor reputation of statistics in that period. Their knowledge of statistics was reduced to very little. Nor was their knowledge of the own profession very much. Otherwise they would not have abandoned it. Thus, statistics represented a marginal activity that did not impress anybody.

The recruitment of staff for government statistics followed similar approaches. The vacancy announcements would put emphasis on education in the subject matter concerned. Should there be no candidates of that type any other education would be considered.

Promotions were based on the same criteria. The implementation of the system of work prescribed is the quality to be considered. If, however, some staff study mathematics or the mathematical theory of statistics - these studies would be considered as a purely personal matter that does not contribute to the ability of a good statistician.

Reference has been made to the classification of statisticians that we took over from the Soviets. This classification was based on the fact that statisticians are employed in agencies dealing with quite different subject matters. Thus, we had "statistician-economist", "statistician-demographer", "statistician-physician", etc. The most common was "statistician-economist" in agreement with the view that statistics is primarily concerned with economic data and economic phenomena.

As to the meaning of this classification, it might reflect the old dispute regarding the relative merit of statistical knowledge versus subject matter knowledge. In other words, if a person is involved in some statistical work, such as data collection or designing of experiments in an agricultural research station, should the emphasis, in the selection of the candidate for this work, be on the subject matter or statistics? Is No. 1 the know-how in statistics or the subject matter?

The problem is very old and will probably stay permanently on the agenda of those who are responsible for the recruitment of staff for statistical work.

A variety of views were expressed on this subject. Morris Hansen, an authority on the theory of surveys, told me: "I feel qualified to take surveys in any field, no matter what the subject matter is". In other words, the essential knowledge is statistics. Experience in the subject matter is contributed by others. Surveys are always taken by a group of persons with expertise in different matters. P.V. Sukhatme, the leading authority in agricultural statistics, was a mathematical statistician. However, he insisted on the priority of subject matter. It is interesting to point out that his successor in the position of the director of the Indian Institute of Agricultural Statistics was an agronomist, V.G. Panse. He also earned a wide reputation for his work. Gérard Théodore, the dynamic chief of French agricultural statistics, was himself a graduate of L′ Ecole Polytechnique, viz. a general purpose school with emphasis on mathematics and physics. He thought that agricultural statisticians should be agronomists with a study of statistics added to agronomy.

It is obvious that the top professional achievements in statistics were made by people with very different backgrounds. Any generalization would probably be in conflict with reality. Sukhatme was involved in agricultural experimentation on small Indian farms whose operators were illiterate in most cases. It was thus normal that he was primarily interested in statisticians familiar with life in villages, farmers, agricultural practices, the psychology of people, etc. This was the condition to develop cooperation. On the other hand, Morris Hansen was doing survey work in the US where the degree of sophistication achieved in data collection was extremely high. This is why awareness was needed of experiences in a wide range of survey problems, the ability to design studies and experiments, skills in the development of new methodological techniques, etc. The emphasis is of necessity on statistical know-how.

In light of that the classification that we got from the Soviets does not seem to be connected with the above dispute. The dispute refers to the relative merits of specialization in statistics versus the subject matter. In our case the knowledge of statistics was reduced to very little. The same was true of the subject matter. Knowledge of the economy would be needed if statisticians were obliged to provide an economic interpretation of data. In fact, this was the primary duty of economists involved in planning. Because of their role, they were supposed to have a broad knowledge of economic problems that could not be expected from statisticians. It seems, therefore, that our classification was primarily based on formal criteria. "Statistician-economist" is the name of a person involved in the production of economic data in a broad sense. It is not an indication of any knowledge. Most professionals in our office had the title "statistician-economist" without ever having studied any economics.

After we broadened our knowledge of the Soviet government statistics we realized that it caused embarrassment to all of us who went through a regular process of education. The Soviet approach reminded me of an experience that I had in the school of artillery. I did my military service in prewar Yugoslavia, at the School of artillery reserve officers. The normal practice was to put in that school the university graduates from a department of sciences, the theory being that the boys who graduated in science would be faster than the others in digesting the artillery matters needed by a reserve officer. The assumption was correct under certain circumstances. Our education was particularly important in the ranging and laying process as we were able to use a large number of methods depending upon the conditions of work. If time was available, we were able to take into account all sorts of elements, such as wind, temperature, humidity, pressure, strength of propellent, degree of wear of the gun, etc.

It took me nine months to graduate from our old school of artilery. On the other hand, from the Soviet instructors I learned the theory of ranging and laying that did not require more than half of an hour. If you see the target, you do this and this. In case you don't see the target, you do this. In both cases the explanation was extremely short, straightforward, and did not require any education.

I realized that my knowledge of artilery was quite above the ability of the Soviet instructors. I made a mistake to report my findings to the chief Soviet instructor. He did not like my words. He put a mask of rigidity over his face and told me: "We use the artillery for mass attacks. In some cases hundreds of guns participate. In such a situation very rough methods of ranging and laying are adequate. The refinements that you are talking about are not applicable. They represent a waste". He left me and never wanted to talk to me again.

The Soviet colonel was right if his assumptions were correct. As the assumptions are frequently not correct, the superiority of a broad education is obvious. It provides the ability to observe the situation, identify the circumstances, and use the method that efficiently solves the problem.

The same philosophy was encountered in statistics. To us, the statistical system of a country was based on a continuous flow of its constituent elements, such as resources, facilities, interest in data, state of the theory, experience, specific know-how, international cooperation, etc. Each stage had its problems, limitations, and inadequacies. In each situation problems had to be identified, solutions worked out and a programme of improvements proposed. The process went on without ever ending. There was nothing that could not be better. This is why we kept observing, studying, and improving. This is a permanent task.

Contrary to such a view of statistics as a product of man, Soviet statistitics was presented as a revelation, a creation of a supernatural intelligence. In none of the books or instructions that were circulated to us was there a single word about problems, difficulties, errors, inadequate solutions, evaluation of work in different areas, etc. The system had to be accepted and implemented without any discussion or doubt as in the case of religious prescriptions.

We found ourselves in conflict with scientific approaches that imply recognition of alternatives and insist on observation and study as the means of making choices. In Soviet statistics there were no alternatives or more or less satisfactory solutions. The imported books brought to us *the* statistical system of a socialist society.

Here again I was slow in understanding what my attitude was supposed to be toward a revelation. I failed to draw consequences from my experience with the chief instructor in the Soviet artillery. At staff meetings I sometimes asked questions about various issues, pointed out dangers that followed from a blind adoption of the Soviet system, and indicated a variety of approaches used in different countries, etc. Some centuries back that attitude was equivalent to saying that the Holy Scripture could be improved by taking away or adding various paragraphs. This was a sufficient enough sin to be burned. Fortunately, that time has gone. However, I developed the reputation of a man who is trying to confuse the others with his questions and references to possible improvements. In the eyes of friendly members of the communist party I was a product of "bourgeois education" who was unable to understand essential matters and offer a constructive contribution to "our statistics". My bourgeois education has certainly helped me to fortify my position at the bottom of the payroll.

Although we were at the very beginning of the process of adoption of the Soviet system, it became clear that a number of fundamental issues needed to be raised. I have in mind the implications of the conflict between the rational and irrational, between faith and reason, between an *a priori* acceptance of a system of ideas and practices on the one hand, and the ability to be critical at each step of work on the other hand.

V In the United States

As an employee of the State Statistical Office, I had the opportunity to go on a mission to the United States on a fellowship of the United Nations Relief and Rehabilitation Administration (UNRRA).

The UNRRA was established in 1943 at a meeting in the White House presided over by Franklin D.Roosevelt. The aim of the UNRRA was to assist the war-ravaged nations by providing relief supplies, such as food, medicines, clothing, etc. The policy of the UNRRA was to help people help themselves. Therefore, in addition to goods and services the UNRRA also operated a programme of fellowships to give a chance to technicians of assisted countries to familiarize themselves with work in the respective fields of developed countries and improve the possibilities of their own countries to speed up their rehabilitation process.

Yugoslavia was one of the assisted countries. In line with its aims, the UNRRA established a programme of fellowships for Yugoslavia. One of them was assigned to statistics to sending somebody abroad to study the achievements during the war and help, upon returning, in the use of these achievements at home.

The UNRRA set several conditions on the selection of candidates. Each candidate had to be reasonably fluent in English and possess knowledge of the subject matter. Both of these qualities had to be tested at UNRRA office by a foreign staff member.

In the fall of 1945 I was summoned to the personnel office and the head of the office told me that I was selected by SSO, as their candidate, for a fellowship in the US.

When I heard the news I could not believe my ears. Going abroad at that time was a privilege reserved for the most faithful members of the YCP. Even in that narrow group many investigations were made in connection with candidates. It was an absolute necessity to make sure that those who were let go with a passport, would return. This was a period when many people attempted to cross the border illegally. Some of them succeeded. However, a large number of them fell into the hands of the police. They were sentenced afterwards to several years of prison. The police did their best to stop the illegal traffic across the borders. The refugees were a source of much stronger propaganda against the communist regime in Yugoslavia than the party was able to counterbalance

42

with its own propaganda. The police also took all possible steps to infiltrate the ranks of guides across the borders. This further reduced any chance of success. A good and reliable guide thus became very expensive.

Against this background, I was unable to understand the reasons that led SSO to select me as their candidate for the passport. Apart from narrow group of people who travelled abroad on government business it was practically impossible for a person like myself, viz. "a nobody", to get a passport, to cross the border without any danger, and use afterwards the position of independence to make decisions about his own future. I did not know anybody who got a passport. Nor had I heard that it happened to anybody.

The head of personnel told me the news and kept quiet for some time. He was looking at my face as if he wanted to read what my reactions would be. However, an outline of my attitude was already prepared. I produced a "poker face". I am sure that there was no sign on my face of any feeling or emotion. I think I looked as a dead body, as if I was not interested in at all.

After some time he said: "Do you accept to go? You are not telling me what your decision is".

My answer was ready before he finished his sentence. I told him: "I have no decision. It is not a simple matter. I have to check first with my wife and see if she would be willing to remain alone. If she says "No", that will be my answer to you. However, if she says "Yes" and is willing to stay alone at home, I have to consider the matter from all possible angles. I will probably need several days to make up my mind".

I did not want to show him any of my cards. I also wanted to gain time and see if anything would happen in the meantime that could tell me more about the situation and thus facilitate my orientation. I was happy with the postponment of my answer. It seemed to me that a flat acceptance of his offer would be interpreted as a desire to leave the country and never come back.

My calculation proved to be correct. I obliged the head of personnel to continue talking. In fact, he said: "I am afraid I am not able to wait for your answer. You are the only candidate from SSO and there is a fixed appointment at the UNRRA office for our candidate to pass a test of English. Knowledge of statistics will also be tested. The test is on the day after tomorrow at 10 A.M. The maximum time that I can afford to give you for consideration is until tomorrow morning".

He had given me a precious piece of information. There would be an exam at the UNRRA office by a person who had an Anglo-Saxon name. I thought that this fact explained the whole story. The director of SSO probably did not want to run the risk of being blamed for the lack of cooperation with UNRRA. I was the only person at SSO able to understand English. Thus, the required test administered by a neutral foreigner made the difference.

I left the office of personnel more excited than before, at the moment when the news was communicated to me. The source of my excitement was in the fact that my chances were quite serious. My name came up because there was nobody else. The

UNRRA's assistance to Yugoslavia was highly appreciated by the authorities. It greatly helped the regime to stabilize. As a result, Yugoslavia was ready to do everything possible to please the UNRRA and offer good cooperation. If the UNRRA decided to provide a fellowship in statistics it was not a matter of discussion or refusal. It just had to be implemented.

Most of my compatriots of that period would have been excited in my situation although the reasons might be different. Many of them envied me because of the possibility to get out of the country without any risk and settle down afterwards in another part of the world. The number of those who wished their life to move in that direction was quite considerable primarily because of childish mistakes of the YCP in the exercise of power. A widespread malcontent developed among the people because they felt at the mercy of a power that left no escape whatsoever. The borders were hermetically closed and heavily controlled. People were in a trap. Within the trap they were persecuted from the morning till the evening by endless and boring political propaganda through radio, speeches at the place of work, in the streets, at the place of residence, etc. No wonder that a large proportion of people started dreaming of a simple and quiet life without politics and speeches. In their imagination the people saw that life at any point of the globe outside the national territory. This is why a large proportion of people kept in their mind the principle: "Let me abandon the country and go over the border no matter where". This was a tragic effect that the YCP has produced.

My new situation brought to my mind the problem of the border, the future of the country, my own future, the confusion on the part of the population and hundreds of other issues. Topics were moving in my mind one after the other as in a movie. I was unable to concentrate on anything else. Nor could I imagine doing some work. I left the office to find my wife and share with her my thoughts. She was at home. I told her the news without any excitement, quietly, as if it were one of hundreds of issues that currently occur to everybody. It was not a calculated attitude on my part. It was spontaneous. I already had enough excitement. It was time to calm down.

My wife did not open her mouth. It was probably too much for her to be able to react. A reaction means a particular type of response. She probably needed time to collect her thoughts. After I saw her serious face, I also realized that I needed to relax. I put myself in a chair, covered my face with my hands and let the movie of my life to travel over memories and past events. I closed my eyes and I saw myself in the village where I was born. I saw the cows and pigs, the creek, the forest, the piece of cheese in my sack, and hundreds of other memories of that kind. I saw myself at the top of trees in my neighborhood. Later on I was jumping into the water of the creek, running barefoot after cows, admiring the flowers in the morning, enjoying the freshness of the air after the rain.....

I always felt I was born lucky. I had so many nice things to think about. My memories were always fresh and alive. They were the life itself. I would say: "Horsy, come to me". And the horse would come to me and put his head over my shoulder. His mouth would be by my ear and he would tell me how much he loved me. Then I would say: "Piggy, come and have an apple". My little pig would come to me, lean on my legs, and eat the apple. There was a communication between us that nobody else would understand. We wanted to repeat each day how much we enjoyed each other's company.

Each human being has memories of this kind. However, they are particularly detailed and strong in the life of migrants, such as those from the region where I was born. In the air they breathe there is something telling them that sooner or later their turn will come. As young children they absorb the idea of migration as life's necessity. They listen to stories about those who left and they know that they will be going away themselves to continue the line of life.

For that big day and the life that would follow in unknown places, they need capital to live on. However, their capital does not consist of banknotes. The capital of poor migrants consists of emotions and memories. In course of preparations for their departure they retain in their mind many insignificant impressions and details of memories that they keep reviewing, strengthening, and absorbing. When they remain alone afterwards in their new world, these memories provid them with company and help them overcome moments of crisis. In case of despair, the memories help cheer up. When doubts arise and energies get exhausted, the memories are always rich enough to bring in encouraging feelings. The memories strengthen the life whenever the need arises.

At an early stage of life, I left my creek, my horse, and my pig. However, I lived with them all the time. Memories were an essential part of my daily reality. There was a physical distance between the place of my residence and the place of my dreams. That distance did not bother me. The memories helped me to suck the substance of life. Whenever needed, they helped me to become fit for life and safe on my legs. I thought I gained that way a sufficient capital for the rest of my life. I felt I was ready to go. I was prepared to start my cycle.

At that moment I realized that a new current of thought was on the way to invade my mind. The head of personnel told me that I would be going to America. It was America that appeared to me now as a new reality of my life. I plunged deeper into my chair and told myself: "Oh, America".

I wished at that moment to speak to people in my village. They would understand my feelings. We are tuned in the same way. America was our obsession, our hope, our dream, and a direction to which our thoughts fly at moments when we felt miserably small and fragile in front of the burdens of life. America is the word that a poor man whispers after he has exhausted all the means of helping himself. America is a source of hope and warmth for a man who looks waryingly at his children and is unable to rear them decently. America is the longing of all those who were humiliated by the power of magnates or those who were deprived of justice or rejected in their desire for compassion and sincerity. America raised our hopes in our misery; America is our base and our resort.

At that moment, the syndrom of America pressed on my mind. America was a part of the blood that circulated continuously through my veins. However, I was never decisive enough to raise the issue of America with myself and formulate, in that connection, ideas about my future. Maybe I was afraid of the consequences. Thinking about America presses on us to accept the voice of destiny and speed up the departure. "Uncle Simon has gone, our neighbors John and George have gone", I told myself. At that moment my mind jumped immediately to a new important matter. My father moved away from the area of his origin but he stopped on the way as he was afraid of too much responsibility for a large family. However, at one of those moments when destiny is being transferred from one generation to the other, he told me: "I started and you continue. You should do what I was not able to do".

In fact, I had no choice. Deep in my conscience I was aware of that. The only real subject of consideration was the date. I knew that.

At that moment the movie of my mind started working violently. I had seen in my mind a long line of people carrying bags in their hands and heading for Ohio, Pennsylvania, and California. In this line was Uncle Simon, John, George, and so many others. I also saw myself standing by as the line was moving. And when the tail of the line approached me I jumped in without any luggage as if I could not miss my chance.

My sudden decision to join the line embarrassed me. "How can it be that you take such a vital decision without considering each aspect of it"?, I asked myself. As soon as I put this question to myself, I rushed with an answer: "All of those whom you have seen in the line have done it under very difficult conditions. They had nothing to help them but a deep hope. You have everything. You have your passport, you will get your ticket. You will also get some money. Nobody who went on this trip from our region was as lucky as you are. You have no reason whatsoever to hesitate".

This argument impressed me. I got the feeling that it was strong enough to speed up the developments. In fact, since my boyhood I had put a lot of time to thinking about migration. Before the war I did not realize my intention as I wanted to finish school and add to my education some knowledge that I expected to be important. After the war quite a new situation appeared. Going away was qualified as a rejection of the "privilege to live in socialism". It meant opting for the capitalist society. Those who would express that wish would immediately be put in the category of the enemy. I of course did not care for that interpretation. However, migration could only be realized illegally. In other words, those who are lucky to realize the idea are going away for good. They have no hope of coming back as long as the conditions in the country remain as they are.

I was not willing to accept that type of trip to the unknown. In fact, I realized that the protective mechanism of my memories was based on the illusion of a temporary separation from my origin. A voice told me frequently: "You go wherever you want. Your memories will enable you to overcome difficulties provided you believe you will go back. You have to have the illusion of an open road back; you have to be able to fool yourself that your return is in your hands. If this illusion is destroyed for one reason or the other you will also be destroyed. The memories will lose their protective power and your existence will become miserable and frightening".

It might be that my people had the same feelings. Most people are not interested in politics nor are they willing to get involved in it. This is why an aggressive propaganda that follows the people like a shadows at every step they make and bores their mind continuously - is generally considered to be a national disaster. The conditions become unbearable if propaganda is combined with various forms of pressure, discrimination, flattery, servility, and the like. The outcome is the philosophy: "Save yourself if you can". People start running around like frightened animals. They abandon their homes,

46

their parents and relatives. They quit their jobs and leave their birth places. They throw away everything they have with the sole hope in their mind to get rid of the pressure, live again in peace and conquer the freedom to follow ones own conscience.

It was barbarous to put people in that situation. It was barbarous to oblige them to make desperate choices. It is sufficient to recollect the events that took place in the sea around Vietnam. Those who survived physically had to experience another tragedy that became a permanent patter of their life. They had to live with the destroyed illusion of being able to return home. The roots that tie people firmly to the ground are thus cut. People are separated from their past, from the source of the substance of life. Gradually they bow their head, their happiness vanishes, and they enter an immense vacuum. They become shadows of human beings.

I had no problem of this kind. My attitude was clear and firm: no matter what happens I shall not leave my country as long as there are difficulties in coming back at the moment I feel the need for it.

I had another point that helped me establish a very definite orientation in the new developments.

In the last two years of high school, I started discussions of political issues with my colleagues. If a single word is needed to designate our orientations, it cannot be anything but socialism. However, that socialism had a very vague meaning. In our understanding, socialism was the society that would emphasize qualities such as justice, honesty, freedom for everybody, respect for human dignity, education for everybody, programmes in favor of the poor, etc. Later on we continued with respect for these ideals. Most of us kept growing in that direction. I was happy about the impact of these orientations on the future of the country.

The postwar developments in Yugoslavia were far from being a realization of these ideals. A brutal violation of freedom created a general and deep concern. The rapid indulgence of the political top in luxury opened up a danger of a new and reckless exploitation of the country by the ruling class. In a very short time flattering, servility, and submissivness became standard behavior with respect to the power. Together with these qualities appeared corruption as a key to a large part of decisions. Dinners, banquets, receptions, abuses of office, reciprocity in favors, and cash as a condition to get the right recognized by the law to everybody - invaded all the pores of the society.

It was painful to observe such a degeneration of the idea of socialism. However, this was the reality for a relatively long period. As a result, I saw myself in a dilemma. On the one side there was opposition to the ongoing programme of the regime in the form of withdrawal from public life and reduction of one's own involvement in survival. On the other hand, I saw participation in the implementation of the ongoing government programmes, hoping that the exaggerations of the regime would be reduced making it possible for the YCP to come, in the future, nearer to socialist ideals. On this road toward a better future, I expected an essential contribution from the younger generation of technicians who were lucky to get their education under regular prewar conditions. I thought that a demonstrated interest in the improvement of work and concrete contributions along this line would develop an appreciation of a cooperative attitude and would help the party overcome the era of slogans and empty formulas in favor of hard work as the only possible basis for the establishment of a socialist society.

In line with these views I thought I had a duty to do my best to succeed in the work given to me, no matter what it was. This is how I interpreted my attitude toward the ongoing political developments. I was also convinced that, by doing so, I would put myself in the service of socialist ideals. In other words, I had to stay on and offer hard work.

I was thus divided into two opposing streams. One of them was in my subconsciousness. It had no theory to justify its course. It was a kind of destiny, an inherited drive toward America. The other was a superimposed rational construction of duty, the responsibility toward my own country, a desire to contribute a share to the construction of the society of tomorrow.

However, at this moment I discovered that the opposing streams disappeared. "They are sending you to America for work reasons", I said to myself. "Your duty and your responsibility take you there. At the same time you realize your destiny. You go to your America without breaking with your past. You get a passport. You will come back and so you have everything".

This new course of thoughts increased my excitement. However, I kept quiet as I was not sure that I took into account all the aspects of the case. I asked my wife to keep me company for a walk. We did not talk. Later on we went to bed. We did not sleep the whole night. However, neither of us opened the mouth.

The next morning my wife told me: "You go now to see your head of personnel. Tell him that you accept to go".

This was probably the result of her long thinking during the night. She was as much concerned about this as I was. Her input was probably much bigger than mine. She was aware of my position. She accepted the consequences. She helped me greatly by accepting the sacrifice of joining the group of wives whose husbands entered the stream toward America.

The attitude of my wife took away from me a real heavy burden. She gave me the wings. I thought I would easily overcome all other problems.

The head of personnel accepted my statement as any other insignificant matter. I said: "My wife has accepted to remain alone. She thought that I should go". He did not show much interest in either me or my wife. He took a piece of paper from his desk and told me: "Tomorrow morning at 10 A.M. you go to the UNRRA office, room ..., and ask for Mr ... He will test your knowledge".

The next morning I went to see Mr ... He was a nice American. He encouraged me by saying that he was neither a statistician nor an expert in English. He said that he wanted an impression about me. He told me that statistics was a boring subject to him. He was in charge of the preparation of different reports and tables in various offices in the course of his career and was never happy when he had to do it. He also told me that my English was good as compared to other candidates. Eventually he wished me a good trip to US. That was all about my exam.

48

From there I went home. I could not work anyway. I was not in a mood to discuss the issue with my colleagues in the office. Their questions would annoy me. On the other hand, I thought that my wife would be at home expecting news about my exam. In fact, it was so. She did not go to work on that day as she had too many things to settle for herself.

I told her about the test. We thought that the test was a step that took us nearer to a successful termination of our adventure. Although it did not have much importance, it introduced peace in our house. It cheered us up. The tension was gone and we became able to talk. In fact, we had a very long talk. My wife checked her understanding of my motives and my position in general. She realized how important this trip might be for our future. She thought that the price of our separation and so many inconveniences was not high as compared to what was at stake. We both had a feeling that our position was essentially clear and we were happy about that.

We decided to keep quiet about my trip. Although the police and the official representatives of the agencies involved decided to give me a fellowship, each communist society is full of "informants", viz. persons who go to the police to remind them of mistakes involved in this or that decision. In my case such a report might be: "It was decided to propose Zarkovich for a fellowship in the US. This was probably done because people do not know him. In fact, he is a great enemy. If you really make a mistake to give him a fellowship and the passport he will never come back. In addition, he will do so much harm to our country in the US. You better stop that fellowship before it is too late".

Such reporting is a powerful means. It does not require any particular effort. Also, the informant remains anonimous. In addition, through their reporting, the informants recommend themselves as "patriots" or "loyal citizens". Needless to say, the prerequisite of the system of informants is a strong police. The operation of the system requires a lot of work. In totalitarian regimes this is not an obstacle. In return, the police would learn all sorts of things about their citizens and contribute to the spread of the belief that police know everything. This belief is of course a means of keeping people under control. This is why it is spread around by the police itself.

The next day I went to the UNRRA travel office to arrange for the issuance of a passport. After the passports were ready and distributed to us, we were told that we had three days to prepare ourselves and report to the UNRRA travel office on the fourth day in the morning.

I went to my office to see the head of personnel, and tell him that I was about to leave. I asked for farewell instructions. He told me that he had nothing to say. I checked with the directors's secretary to inquire whether he wished to tell me something. Later on she rang me up to say that he had nothing for me. As a result, I left the office puzzled and sad. I expected that, as a part of the agency, I would get at least an expression of good wishes and a friendly smile.

I kept in mind this treatment by the office and I always felt bad about that.

On the day of the planned departure, I reported to the UNRRA travel office with my suitcase, coat, and everything else that I needed for a long trip. However, we were told to come the next day at the same time. The next day we got the same information. There was no plane coming from the West. This is how I kept coming to the UNRRA office each morning and going home after an hour or so. After about two weeks of unsuccessful departures the day came when we were told that an aircraft was available for us. Each of us was given a letter "To whom it may concern". It contained our respective names and information about the purpose of our trip. At the end there was an appeal to all the allied military authorities to provide us with any help needed. After that we boarded a DC-3 military aircraft. Our destination was Vienna.

In Vienna we were taken to a military camp. There we stayed for about a week. In Vienna we again boarded a military aircraft and landed in Frankfurt. Again a camp. Some days later we continued to Paris, where a kind of UNRRA office was located that was responsible for all the operations in Europe.

The UNRRA office in Paris was located at the Hotel Moderne, Place de la Republique. There we got our "godmother", an elderly British lady whom I still remember very well because of her intelligence, skill, and patience. Most of my colleagues were not able to understand any word of English. It was only because of the intelligence of that lady that these people overcame all the difficulties and felt happy.

I was in the group of fellowships who were planned for US. We were told that our curricula had to go to Washington to obtain the authorization for the issuance of visas. It was obvious that our stay in Paris would be a long one. In fact, it was so. The first week passed in filling out forms, talking to officers, preparing photographs, writing study programmes, etc.

After the first week was over, we became a burden for the UNRRA office. They did not expect to keep people for long periods as they were not equipped for that. The problem of visas added to their trouble. Obviously the office did not assume that it would take such a long time. In that situation I proposed that they send us on trips to different parts of France. The proposal was accepted with pleasure. I made my first trip to Nancy, Alsace, Lorrain, etc. I saw the provincial post-war statistics. After some time I came back and planned my next trip to Marseille, Toulouse, Bordeaux, Lion, etc. Afterwards I went to Normandy.

After I covered France I proposed a visit to the statistical office in London. The trip was arranged and I stayed about two weeks in London.

After an additional period in Paris our visas eventually became available. On our way to the US, we went to Bordeaux. We took one of the Liberty ships that was going back to the US. However, our destination was not known. The ship was unloaded at Bordeaux and was available to whoever was ready to rent it. The company decided to sail toward the US without a fixed destination. We were told that any port between Central America and Labrador would be considered. However, we were lucky. We landed in Baltimore and moved the same day to Washington.

The next day I was at the UNRRA Headquarters in Washington.

At that time I was not able to appreciate the organization, the decisions that were behind it, and the statesmen who had the courage to start building something quite new

50

in human history. A large crowd of fellows including myself came from many parts of the world to absorb the know-how and make it available afterwards to so many different parts of the world. The resources were secured to operate a large organization as the UNRRA was. And above all, the cooperation was secured from thousands of people in agencies, factories, universities, and so many other places to devote their time and attention to fellows from other countries and help them as much as it was possible. When I go back in my mind to these days I remember with gratitude and admiration the dedication of many people who did not spare time and energy to help us in our studies. Only now that I look at UNRRA from a distance of time I realize how lucky I was to enjoy the benefits of that organization.

The attitude of the UNRRA officers in the organization of my studies was as good as I could wish. They did their best to find useful places for me to see. However, they also accepted my own views. As I had rather firm views, they concentrated their effort on the steps needed to implement smoothly my own programme rather than trying to impose their programme. In this way I achieved everything that I had on my own list and quite a few additional matters that I was not aware of.

As a result of that programme I started with studies of agricultural statistics at the US Department of Agriculture. A good part of the methods of agricultural statistics that I had a chance to see was not applicable outside the US. The methods assumed large fields of the same crop, the availability of roads, use of cars by the field staff of the Crop Reporting Board, detailed maps with farm houses introduced on maps, etc. More useful was the study of censuses of agriculture. The rich programme (number of questions) used in the US offers to census takers from other countries an excellent basis for their choice. Equally useful was the methodology, viz. the formulation of questions, variations of census programmes by states, the tabulation of data, the content of supporting documents, such as instructions for the enumerators and supervisors, etc. I particularly appreciated the information regarding the uses of data. In that respect there was something spectacular in the current practice of the Crop Reporting Board. A day before the release of important reports, the staff of the Board would work the whole night and nobody was allowed to leave the office. All communication with the office was controlled by the police. After the release is distributed the next day at a time fixed in advance, a big crowd of journalists, reporters, business people, etc. would precipitate to telephone boxes and inform their respective agencies of the news released. This is a spectacular aspect of the use of data and public interest in statistics. I have not seen anything similar in any other country. Some implications of that practice were obvious at the time when I first saw it. The statistical work that is accompanied by so much public concern is able to count on all sorts of facilities that are needed to carry out the work adequately. The use of data is also a pressure on statisticians to keep thinking about improvements of their work. Uses of data thus represent a stimulus that is as important as resources. At that time I became aware of that. Many years later, on the basis of our own experiences in Yugoslavia, I had another chance to appreciate fully the relationships between the quality of statistical work and the public concern about data.

After I was through with the USDA, I went to the US Bureau of the Census. My studies there had a decisive importance for my subsequent work. The Bureau of the Census was at that time an ideal place for studies of government data collection work. The Bureau was a leading place in the methodology of data collection. The period when

I went there was the beginning of a revolution in statistics created by the introduction of a new statistical theory.

At that time, quite a lot of literature on sampling was already available. In addition to being a pioneering place in sampling, the Bureau of the Census closely followed developments along that line in the whole world. It was thus very well equipped for guiding students of sampling. I used the opportunity and started systematic studies of sampling. It gave me a chance to broaden my understanding of sampling that followed from earlier studies of German literature.[5] Sampling was the way how I interpreted my duty toward both the statistics in Yugoslavia and the UNRRA.

The further I went with these studies the more enthusiastic I was about the possibilities that sampling introduced in data collection.

Sample surveys meant the introduction of science to data collection. Sampling rejected assumptions, took the orientation toward facts, and offered the theory of objective conclusions from facts. The theory of sampling operates with concepts, such as minimization, maximization, optimum, efficiency, measurable errors, etc. The philosophy of modern developments was thus introduced in data collection. Sampling also facilitated the introduction of objective procedures in countries with extremely difficult conditions for data collection. Also to mention was the practice of pretesting and experimentation with the aim of avoiding guessing and the related waste of resources. This is how the possibilities arose of getting more and better information within the available amount of resources.

Needless to say, sampling is the philosophy of modern technology transferred to data collection. The language of sampling is the language of science. This is what I thought we badly needed in Yugoslavia. I considered that I had a duty to help flourish science in data collection. In line with this, I talked to many people about future contacts. The names of many important US statisticians were on my lists as persons who were likely to help in the effort to improve statistics in Yugoslavia. I also asked for available literature in all the places that I visited. I sent home many parcels of books at my own expense. We were thus ready to start a center of statistical development in Yugoslavia with support of that development by many of those colleagues in the US who were at the top of statistical centers.

At that time textbooks of sample surveys were not yet available. F.Yates' book *(Sampling Methods for Censuses and Surveys,* Charles Griffin) appeared in 1949, W.E. Deming's book *(Some Theory of Sampling,* Wiley) was issued in 1950 and the one by W.A. Hendricks *(Mathematics of Sampling,* Blacksburg) in 1948. Later on, in 1953 appeared the book by Hansen, Hurwitz, and Meadow *(Sample Survey Methods and Theory,* Vol. I and II, Wiley), W.G. Cochran *(Sampling Techniques,* Wiley) and P.V. Sukhatme *(Sampling Theory of Surveys with Applications,* FAO, Rome). However, with the help of contacts between colleagues it was possible to know what issues were on the agenda of different centers and different authors, what were the books in preparation, etc. While at the Bureau of the Census, I had a chance to see parts of the manuscript of Cochran's book, pieces of the *Chapter in Population Sampling* that was published in

---

5 Gebelein, H.: *Zahl und Wirklichkeit,* von Quelle, Leipzig, 1943.

1947. Later on I also got hold of a copy of P.C. Tang's lectures on sampling. However, I do not remember how I got these lectures. I met Tang later on. This is how I entered the sampling family that kept me informed subsequently about all major developments.

Colleagues from the Census Bureau introduced me to statistical quality control. Needless to say, the Bureau of the Census was not officially involved in the industrial application of statistics. However, the quality control was a very interesting part of the application of statistics. A familiarity with it was a part of modern statistical education. The first class research staff of the Bureau, with whom I was lucky to keep in touch, were competent to talk about quality control.

Quality control refers primarily to some specific techniques, such as acceptance sampling that makes possible an objective estimation of characteristics of goods submitted for inspection. For example, the aim might be the percentage of defective products. Another technique is the control chart that makes possible to follow in time the variations in the process of production with respect to selected characteristics. Generally speaking, quality charts represent a means for a rational supervision of the process of production. They show the characteristics of the process of production "under control", the changes that arise in time with respect to various characteristics, economic effects of these changes, etc. They also indicate the need for interventions to bring the process "under control", the effects of steps taken, and the economic meaning of these interventions as well. It is easy to see that statistical quality control is the introduction of science in the organization of mass production. It speaks the same language as the theory of sample surveys. It represents another contribution that statistics has made in the recent period to improve man's endeavor.

The statistical quality control impressed me very much. It seemed to me a tool that deserves the full attention of the authorities of the country that declared serious ambitions for industrial development. I thought I should be prepared to assist in this direction if the chance arose. Therefore, I went to different places to broaden my information. At Columbia University in New York I studied sequential sampling. At the National Bureau of Standards I studied the role of statistical quality control in industrial standardization. This is what further strengthened my views about the importance of quality control in any country that wants an orientation toward modern efficiency in its own industry.

At the Bureau of the Census, the discussions among colleagues touched frequently on the topic of statistical education. At that time the essential changes in the statistical education had already been made. The basic lines of recent progress resulted from mathematically oriented statistical theory. The education followed this line although there were important differences in the content of courses at various educational centers. This was a period of rapid changes and many new ideas. It was normal that different universities emphasized different sectors of statistics.

On the other hand, European universities were largely moving along the line developed in the last century. Needless to say, some universities were influenced by developments in the Anglo-Saxon countries. However, the bulk of education consisted of a limited amount of descriptive statistics and a great deal of specialized statistics, such as demography, industry, agriculture, labor force, etc. In these areas again the emphasis was not on methodology, viz. the methods of the collection and analysis of data but on the conceptual framework in the respective fields that could better be presented in economic courses. In this type of education neither students nor their teachers had any serious mathematical background. They were obviously not ready to follow new statistical developments in the world.

It was thus clear that statistical education in Yugoslavia was an urgent issue on the agenda. Before new types of curricula are introduced and fresh generations of students brought up, the country will not be able to make use of so many advances that were made recently.

In order to get more detailed information about the state of statistical education in the US, I visited statistical departments of several universities and collected documents that reflected their respective views of statistical education at that moment.

It was also obvious that improvements in Yugoslav statistics could not be carried out unless a reasonable supply of new literature was secured that would give a chance to a larger number of statisticians to familiarize themselves with the new ideas. This was not an easy task to achieve as our fellowships were not sufficient for this purpose. The UNRRA was aware of that shortcoming. They were equally aware of the need to provide us with literature to continue working at home. We, therefore, got an authorization to prepare a list of books that the UNRRA should purchase and ship to Yugoslavia. I collected additional books and documents at the agencies that I visited. In this way a supply was built up that was reasonably complete for a person who wanted to get a view of recent developments.

There was another duty that I imposed on myself. I thought that I had an exceptional chance to live in the US at a moment of transition from war to peace. Big changes were visible everywhere while their impact was difficult to predict. Any observer of world developments had to look at the US. It was obvious that the future of the globe depended largely upon the US, their technology, and the impact of that technology on the social and economic aspects of modern society.

I had particular reason to observe as many aspects of life in the US as I could follow. By coming to the US I realized my dream. It remained to see what was America. Is it able to provide leadership to the world that would include, in addition to technology, political, intellectual, and moral patterns that people would appreciate as their guidance toward future? I read some time ago what Alexis de Tocqueville wrote about America. It filled me with enthusiasm. I found myself in the situation to see where matters stood with America and what my own attitude should be in that respect.

I was aware that my attitude was in conflict with the practices of the YCP. At that time the YCP considered itself a leading force in revolutionary world politics. From that point of view the US was enemy No. 1 of the progressive hopes, protector of capitalism and slavery, the source of all the devils of the capitalist society. Everything was negative. There was nothing to study. I was thus aware that my attitude was at variance with the standards imposed by the YCP. However, I couldn't possibly do otherwise.

No wonder that my position at home has become bad. Some events have taken place that are typical of the conditions under which we lived. Soon after I left Yugoslavia the news speard around that I served for years as an agent of the communist police.

"As a prize for the service that he had made to communist police - say the rumors - he was sent to US". The rumors also offered "proofs". There were probably many other revelations of a similar type. One of them reached me while I was in the US. Namely, some friends of mine, a couple, wrote to me to say how much they were disgusted by hearing that I worked for the police and sent, in that capacity, several people to jails.

Needless to say, there were many interventions from the other camp. One of those who made a fuss about my departure was Radovan Zogovich, the glorified poet of the communist party during the war. His hatred ruined him some years after the war. He also entered the class of people called "nobody". However, while he was at the peak of his power he made an investigation to find out the names of persons who had recommended me for a fellowship and a passport. I heard that he said: "Don't you know what is going to happen? This man is an arch-reactionary and a "provocateur". He hates socialism. He will never come back from the US and will do there a lot of harm to us".

He was not alone in protesting. Nor was Zogovich's language the worst one.

I of course did not care for this interest in me. Instead of paying attention to the gossip, I continued using my leisure time for a study of the US. I had a wonderful opportunity and I decided to make full use of it. I pretended to be a typical European intellectual. I could not miss the chance of looking around, reading, getting explanations, digesting the collected material and attempting some conclusions that my numerous friends in Europe would want to hear. Obviously, I could not pretend that my views and projections would always hold. However, the important point for me was to have my views.

In order to build them up I remember I attended many lectures on topics of interest to me in all the cities where I happened to live. I was buying several newspapers a day, periodicals, magazines, booklets, etc. I bought myself a radio to be able to follow the news. At that time it was not a transistor but a big box that gave me a lot of trouble whan I had to move. I also went to churches to see how people behaved. I talked to common people in the streets, to messangers in offices, elevator operators, etc. I would also accept invitations by my colleagues whom I contacted in the course of my trip to come to their house and see how they live. Quite a few of these contacts are still active.

The study of social and political developments in the postwar period helped me more than anything else to establish a peace of mind and carry out successfully the mission that I had in the US according to my interpretation of the UNRRA's aims. That study told me that a great period of history was over. All over the world people wanted peace and a return to a regular life. Needless to say, it did not mean that all the problems were solved. Between the US and USSR there were many open issues. They might generate major trouble sometime in the future. However, one big war was over and nobody was thinking about another war to settle the remaining issues. Let the next generation worry about the future situation. Our generation has done its duty and it deserves a period of peace.

The message of my studies was clear. It left no alternative to the orientation to go back, roll up one's sleeves and engage fully in the work for the improvement of our conditions. This was the way to be useful, this was the contribution to the chance that a catastrophe of another war be replaced in the future by a less terrible alternative.

This is what I did. I also advised the others to follow this philosophy. I flatter myself that in this way the tragedies and sufferings among my friends and acquaintances were avoided and replaced by constructive effort.

VI An announcement of crisis

In the spring of 1947, while my studies in the US were moving toward an end, the news came to me that Dolfe Vogelnik, the head of SSO, was transferred to another job. The news was interpreted by my colleagues as a shake-up of the whole statistical system. In fact, the news came unexpectedly. No public discussion of any problem ever appeared before. It was thus possible to interpret the removal of Vogelnik as a public recognition on the part of the YCP of a collapse of party views and approaches in statistics.

What happened?

After the YCP took absolute power in its hands, party ranks started broadening rapidly, as is normal in similar situations. The party in power means the right to appoint people to high positions and give them an opportunity to get recognition, prestige, money and everything else that money can buy. New members were pouring in from all directions. However, most of them were just newcomers, viz. people who cannot count on getting more than cramps from the seat of power. The decision making process was held strongly in the hands of a small number of members who joined the party as youngsters and went with it through the hardship of jails, illegal activities, fights, strikes against the prewar bourgeois class, participation in the ranks of war partisans, etc.

Within the narrow group of dignitaries, there were several strata resulting from the application of criteria, such as unconditional devotion to the party line no matter what the issue is, willingness to attack the enemy whenever party matters are at stake, prompt reaction to any form of weakness or tolerance, readiness to inform superiors of any event that might have a bearing on the success of the party line, keeping the party above relatives or friends, etc. On top of that a good party member is obedient, ready to accept orders, carry out instructions, accept the matters as presented, etc. Particular importance is attached to special merits, such as prewar membership, years in the jail, exile, illegal activities abroad, participation in the Spanish war, wounds in party activities, etc.

From the point of view of these criteria, Vogelnik was a good choice for the position of director of SSO. His appointment was probably the best solution available in the party. Vogelnik was a prewer communist. He adopted the communist ideology as a youth. However, he combined his communism with the usual approach to life on the part of young people who plan to get a job and live on the money they make. He studied at the school of law. His studies included statistics. He also learned a couple of foreign languages and took his Ph.D. degree in law and thus completed his education. Afterwards he continued studies of statistics and became a statistical professional. In addition, he was extremely devoted to his supervisors and particularly to Kardelj and Kidrich. Whenever he made reference to their names, it was always with high respect and admiration. Whenever a problem arose in discussions he would always express the wish to have a chance to consult with Kardelj and Kidrich.

Vogelnik was also anxious to make publically known his absolute acceptance of everything that was going on as communist ideology including the points that were just empty slogans. By listening to him I frequently asked myself whether he was convinced of what he was telling us or, on the other hand, he was just building himself by collecting points wherever a chance arose. It is useful to go through his paper "Recording and Statistics"[6] that is a kind of theoretical justification of his work while he was director of SSO. There he says: In the prewar Yugoslavia "there was no use of statistical data. The economy was governed by anarchy and chaos. Revolutionary changes of the new social order and the transition to planned economy have created, almost overnight, a huge need for a variety of data". He aslo says: "Such an increased need for data was confronted with an almost complete lack of statistical tradition and experience, a poor state of statistical institutions that were inherited from the old Yugoslavia, and badly organized recording, that was in the service of private interests if it existed at all".

This is obviously in line with the standard expression of disdain for everything that existed before the war, in the non-communist Yugoslavia, and an *a priori* confidence that in the socialist society everything will be fine and superior to the respective achievements of old statistics.

Regarding the accuracy of data, Vogelnik had to tell us the following: "Statistical data of the old Yugoslavia were full of errors. These errors, such as non-response, refusals, and response errors appeared because of the lack of confidence on the part of the working masses in the state and all its practices. The outcome was a refusal to fill in the statistical questionnaires or a supply of inaccurate data". Generally speaking, in capitalism data are inaccurate. "The action against the supply of accurate data comes from the masses of workers. They deeply mistrust the state and the governmental statistics. From their own experience the masses have become aware that statistical censuses do not serve their interests".

All those who have engaged in studies of the accuracy of data will certainly appreciate these statements. Shortly after these statements, we went into systematic studies of errors and found out that they were arising in Yugoslavia in the same way as in capitalist countries. In other words, the confidence of working masses in the operations of a socialist state did not have any effect.

Needless to say, the accuracy of these statements was not the aim. They were obviously declarations of faith.

Vogelnik was thus nicely equipped for the leading position in Yugoslav statistics.

---

6 · *Statististical Review* (in Serbo-Croatian), Vol. I, 1951.

Nobody else was his equal. He also enjoyed the full confidence of his superiors. From time to time, he was able to see Kardelj and Kidrich, get their opinion, and secure conformity of his views with the advice that he would get from his superiors.

As to his mandate, there was no confusion whatsoever about its content. Yugoslavia was a socialist state with the ambition of moving in the same direction as the USSR, building the same institutions, and using in that work the experiences that existed in the USSR. Needless to say, all these experiences had a common denominator, viz. a strictly centralized power. All the important decisions were made in the central administration. The republics existed as the executive authority.

The statistical work had to fit this context. The Central Statistical Office in the USSR was responsible for the establishment of the programme of work, the methodology of various projects, instructions, preparation of the calendar of operations and anything else that should prove useful. The implementation of the centrally planned projects was in the hands of the authorities in the republics and autonomous provinces. The best staff should thus be in the center. The performances of the statistical services primarily depended upon the quality of the staff in the center.

This is what Vogelnik was doing successfully. It has already been pointed out that he recruited for the work at SSO all the staff who had some experience in statistics no matter where they lived. He had no embarrassing limitations from the respect for geographic distribution of the staff. He put as his Assistant Director another Slovenian, Boris Debevec. Some other people were even taken out of the category of semi-enemies.

Vogelnik had no particular difficulties with the staff. He was not a talkative man who would seed around his views about people and events. His contacts with the staff were brief, reduced to necessary words. He never went into that type of friendly chat that takes place after business is over or in the corridors, streets, etc. Vogelnik was a rather isolated man without any sign of willingness to have any contact outside business. He considered the staff as subordinates. He was polite although never friendly. He did not care for consultations with the staff. Consultations imply a kind of equality: in the exchange of arguments the subordinates might have stronger points. Quite a few colleagues had the feeling that he had an ear for everybody and the necessary respect for his collaborators. Although I am not sure that such a conclusion is correct, I would agree that he had no problems with the staff.

However, there were many conflicts between Vogelnik and Boris Debevec. It is difficult to recollect the reasons of these conflicts after so many years. Broadly speaking, at a number of points, Debevec was right. In the reconstruction of prewar data, Debevec frequently pressed for as good work as possible, examination of the assumptions before they would be used, courses for the staff to improve their technical skills, systematic discussions of the practices presented to us in the Soviet literature, etc. I would say that he was mostly right with his requirements. I also think that he was aware of the defects of the new Soviet literature. He realized that it eliminated theory altogether in favor of ready-made recipes. In opposition to that, Debevec insisted on the need for statistical theory as dealt with in the books of statistics published in Western countries. In that respect Debevec earned quite a lot of respect among his senior colleagues. They were convinced that this was the line for us to improvement of our work.

Vogelnik overestimated his power over Debevec. He could have handled Debevec easily. Debevec was a proud man. He was convinced that his cards were in order for a leading position in statistics. On this ground Vogelnik brought him to SSO as his assistant. This was a good step and I think that it could have solved Debevec's case had Vogelnik been able to understand that an intelligent man like Debevec, who also had a good knowledge of statistics, had to be given some authority and recognition. Rather than moving in that direction, Vogelnik was too convinced of his superiority and the power of his contacts with the top. He thus committed great mistakes. He never consulted Debevec. Debevec was mad about that. He felt offended. He developed a kind of emotional opposition to Vogelnik. He was against everything that came from Vogelnik. He generalized his opposition to Vogelnik in the form of a negative attitude toward all the characteristics of Vogelnik's work. Vogelnik became an obsession for Debevec.

In his opposition to Vogelnik, Debevec went to see the Soviet advisor to SSO, inform him about Vogelnik's mistakes, and suggest somehow an intervention. However, our advisor was an experienced employee of a communist government. He advised Debevec: "I see that you are quite excited about Vogelnik and his work. You talk too much about it. I think your attitude is wrong. Vogelnik is a very strong man at present. As long as he is that strong it is foolish to disagree with him. Keep quiet and wait. Sooner or later he will fall down. When you see him on the way down you also raise your voice to help push him till the earth's center so that he disappears for ever. Your attitude will then be appreciated as you will have helped that way the new ruler to rule".

After his visit to the Soviet advisor, Debevec came to inform us of what happened. He took the advice as an expression of scandalous ethical standards. The principle presented was quite new to us. We were not used to the attitude of keeping quiet in the presence of strong ones. Even less we were able to follow the advice to attack somebody who was already moving down because of his mistakes. What is good in the elimination of people forever because of some mistake or wrong steps in the past?

With his opposition, Debevec certainly contributed to Vogelnik's end. This was what Debevec probably wholeheartedly wished. However, Debevec also moved another process that he did not want. This was his own removal from SSO. He failed to understand that he had to take the same train as Vogelnik did.

In spite of these developments I would say that Vogelnik was the best director of statistics that Yugoslavia ever had during the communist regime. He had many defects. His greatest shortcoming was his inability to consult with the staff. However, he was intelligent and knowledgeble. In a democratic society he would have probably done a good job. He could not have neglected the staff as they would have imposed themselves through their writings and public interventions. In a communist society people are unable to make their point. Vogelnik realized that. He was aware of the extraordinary power of the political top and he, therefore, concentrated his attention in that direction. This is probably the explanation for his servility.

Some people considered Vogelnik as a man who unnecessarily exaggerated with a political interpretation of all events. He would never fail in doing whatever would contribute to his standing in ideological and political matters. He would talk with enthusiasm about Lenin's contributions to statistics although he kept quiet about so many achievements of people from capitalist countries that were known to him. His statements about the accuracy of data in socialism and the inaccuracy of capitalist data were scandalous. While talking and writing that way, he was obviously aware that his words had nothing to do with reality.

I mentioned that he put me at the bottom of the payroll as he was aware that he could not gain anything by giving me a higher salary. Nedeljkovich introduced me as a man who had to be taken with reservations. Vogelnik did so. However, he was also quick in changing his mind if he found it useful. After I was in SSO for quite some time, I saw in a corridor, by pure chance, a strong party man, Vlajko Begovich, who was at that time one of the Vice Presidents of the State Planning Commission. It seems that he was responsible for party control of all operations of the Commission. He asked me where I was working. I told him. He added that he would like to organize some studies and wanted to know if I would be willing to change my job and join him. After he heard about my salary he told me that he could see to it that I get a transfer. In fact, he called Vogelnik, explained the reason of the call, and proposed my transfer. Vogelnik understood the situation. He realized that a strong man wanted my services. He answered that I was his hope, a man at the center of his plans. He said that he could not possibly afford to lose me. As to the salary, he said that it was a mistake that he was not aware of. The next day my salary jumped from 2.000 Dinars to 4.500 Dinars a month. In other words, if you meet by chance a strong man in a corridor and you happen to know him, it contributes more to a career and salary than any amount of hard work.

Needless to say, that flexibility in moral standards had helped Vogelnik to survive. He was equipped for life in his era. His removal was, in fact, the collapse of the approach used by the YCP in handling matters of social life, the economy, and the organization of government agencies including statistics.

One of the best trumps of the propaganda organized by the YCP was the transition to planning as a way to rationally organize social and economic activities. The arguments used had an appeal. However, the theory did not work in its implementation. Planning requires a lot of data that we did not have. In order to know the production capacity after so many changes that took place in the course of the war, it was necessary to have a series of censuses with a tabulation of data by small administrative units. We did not have these censuses nor had we the ability to take them. SSO had neglected the development of skills for the organization of censuses. It also neglected the cultivation of statistical theory that was a prerequisite of the ability to embark on modern large-scale surveys. However, this was only a small part of our problems. Planning requires current statistics. In some areas it was essential, such as agriculture, trade, transport, etc. The establishment of current statistics meant work that takes a lot of time. In 1947 we were very far from any systematic effort in this direction. Nor does planning have much meaning without a block of household surveys that should provide fresh data about income, expenditures, food consumption, prices, etc. We had none of them. In other words, whoever wanted any serious involvement of the country in economic and social planning must have come to the conclusion that a different and much better system of statistics was essential.

Other problems arose independently of data. Assuming all the desired data available, we did not know how to put together the facts, the requirements, the wishes, and work out a coherent plan of the national economy. We did not cultivate studies of planning techniques nor did we follow the related developments in the world. The planning exercise was reduced to a system of guesses based on various more or less arbitrary assumptions. In addition to that, the impact of the current politics was terrific. Somebody wanted an emphasis on targets from the point of view of the country as a whole while others showed a clear preference for the strengthening of republics and provinces. There were also people pressing for military priorities and the development of an economy that should be satisfactory for military purposes. Some groups pressed for projects in regions of their origin. The others favored some specific branches of economy, etc. Thus, there were many approaches, many different lines of interest and no common philosophy of what could be called the social and economic planning of Yugoslavia. As a result, the compromising approach appeared as the main wisdom and the most satisfactory technique.

Once we had a plan, no matter what it was, the question also arose of how to express that plan in quantitative terms so that its fulfillment could be followed. According to the declared politics, people had to be involved in all aspects of the decision making process. In other words, reports about the plan had to be made available so that many thousands of bodies get a basis for discussions of the progress achieved. A restricted reporting of the completed projects, such as new factories, was unsatisfactory as the "work in progress" might mean anything between one and ninty nine per cent of work done. If the reporting referred to some basic quantitative indicators, as cubic meters of soil removed, tons of cement or iron used, amount of money spent, labor employed, etc., an unsatisfactory evaluation of work done followed. In some cases various machines were missing and they kept the project half completed although the majority of quantitative indicators are at 100 per cent. Additional complications arose because an infinite number of unexpected motives became components of reporting. Some units reported non-existing achievements for reasons of prestige. Others reported less work and asked for additional resources to secure some other effects. Other reports were inaccurate because the investors did not want to be blamed. In other cases, the reports were meaningless. Area planted in agriculture has no meaning unless the crop involved is known. However, within the same crop the information is misleading without an inspection on the spot to ascertain if the work was done on time and in agreement with existing standards of quality.

Thus, extremely complex problems arose in the exercise of planning. At various places and by various responsible personalities these problems were felt in different ways and to a different extent. However, the feeling was wide-spread that we were not prepared for a colossal undertaking of a rational control of the national economy. A part of these feelings was the idea that a different and better statistical service was needed.

However, the most important element of unhappiness with the direction of social and economic life was the negative experience with the excessive power of the central government. In fact, the YCP learned quite early that the Soviet model of the central control of the flow of economic processes leads to the establishment of a huge bureaucratic machinery that grows at the expense of efficiency. Instead of quick decisions, an extremely complicated system developed of reporting events and problems to a series of bodies and agencies, organization of meetings, efforts to coordinate views, search for additional information, negotiations regarding the content of collective decisions, etc.

This lengthy process led to many inadequate decisions, delays, lack of responsibility, apathy, etc.

The YCP learned that lesson very early. However, it was not opportune to talk about it to larger audiences. The lesson was kept within the inner circle of top party personalities. But, the increasing tension in the relations between the YCP and the USSR broadened that circle and the lesson became the basis for general doubts about the Soviet model.

Vogelnik's transfer to another job is probably associated with these developments. SSO was not adequate. Better statistical services were needed as an instrument of improved methods of planning. In addition, he was a symbol of a strong central statistical office with a commanding position in all statistical matters. His removal from the position of director of SSO was a way to announce the end of an inadequate period and the beginning of a search for new ideas.

As a result, in April of 1947 Vogelnik was transferred to the position of Vice President of State Planning Commission with responsibility for the methodology of planning and the coordination of plans for the republics. However, before he had time to warm up his new chair, he was obliged to pack his suitcases again. After some months he lost his new job and was sent to teach statistics at Belgrade University.

In is not easy to say what actually happened in this period and what was the reason to put Vogelnik out of government office. His new position gave the impression that he was not bluntly fired out. However, he lost that position after some months. In other words, there was a lot of rush in his removal.

Some people have related Vogelnik's removal with Andrija Hebrang, who was President of the State Planning Commission. Between Hebrang and the ruling group in the YCP there were many frictions. Later on Hebrang was executed on ground of charges of cooperation with Germans during the war. I of course do not know what happened. Some people pretend that Hebrang was critical of the political line adopted by the ruling group of the YCP and had to be removed to clear their way.[7] In favor of some such explanation goes the fact that Hebrang was minister of the central government. If he were a German spy he would have been eliminated at an earlier stage.

According to a number of indications that were in circulation at that time, the ruling part of the YCP was afraid that Hebrang would be able to seed friendship and respect for his personality and his ideas. It was also probably assumed that the largest danger existed at State Planning Commission viz. the agency under Hebrang's influence. In order to make sure that any influence of that type be radically exterminated, it was apparently decided to kick out of work from that agency all the senior staff who were Hebrang's potential allies no matter whether they were in contact with him or not.

In this period several events occured that made difficult judgements about the impact of various tendencies. In the second half of 1947, preparations were going on for a new organization of both the country and the government. The termination of SSO

---

7   Supek, I.: *Andrija Hebrang,* Markanton Press, Chicago, 1984.

was on the way. The outline of the arrangements for the establishment of a new statistical setup was already in discussion. Personnel changes were thus unavoidable. However, it so happened that in this period a group of people lost their jobs who should never have been touched if there was any respect for education, experience, achievements, and skills. Vogelnik was one of them. His Assistant, Boris Debevec was another. Debevec was sent to Slovenia to become director of statistics of the republic of Slovenia. In fact, there are many reasons to believe that it was a purge.

After Vogelnik left, Mrs. Veda Zagorec was in charge of SSO till the end of 1947. In 1948 a new setup started operations.

Vogelnik's departure from SSO meant, in fact, his elimination from statistics for ever. From the University of Belgrade he went to the University of Ljubljana. In Ljubljana he was Rector of the university for some time and a member of the Yugoslav delegation to UNESCO. For some time he was also Chairman of the Federal Committee for Culture, viz. a government agency for the coordination of cultural activities. The Committee is the name for agencies in communist countries that do not have the rank of a Secretariat (that corresponds to a ministry or a department).

In communist countries the university is probably the best hope for "reactionaries". University teaching is the highest position that a non-communist can achieve. It gives a bit better salary than the average and a degree of independence that is higher than in other jobs. However, for a communist, university teaching is an offense. This is how the university position is interpreted by a communist with recognized seniority from revolutionary activities when the party was fighting for power. The university is outside the power. Within the university there are no commanding positions. The university does not issue instructions to party cadres, it has no power to appoint people to influential positions, nor does it offer a chance for publicity, public recognition, or an access to jobs where the incumbent is entitled to have a car, a driver or an office with secretaries and staff who help overcome problems of daily private life. The university is thus a place for low ranking party members who cannot aim at higher than a dean, director of an institute, etc.

The university is also the place where people are transferred after they make some mistake at a higher position. This was Vogelnik's case. At a university they have all the time to think it over, correct their behavior, and thus hope for re-appearance that usually never comes.

The third group consists of people who are pushing too hard or are too loud in selling their devotion to the cause of communism. The party rulers do not like to put these people at any position of power as it would be too risky. The university is thus a safe prize for their decision to join in.

My last contact with Vogelnik took place many years later on, viz. at the time when he was Chairman of the Committee for Culture. I called on him hoping to get his support for the efforts to build up in Belgrade a center of statistical education and research that had to serve as a basis for the improvement of statistics in the whole country. Being a statistician himself, I thought that he would have a genuine interest in the subject. I also expected that his official position would make it easy for him to intervene. In order to strengthen his support, I pointed out that the applied research in

64

data collection required a great deal of resources. Therefore, it could only flourish at special places established and supported by governments, such as the Bureau of the Census in Washington, Indian Statistical Institute in Calcutta, Statistics of Canada in Ottawa, etc.

His reaction frightened me. He was up to his neck in the mood of the current politics. At that moment the authority of the central government was already eliminated. All the necessary institutions had to be established in each republic. A good party member had to be "republic-oriented". This is why Vogelnik told me that he would vehemently oppose any idea of building anything in Belgrade unless the same thing was done in each republic. Even more. He spoke of the need to have a center of statistical education and research at each university in the country.

I was frightened by his philosophy. I told him that such a solution was neither possible from the point of view of the staff nor would it be economical. He gave me a lecture about "socialist approaches". He said: "In the Middle Ages the students used to go away and flock around famous teachers. In socialism the teachers will travel around and become available to students on the spot".

He was aware of what was going on in statistics in places, such as Washington, Calcutta, etc. He knew that it could not be done otherwise. He was equally aware that a travelling teacher was just impossible when facilities were needed, such as laboratories, various aides, assistants, computers, etc. However, he was strongly tuned to politics of the moment. He preferred defending impossible approaches than exhibit doubts as to the value of the current party line.

He might have also been guided by the hope of regaining power through obedience.

I left him forever as a tragic case that politics can produce in the behavior of a person.

VII Upon the return

In the summer of 1947 I was ready to go back.

While in the US, I was living in a world that was moving decidedly away from war in every aspect of life. The people were hungry for a normal life, regular work, and care for the future. I was taken by that atmosphere. I developed a terrific desire to engage in work.

The idea of work led me to the UNRRA. In fact, at that time my thoughts were frequently with the UNRRA. I admired the philosophy behind the UNRRA and the efforts made to implement that philosophy. To me, the UNRRA was one of the history making events; it was a source of hope that people would be able to solve their fundamental problems. The UNRRA appeared to me as a victory of great ideals. I enjoyed myself in seeing in it the beginning of other developments in the same direction. I felt very happy that I had a chance to participate in this historic event. I also thought that I had an obligation to carry out the commitment assumed in my fellowship, viz. do the work that I was studying in the course of my trip and thus contribute what I could so that the UNRRA seeds bring fruit.

Part of my excitement about work was based on news coming from Yugoslavia. Nobody was giving me systematic information about the events at SSO. This is why I concluded that a serious search must be going on for new ideas and a redefinition of our task. Although it might be foolish to say so, I developed an idea that I had a mission in that situation of Yugoslav statistics. My attitude was based on the fact that I had a chance to visit the most important institutions for statistical work in the US, talk to hundreds of statisticians of different varieties, and keep in my pockets many addresses of people and agencies who would never fail to answer if requested to assist. I thought that I had a huge capital at my disposal that should be of some help in a situation where fresh ideas were needed.

More foolish was another idea of mine. No matter how much horror my words might provoke, I felt that I had a mission in a world of hatred that had penetrated the hearts of many of my compatriots. Alarming signs were available at almost all the places that I visited of deep political division between Yugoslavs. Some participation in the conflict between the supporters of the communist regime in Yugoslavia and the oppo-

66

sition to communism in any form was almost physically imposed on everybody. The two groups were separated by a deep gap of hatred that made impossible any contact let alone cooperation in the pursuit of ideals above the current politics. Both sides were equally submerged in hatred.

On one occasion a group of us, who came to the US as fellowship holders from the UNRRA, were invited to the Yugoslav Embassy for a discussion of our plans, progress made, and problems to solve. Toward the end of our meeting the person who conducted the discussions wanted to give us help and advice. We were in a half-dark room with the curtains closed. The speaker said in a whisper: "You have to be very careful at every step. You are in the country of the enemy. The enemy is all around. He is watching you. He will do his best to put you in trouble and harm you personally and our country as well".

As he was talking, I asked myself: "What future can Yugoslavia hope for with this type of person in important positions. All the senses of this man were blocked by a hatred that transformed everybody around him into an enemy. While I was looking at him, my memory went over the faces in a long line of people at the various agencies, universities, etc. who were more than kind to me, who helped me more than I could expect, who took me to their homes to live with them and their families, etc. I would say that I experienced more interest in making me happy than I was ever able to expect. I do not think I experienced something similar in any other country.

I was equally embarrassed by the treatment from the other side. From among hundreds of experiences the following case is a good illustration. I was living for some days in a small provincial city. In the evening I asked the receptionist to give me the key of my room. When I got it, I saw a piece of paper in my pigeonhole. I thought it was a message for me and I asked for it. It was a message in Serbo-Croatian language. Somebody wrote: "Tito excrement". The following two evenings I found the same message. The next day I asked the receptionist if there was a Yugoslav on the staff of the hotel. He told me that their bell captain on the morning shift was a Yugoslav. The next morning I found him and told him in our language: "I am your compatriot from room No ... I learned from your messages that a Yugoslav was working in the hotel. Why did you not ring me up"? He stood for a while without words. Suddenly the blood filled his face and he said: "You are a communist son of a bitch. Don't talk to me. Unless you go away I'll knock you down".

This is how far we had gone. This is also a measure of our inability to settle down, achieve peace of mind, and do some constructive work. An excited mind and a heart filled with hatred can not achieve anything appreciable on the constructive side. How great was the UNRRA with its insistence on the importance of work as a road to peace. The return to work seemed to me the best psychiatry for many individuals and whole nations.

There I saw my mission. The world of hatred needs people who are not capable of hating; it needs people who will fully engage in work and thus offer an alternative to hatred. The alternative is the involvement in cooperation and constructive contributions to the future.

I was ready to return to Yugoslavia, roll up my sleeves, and try to make my contribution. I shipped all my books and documents and requested the UNRRA travel office to make arrangements for my return trip.

At that moment I got my first and last official communication from SSO since I had left. It was a cable saying that SSO decided to extend my stay in US for another six months and pay my fellowship, if needed, from its own resources. I cabled back saying that it was too late to change my arrangements. It is obvious that I could have done otherwise. However, it was too late to change my thinking and my decisions as to the future.

In the summer of 1947, I took a boat for England. After a long trip through different countries I eventually reached Belgrade.

The next day I went to my office. My head was full of various projects of work. I was anxious to enter the office and talk to somebody who would have the authority to consider my plans and do something about their implementation. I went first to the office of the head of personnel. He told me that he was busy. He had to attend a meeting. I stepped out. I reported afterwards to the secretary of the new director. She told me that she would inform the director about my arrival. The rest of the day I spent sitting in the library and waiting to see the director. At the end of office hours I would go home. I stayed in the library for the whole week and nobody called on me to say "Welcome back" or "How was the trip"? let alone something more than that.

After a week I saw the staff going to a conference hall to attend the staff meeting. I joined. There I learned from a document that there had been a reorganization of the office in the meantime. I was put in charge of investment statistics.

Five or six persons were included in my new office to work with me. Our duty was to follow the fulfillment of the investment plan on the basis of reports sent in at the end of each decade by establishments responsible for the related investments. Our task was to compute the percentages of fulfillment of investment plans. Our report was supposed to be the basis for interventions in case that progress in some areas was below expectations.

My work was very dull. There was no correspondence between the investment units included in the current reports and the projects in our plan. Our inquiries showed that the original plan was sometimes abandoned in the meantime or modified. In some cases the work started on something quite different than the original plan. Thus, our reports contained a great amount of arbitrariness.

In addition, there was confusion about the meaning of our data. Our plans were spelled out in quantitative terms. The related information about the progress of work was a very dubious indication of achievements. However, our reports were made as we were instructed. I was convinced that the responsible officers would never accept our reports as a basis of their judgement.

This is why I felt unhappy. It is very unpleasant if you keep putting time in the work that you do not consider useful. I continued my responsibilities without much attention to what was going on.

My work had nothing to do with my views about modernization of our statistics.

In the course of the several months that passed since my return, nobody has ever raised the question of using the results of my studies for any purpose or in any context. I frequently thought that my office proposed me for a fellowship because they had no other candidate with qualifications required. Some confirmation of that view came soon after a reclassification of all the staff. We had five categories of professionals. I was put in the lowest class called "junior statistician-economist".

In addition to this confusion with the work, the atmosphere in the office and contacts between colleagues were far from satisfactory.

At that period, the members of the party had already developed a great degree of isolation from non-party staff. Contacts between the members of the two groups were correct in the sense that a party member would say "Hallo" in the corridor to his non-party colleague. It was a typically cool attitude. Real friendship was a privilege of non-party staff. They meet from time to time outside the office, cultivate common interests, and talk freely about anything they wish. Between the party members there were frequent contacts in connection with party activities. However, there was no friendship. Party members could not afford to talk freely in the presence of other party members as somebody might report the statements made. These reports usually lead to investigations and could become unpleasant. This is why the best attitude for a party member was to keep quiet and use his mouth for answering questions. A typical party member did not like situations that gave rise to frank discussions. Thus, a typical party member was a reserved person.

The isolation of party members also followed from their commanding role. They discussed the characteristics of their colleagues, made decisions about salaries, promotions, decorations, prizes, fellowships, leaves, financial support, etc. As a result of that position, they felt embarrassed in the presence of those whom they ruled. This was particularly so in the case of people whom they hurt for one reason or the other.

In that respect there are different categories of party members. The low ranking members who joined the party for the sake of its benefits, such as promotion, career, housing, better salary, etc., did not feel as the ruling class. Therefore, they mixed with other people in a way similar to the non-party staff. The higher ranking party members were very isolated. They themselves avoided company. Nor did the others care for their company as it imposed some limitations in the choice of topics for discussions, words to use, etc.

My contacts with non-party members at that time were rather formal. When I left for the US, some of them thought that I was an agent of the communist police. Some of them engaged in spreading that reputation for me. My return from the US added fuel to that attitude. One of them said: "If any doubt existed as to his association with the communist police at the moment of his departure, the matters are now clear. He preferred to live in communism than to enjoy freedom in the US. Communism is his choice".

At that time, this argument had a great deal of appeal to people. Some months after my return, I went for my usual shopping. As there was a long queue, I stood in line to wait my turn. After some time, one of my acquaintances was passing by. When he saw me he stopped and said loudly: "Fellows, this man was in US and he has come back. I invite you to have a look at this fool". All the people turned to see me. Some of them left the queue.

For that reason I was a bit reserved in my behavior. I refrained from starting conversations. If somebody approached me, I was always kind and friendly.

At that time I developed a friendship with Boris Debevec. Before the war, he was a school teacher. In the course of his studies of psychology and education, he started studying statistics. Later on he used statistics in the analysis of experiments that he conducted in the schools where he was employed. In addition to his interest in general statistical theory, he had some experience in experimentation, designing of surveys, data processing, etc. While my knowledge was purely from books, he had several years of experience in statistical research.

Debevec was a statistical enthusiast. He loved statistics to the extent that he was hardly able to talk about anything else. The literature that he was using in his studies was almost exclusively in German. When he saw the books that I brought from the US he became crazy. He wanted all of them and pretended that he would start reading all of them at the same time. Of course, we shared the supply. However, it was a pleasure to look at a man who was losing control over himself in the presence of books.

I realized soon that he was quite superior to me. I particularly enjoyed his ability to participate, with strong arguments, in discussions of various surveys, censuses, and other current issues of a government statistical office. This is why I gladly responded to his invitation to discuss the problems of the office, the issues encountered in books, the plans for the future, etc. After office hours we used to meet and go into endless discussions.

In course of 1947 our company got the third member. This was Juraj Echimovich who came to Belgrade from Zagreb to work for Social Security.

By his education Echimovich was a mathematician. However, he added to that a degree in economics. I knew him for quite some time. In 1938 we did the military service together in Sarajevo. Later on I found him in Paris where we both had a fellowship from the French government. Echimovich was studying probabilities and actuarial sciences. In Paris we were frequently together. During the war I lost trace of him. After I joined SSO and started correspondence with various government agencies about labor force statistics, I got a letter from Social Security in Zagreb signed by Echimovich. Later on he moved to Headquarters of Social Security in Belgrade.

I introduced Echimovich to Debevec. Echimovich was familiar with German and French statistical literature. It was easy to achieve an understanding between us. We had read a number of books independently of each other. It was primarily German literature. The books that I brought from the US had a great effect on our group. It was a new orientation in both our reading and our views about statistics.

Echimovich was the fastest in picking up new ideas. His education was just of the type needed as a preparation for the new statistics. He was thus the most advanced member of our group.

During our discussions we worked out an action programme. In fact, we had a joint programme and three specific programmes for each of us separately. The joint programme included the preparation of a textbook that we called *The Theory of Statistics*.

The Theory of Statistics had to be the first treatment of statistics based on recent views. It emphasized sampling distributions and estimation. We divided the work into three parts and expected to publish the volume in 1949. However, the progress was not as expected. The delay was due to Debevec. In fact, he got involved in politics that we were not able to understand. It was not the usual involvement that would imply discussions with friends. In fact, we did not know anything about what he was doing. However, his contacts with us started fading. His part of *The Theory of Statistics* was not making progress. It was particularly so after he moved to Ljubljana. At that point we lost contact entirely with him. He came to Belgrade from time to time. However, he was in a state of extreme excitement and very suspicious about everybody and everything. He would come to my house and, before he would open his mouth, he would make a thorough inspection of the room to check if somebody was hiding. We could not understand his behavior. He did not give us any explanation. However, he frequently repeated: "You don't know what is going on". After some time we got news that he was put in jail. His wife had the chance to see him from time to time. She was the source of news about him. At one point he asked for books and an English dictionary. The last news was that he committed a suicide in the jail.

Debevec was not the kind of man to commit suicide. He had a strong character and was firmly attached to life. We made several attempts to get in touch with his wife and learn more about his end. However, she avoided contact. Even now we do not know what happened. The only thing that I should say is that a very intelligent and able man lost his life in the stupidities of politics.

Debevec's destiny also burried our *Theory of Statistics*.

In this situation I diverted my attention to quality control. While in the US, I considered the promotion of this area of work in Yugoslavia an important task. I had in mind doing something about that. However, upon my return, I thought that my involvement in the responsibilities of SSO had priority. I expected a major programme of improvement of the methodology of data collection, an orientation of SSO toward studies and analyses, more interest on the part of the responsible people in statistical training and education, etc. Reality proved to be different. I was put on work that had nothing to do with any of the activities that I had in mind. Nor did anybody show any interest in having a word with me to check if I brought home anything useful from my trip. I, therefore, expected that effort in the direction of quality control might be more promising. In my interpretation of the situation, quality control would bring me in touch with the engineering circles who should have a more attentive ear for contributions to the organization of production and the improvement of quality. I expected definite achievements and an appreciation of methods of work that lead to these achievements.

In order to be able to organize the work on the promotion of quality control I thought that I had to start with some presentation of the related techniques either in the form of a book or in a series of documents. That would give me an opportunity to disseminate the essential ideas about quality control in all the places where people might be interested in it.

While I was fully involved in the studies and drafting, an event occured in the office that changed my plans. At the end of 1947, I was summoned to the office of the head of personnel of the State Planning Commission. The head was a woman, the wife of a general who was quite strong at that time. She told me: "You go home and do not come to the office any more". As I was not able to understand the situation, I said: "I won't go home before five o'clock". She said: "No, no, you go right now. You will not work here any more". I realized that it was something more serious. I said: "Let me start packing my books. I hope I shall be able to quit by five o'clock". She said again: "No, no, you go right now and we shall send you all your stuff". I asked: "Do you mean that I am dismissed? How about my salary"? She said: "You go home and stay there. Somebody will bring you your salary. You will continue getting your salary".

After the first shock was over, I realized that the matter was serious. I was obviously a part of a broader group of ousted employees from the building of the State Planning Commission. Vogelnik and Debevec were in the group. My friend S.Stanich was there. The whole group of higher officers of the Planning Commission was also fired.

After several days I got used to my new situation. Human beings have the remarkable ability to adjust to any situation, no matter how unpleasant or dangerous it might be. In my case it went that far that I considered myself very lucky to be a dismissed employee with unchanged salary and other benefits of government officers. I continued taking my lunch in the government operated restaurant for employees of our group. At home I organized my life. Most of my time was devoted to quality control. I decided to write three booklets about the related issues. I had a feeling that my position as a dismissed employee would continue for some time thus giving me a chance to produce more work than I expected before.

In fact, I enjoyed my position. However, my wife was terribly afraid for the future. She was convinced that my case was a part of some kind of plot. She thought that I would not survive. She insisted that I ask the head of personnel for a job, as other people from the same group had already been given jobs. I did what she wanted and after some time, in April 1948, I got the job as supply clerk in the Committee for Scientific Institutions. My job was to secure a sufficient quantity of old clothes for cleaning machines at the School of Mechanical Engineering.

This was the best job I ever had in my life. There was one single shop specializing in old clothes. The man in charge would ring me up once a week to fix the time of delivery. I would call the School afterwards to tell them to send their pick up and collect the parcel. That was all. The rest of the time I studied survey techniques and wrote my books about quality control.

I lived like that for several months. Then I made a mistake that spoiled my life. I went to my office and saw there my boss, a young student who had never passed any exam. He was sitting at his desk with a slide rule in his hand. I said: "What are you doing"? He said: "For the past three days I have been studying this damn thing and we cannot discover how it can be used for the calculation of percentages of fulfillment of our plan". He showed me a table in front of him with absolute figures introduced and percentages missing. At that moment the telephone rang. The call was for him. He had to go and see the Vice President of the Committee. In the meantime, I did the percentages and left. About two hours later he came to my house. He said: "Who did those percentages? Do not tell me that you did them?". I said: "Yes, I did it". He stared at me for some time and left without a goodbye. After an hour he came back and requested me to go immediately to the office. After some minutes he took me to a meeting hall where all the senior staff were sitting together with the President, the wife of a Serbian party man. He took me to the center of the hall and said: "Comrades, this is the comrade who knows how to use the slide rule. He computed all our percentages". They were all looking at me in astonishment. None of them had ever seen me before. I gained quite a reputation. People came to see me. They asked for me. As a result, I had to be in the office. I lost my wonderful freedom. My job at the Committee lost its attractiveness. Needless to say, I continued working on quality control. However, it had to be done in the office.

VIII The new setup

In democratic societies, institutions are man-made. As such, they reflect the limitations imposed by circumstances. More knowledgeable people and/or more experience might have created quite different institutions. The impact is also obvious of the degree of general development of the country, characteristics of the population, resources available, etc. The state of technology is another important factor.

In order to adjust the work of the existing institutions to changes in the underlying circumstances, democratic countries maintain an appraisal process of the performance of their institutions. The process takes the form of public discussions with particular involvement of professional associations, their meetings, and their publications. A continuous review is thus secured of problems, experiences, needs, ideas, and proposals. The discussion forum is always open.

On the contrary, in communist countries there are no problems, no criticism of the line adopted by the government, no suggestions for improvement, and no identification of inadequate solutions. Everything is fine, the best that could have been done. No government office is shortsighted, unaware of the course of developments and the solutions required. All the staff are doing the job adequately; all of them are qualified. Particularly qualified for the direction of activities entrusted to them are those at the top. This is also true in cases when the qualifications imply a high level professional standing, experience, and skill.

While everything is thus moving fine and to everybody's satisfaction, thunder comes from the clear skies to blow up the whole structure. After the thunder is over new persons in charge come in, old approaches are rejected, and the work moves in an entirely new direction. Another cycle of history starts. In the new course everything is again fine, the best that can be done. The silence continues; no examination of alternatives, no recognition of any possibility of errors, wrong views or inadequate solutions.

In this way changes take the form of catastrophe, a sudden reshuffling of everything. A catastrophe is a way to adjust the work to new conditions, make it more adequate, and introduce to it the changes that are unavoidable in life. The communist society improves its operations as any other society. However, in a communist society, improvements are made without mentioning failure and the inability of the top to direct the work properly. The catastrophe comes on a sunny day, without any preparation.

In line with this, no word of criticism was ever said about our earlier organization of statistics. No discussion whatsoever took place with statisticians with a view to asking their opinion before the implementation of the starting design. There was no discussion with users of data to ascertain the degree of their interest in the information that they were promised. No study was ever made of the financial implications of the organization proposed. The establishment of a special staff responsible for recording in each unit of work was obviously a huge financial burden. However, there was no study of the feasibility of the design made. The assumption was that the victorious socialism could do nothing better than take over the ready-made model that was developed in the USSR. If the model was adequate in the USSR, there was no reason to think that any problem would arise in Yugoslavia. Therefore, the model was implemented. The staff had nothing else to do than to transfer the ready-made institution. They were not asked to pause from time to time, think it over, and examine if any problem has arisen. Yugoslavia was lucky to get *the* solution. The YCP had to be grateful to the USSR for its big help. It had to praize the quality of the help and the ideas incorporated in the model. And we did so. The admiration for the model was expressed on every suitable occasion.

All of a sudden Vogelnik was transferred to another job although nobody has ever heard a word of criticism of his work. Mrs. Zagorac was put in charge of SSO although she had never heard of statistics before she got the appointment to the post of director. After the matter of the director was thus settled, everything was all right again. No discussion whatsoever took place to examine what was wrong, what were the characteristics of the line toward the future, and on what ground it was expected that tomorrow would be better than yesterday.

In line with her instructions, Mrs. Zagorac announced that SSO would operate within the State Planning Commission because the main purpose of data collection is to facilitate planning and control of the execution of plans.

This was a big blow for the professional staff of SSO. They considered themselves technicians in the activities that were going on all over the world. The newly proclaimed orientations did not need that type of staff. Although it was not quite clear what qualifications would be needed in the new office, the first experiences were not encouraging. New faces appeared without any knowledge of statistics and without any appreciation of that knowledge. They occupied the key positions and pushed the old staff to wait in the corner if any work would be available for them. Thus, the old staff expected an unpleasant future and they started looking around to find some other employment.

In the meantime the new statistical setup was prepared.[8] At the end of 1947 the State Statistical Office was abolished. In the new organization, a separation was announced between the collection of data for general purposes and the collection of data needed for the government administration in both the formulation and the implementation of planning.

---

8 More details about changes introduced can be found in *Thirty Years of Statistics in SFR Yugoslavia*, Federal Institute of Statistics, Belgrade, 1974.

The first task was to be carried out by the Federal Statistical Office (FSO). Its main activities included the preparation of methodology and the execution of statistical surveys, organization of data processing, analysis of data collected, supervision and co-ordination of statistical activities, publication and dissemination of data, cooperation in statistical matters with domestic and foreign institutions, care for statistical education and training, etc.

FSO was an independent institution in the Presidency of the Government.

The needs for data related to planning and the operational decisions in economy had to be taken care of by two institutions, viz. the Secretariat of Operational Recording ("Sekretarijat za operativnu evidenciju") and the Bureau of Recording for Planning ("Biro za plansku evidenciju"). The Secretariat was a part of the Economic Council, a powerful government agency for operational economic matters. The task of the Secretariat included the preparation of reports about production, use of stocks of material for reproduction, deliveries, labor force, etc. The essential information along the line was a subject of daily reports while more detailed information had to be made available once in ten days or at longer intervals.

The task of the Bureau was the organization of a similar reporting system aimed at following currently the fulfillment of plans. This part of reporting was made obligatory for all the items included in the plan.

The same organization was made at all levels of the hierarchy. Each republic, each district, and, in most cases, each commune had the same institutions. In this way three different networks of data collection agencies were established.

It should also be pointed out that the attribute "Federal" in the new name of the statistical office does not mean a decentralization of the decision making process. In fact, FSO was a highly centralized organization. The period involved was called later on the "era of administrative direction of economy".

Regarding the last two institutions associated with planning, the first thinking was that two separate agencies were needed. However, later on it was found that their activities overlapped in many sectors. It was, therefore, decided to join them under the name of the Federal Directorate for Recording and keep within it two main lines of work that corresponded to the aims of the separate agencies.

There should be no surprise about the confusion that arose in connection with planning and management in the societies with a large sector of public property. Historically, this was a new issue that represented a great challenge to the human mind and its courage. Many people all over the world would have appreciated a chance to participate in the effort and see the results achieved. However, for that purpose the work had to be done with an open mind and with a right for the brain to follow the developments critically. In other words, the emphasis was on the process rather than on recipes. The process would lead to questions: what kind of planning is possible without running the risk of inefficiency and the establishment of clumsy administrative machineries, what institutions are needed for the purpose, what should their techniques of work be, what data do they need for their work, etc. The challenge faced required a real concentration in the search for new paths toward the future.

However, the idea of the process was rejected. The process requires a position of open doors to everybody guided by an interest in the problem and, essentially, a kind of democratic cooperation. Instead of that an organization was created that anticipated answers to all the fundamental questions of the moment. In other words, the authorities do know what the planning is, they do know what institutions need to be created for the purpose and what their methods of work should be; they do know what data are required for the purpose and how the related work is to be organized. The answers to these questions are incorporated in the established organization as their assumptions.

The Federal Directorate of Recording was nearer to the heart of the political top of the country. It was understandable with respect to its role. The Directorate was expected to be their instrument in the process of current decisions. This is why it was located in the center of Belgrade, in the same building that housed the Federal Planning Commission. On the other hand, the FSO was involved in the collection of data that were not urgently needed. As a result, the FSO did not have powerful protectors. This was known to the housing authorities. Office space for FSO could not be found in Belgrade. The FSO was obliged to go to Indija, a small place about 40 km from Belgrade. In this way the physical circumstances anticipated the future of FSO. At that time, communications were extremely difficult. The office had a bus for its employees. However, on the way it frequently broke down and reached its destination with a delay of a couple of hours. Equally unpleasant was the problem of staff. Many candidates from Belgrade for job at FSO did not want to accept the hardship of the adventurous trips to Indija.

The head of the Federal Directorate of Recording was Ante Novak.

As any other manager in that period, Novak was a prewar communist. As a result of his involvement in illegal activities of the YCP before the last war he was put in jail. There he attended a school for revolutionaries that was established by the inmates themselves to improve the knowledge of those who were serving different sentences. One of his teachers was Mosha Pijade, a member of the Politburo of the YCP. After the war, Pijade was responsible for the organization of government agencies. It gave Novak a chance to call on Pijade when he badly needed his help.

Novak was one of those prewar students who played a great role in the party. He never graduated nor he made an attempt at getting a degree after the war, when it was easy for people in high positions in the government hierarchy. However, in matters of formal education some bitterness remained forever in his mind. He probably suffered from some complexes. He would frequently ridicule "people with qualifications", certificates, schools in general, etc.

However, Novak was intelligent. He was quick in understanding the situation around him. He would quickly define his position and would move into various discussions without hesitation. He also had a lot of selfconfidence and courage. He made an effort to pick up the basic ideas of work in various fields. None of the other directors had that courage. He was thus attracted by graphic presentation. He even published a book on this subject.

Novak was a short man with a tiny body. In compensation, said a colleague, he got a double ration of nerves. He was a man of strong passions. He would frequently go to extremes in love, hatred, protests, and excitements. In defending or attacking somebody or something he would go beyond measure. His reactions were out of proportion with his body. In his views, he was exclusive. In the presentation of his own arguments he was aggressive, without any space left for tolerance or compromise. He was never ready to give up. The way to stop him at a meeting was to take him away physically. He was the incarnation of a fanatic.

Some of my colleagues from that period pretended that Novak's role in Yugoslav statistics was the result of his nerves. There is certainly some point in this opinion. Whatever Novak was doing, his work always mixed with passion, drive, aggressivness, and similar qualities of his character. While working on the establishment of universal record keeping, he showed a great working capacity and a readiness to tackle any problem at any time no matter what the effort needed would be. Such a behavior is obviously not possible without passion.

Novak made an attempt at outlining a general philosophy of recording as opposed to statistics. To him, statistics was a product of capitalism in which the reason of profit, private property, competition, and secrecy of operations led to a collection of data for summarization purposes. The end product of statistical work consists of averages, proportions, and totals, viz. the measures of the population as a whole. As opposed to that, in socialism there are no secrets. Each unit of work generates accurate data about its own work for its own use. The same information is aggregated later on at different administrative levels and for different types of groupings of units to help in the direction of social and economic activities. Statistics is thus a source of information at a relatively low stage of social development. The transition of the society to its higher stages of development, viz. socialism, implies a disappearance of statistics and a domination of record keeping.

Novak involved all his passions in various fights for the recognition of his work. As the future society was going to be based on recording, he thought that the agency headed by him had the noble task of building the society of tomorrow. The task required a new breed of people who would do their work with the enthusiasm of conscious masons of the future. A prerequisite for a role in that task is the staff with membership in the communist party. The prerequisite of enthusiasm and passion is the young age. This is why Novak filled his office with young zealots. They lived in the office day and night. A restaurant was available with free food at any time. The work was carried out in secrecy. The enemy of socialism was all around keeping an eye on each piece of paper containing figures that could reveal information about the course of socialism. The entrances of the office were constructed of iron bars. Heavy metallic treasuries were placed in all the offices to lock in the data before and after use. All the pieces of paper used in the course of work were collected twice a day and burned under control to make sure that every bit was destroyed. As the enemy could make use of the burned paper and reconstruct the information from pieces available, the practice was introduced of walking over the burned paper in order to destroy everything into the smallest ashes. After that none of the enemy's witchcrafts could be used any more. As to the results of data processing, the practice of top secret was applied. The statistical reports were made in twenty copies only and distributed to the political top. Each copy of the report had a serial number. In the evening all the reports would be withdrawn and fresh data introduced during the night. The next morning the reports are distributed again. The top politicians thus started their day with up-to-date information.[9]

Novak considered the parallel statistical office as a remnant of capitalism. A disdain thus developed among the staff of his agency for colleagues in the statistical office. The staff of the statistical office consisted of prewar professionals with experience and seniority in the service. They were mostly non-party people. On that ground the staff of statistical office was considered in Novak's agency as nothing else than a bunch of "reactionaries" who should be ignored together with their work.

Credit goes to Novak for the effort to formulate a justification of recording, help solve numerous problems that were arising all over the country, and provide his staff with a feeling that they were involved in an essential activity of the socialist society. He established a periodical *Record Keeping* (Evidencija). Its publication started in 1950 and ended in 1951. There was no substance to publish. The greatest contribution published in *Record Keeping* was an article about dictation of numbers in reporting data by telephone.

Novak did his best to secure the success of recording. He knew personally Kidrich and Kardelj, the political top of the country. In might be that their intervention or the action by some party committee or both helped him to push through the recognition of the identity socialism-recording. The identity is due to Lenin. However, Novak used it to secure party support of his recording as the essence of socialism. All those who neglect recording at the place of work would run the risk of being accused of negligence toward fundamental principles of socialism.

It might be that he overdid it in his search for support. Nobody wanted to be blamed. Very soon recording was everywhere. As there was no firm guidance as to what had to be done and what the recording really was, it so happened that various units of work did it in the way they thought that it was the right manner to do it. In fact, after a very short time the recording became a mess of solutions, approaches, number of questions, subject matter, etc.

In fact, the task was not simple. In a factory of bricks the task of recording is very simple. One has to count the number of workers and the number of bricks produced. However, there are many other situations where the task is very complex. Take for illustration the Ministry of Justice. They construct a new annex to the main building. This is part of their investment plan. In the financial plan they have the furniture and the equipment for the new building. Their plan of current work includes preparation of a number of new laws. A section of the ministry is responsible for a revision of various categories of sentences. This is part of the ministry's plan. In other words, the ministry is responsible for a large number of different activities and all of them are included in the ministry's plan of work.

---

9 More details are available in Novak, A.: "Statistics and recording", *Thirty Years of Statistics in New Yugoslavia,* Federal Statistical Office, Belgrade 1974.

What kind of recording is necessary to make it possible for the ministry itself and for other agencies as well to follow the fulfillment of the plan, identify problems, and detect points that require interventions?

It is obvious that there is no simple solution as in the case of the brick factory. The ministry will, in fact, be obliged to break down its work into homogeneous activities and organize for each of them a separate system of recording that will reflect adequately the nature of work.

This is what happened all over the country. In the organization of recording each office carried out the task in a way that reflected the specific properties of the work. The outcome of this attitude resulted in an extreme diversity of recording either from the point of view of the subject matter or the number of data to be included in the related reports.

The authorities realized the danger of the mess. They took steps to "simplify" the system and reduce it to a programme that could be called an essential minimum. In this connection Novak proposed to distinguish "general recording" and "differential recording". The first group should consist of an obligatory recording for all the units of work while the second category makes it possible to legalize deviations from the common programme in order to meet the needs of specific agencies.

The task force established for the purpose of simplification of recording produced a list of obligatory forms. The list was published in *Record Keeping* (Vol. I, 1950). The accepted minimum programme varied from one branch of industry to the other. An illustration is provided of the accepted minimum programme used in the reporting in industry. The establishments were obliged to make the following reports:

i)	Monthly production programme in financial terms,
ii)	Monthly production programme in physical terms,
iii)	Monthly production programme by days (in financial terms),
iv)	Monthly production programme by days for each product separately,
v)	Daily report of production in financial terms,
vi)	Daily report of production in physical terms,
vii)	Report of personnel employed (once in each decade),
viii)	Basic monthly report of production in financial terms,
ix)	Basic monthly report of production in physical terms,
x)	Monthly report of the use of raw materials and stocks,
xi)	Monthly report of deliveries,
xii)	Monthly report of deliveries by republics,
xiii)	Monthly report of fulfillment of the plan of distribution,
xiv...xx)	Report for six month period,
xxi)	Daily report of deliveries of fats by recipients and type of trade,
xxii)	Daily report of use of fats from production,
xxiii)	Report of deliveries to retail stores,
xxiv)	Monthly report of employed labor.

In other sectors of work, such as retail trade and agriculture, the programme of reporting was considerably broader.

Novak was frequently pointing out the superiority of socialism over capitalist societies from the point of view of the facilities for the collection of data. Capitalism has no alternative to surveys that require a huge budget. In socialism the information about work is generated by the work itself. It is thus costless. As a result, the budget of data collection agencies is very modest.

Needless to say, in his calculation incomparable matters were compared. The real issue is the total cost of data collection.

As to FSO, it was also headed by an ambitious man of quite a different character than Novak. His name was Stane Krashovec, a Slovenian from Ljubljana. He studied economics before the war and got a degree. He joined the communist movement as a youg man. He served in jail for some time because of his communist activities. In jail he continued his studies of marxism, although economy remained his preferred field of interest. In the prewar period he published some papers and translated Marx's *Capital* into Slovenian language. In this way he earned some authority in the communist circles of Slovenia. In his young days he came in contact with Kardelj and Kidrich. He kept these contacts later on and made good use of them in different situations.

After the war, Krashovec started as Assistant Minister of Heavy Industry. This was a very influential position as his boss was one of the strongest personalities of the YCP. From that job he was transferred to the position of Economic Advisor of the Yugoslav delegation to UN. While travelling around in the US, he had a chance to see many aspects of statistical work. He greatly depended upon these impressions. He also learned that mixing with foreigners and working with them is not necessarily dangerous for one's own country. He was convinced that many foreigners were quite knowlegeable people.

From that position he came back to Yugoslavia to become director of FSO.

Krashovec was an entirely different director than Vogelnik or Novak. He insisted on consultations with the staff. This was his strong point. Before any decision, he would have consultations with many people. In this way he was able to overcome many difficulties that he had to face.

Although his political biography was in order, Krashovec had none of the characteristics of Novak's zealotry. He was quiet, calm, unwilling to attack people for differences of opinion and even less so in case of political differences. When the work had to be done, he did not care for political slogans and words without support in work. This is why people appreciated him as boss

His initial period at FSO was used for consultations. He depended very much upon Debevec. It was primarily Debevec who put in his mind the idea of building a modern statistical service based on cultivation of theory and research. At an early stage, Debevec advised him to get in touch with me. He immediately did so. We had very many talks about statistics, the state of statistics in the US, my experiences in the US, my views about the programme of modernization of statistics in Yugoslavia, etc. In most of these matters he accepted my wiews and decided to move in that direction.

After long discussions were over he asked me to join FSO. I accepted after I realized his determination. One condition was the understanding that my recruitment was a part of the effort to rebuild the old statistical office and get together the staff dispersed in course of the reorganization. The other condition was the necessary freedom in the programming of statistical modernization and the formulation of the related proposals. Everything seemed all right. I decided to join him. He kept his promises. In a very short time we made a step ahead in the development of statistics in Yugoslavia.

However, my transfer to FSO did not go fast. Krashovec wrote a letter to the President of the Committee where I was working as a supply clerk and requested my transfer. The request was turned down. As is usual in these situations, the Committee replied that my services were essential for smooth operation of the university. After some weeks, another letter arrived requesting my release. It was signed by Boris Kidrich, the new President of the Federal Planning Commission. This time, however, it was spelled out in the form of an order.

This request was a shock for my Committee. The leaders of the Committee were afraid of the consequences. The man who was entirely unknown and unused in the Committee suddenly became an important person to such a high personality as the President of the Federal Planning Commission. I got a farewell party. They all looked at me as if they wanted an answer to the question: "What is going on"?

This is how I returned to statistics under favorable auspices.

IX The achievements

Unlike the Directorate of Recording that was involved in a very broad range of vague responsibilities, FSO was lucky to be responsible for the best pages of the history of statistics in Yugoslavia.

The circumstances under which FSO had to work were extremely difficult. FSO had none of the facilities and privileges of the Directorate of Recording. In spite of that, it made many lasting achievements. It shows that money and facilities do not necessarily buy success nor are the doors to success closed to those who are working under difficult conditions.

The key to FSO achievements was very simple. It could be summarized in the precept: "Let people work".

In fact, the recipe followed by FSO was very straightforward and in line with fundamental experiences from work all over the world. These principles, as interpreted by all of us who were involved in the story of FSO, are as follows:

i) It is not true that the ability to do work is correlated with membership in the communist party. Therefore, one has to let people work and press for support of those who are able to show achievement;

ii) It is not true that the leading impact on work should be a privilege of members of the communist party. Politics of preferences in favor of party members has a negative impact on work. It means discrimination against creative abilities; it leads to frustration; it kills initiative and drive; it paralyzes work;

iii) It is not true that involvement in hard work and the desire to see one's country progressing is correlated with membership in the party. Contributions are measured by achievements. "Patriotism" reduced to political formulas and slogans is shallow.

It is obvious that full respect for these precepts was not possible at that time. However, Krashovec showed serious determination to put them into practice to the extent possible.

The impact of that attitude will now be presented.

Krashovec was a sincere and devoted member of the communist party. However, he interpreted his mandate in a way that was quite different than the approaches used by others in a similar position. Vogelnik and Novak, both intelligent, took from the party the essential orientation of their assignment, the framework of their task. Krashovec interpreted his duty as a search for ways that would make it possible for communism in Yugoslavia to make the best use of the progress achieved in the world. He thought that he had to open doors to all important developments and use them for the advancement of work in Yugoslavia to the extent they prove to be useful tools. He was thus open, without prejudices. He never hesitated to open doors if an achievement from Western countries was referred to as a line worthy of attention. Nor did he consider himself obliged to accept certain approaches for the mere reason that they were used in the USSR.

This is what we interpreted as a satisfactory atmosphere for work. We decided to engage in work to the maximum possible extent in order to secure for the country the benefits of new developments in statistics. We interpreted our involvement as our duty toward both our country and the promotion of the statistical profession in an area of the world where much had to be done to secure the level already achieved by more developed countries.

The achievements that will be presented include primarily the work done within FSO by four persons, viz. Debevec, Blejec, Echimovich and this author. Debevec was not an employee of FSO. However, he had a great influence on Krashovec. Therefore, his role was essential for the course of subsequent developments. In addition, Debevec kept consulting with other members of the group whenever some new problems arose and discussions were needed to shape our views and formulate our projects for subsequent action. Nor did Blejec ever join FSO. He was associated with the Statistical Office of Slovenia, in Ljubljana. Later on he joined the Department of Economics, University of Ljubljana. However, he frequently came to Belgrade and we thus kept in touch in connection with all major issues. I was the only permanent staff with FSO throughout the period of the duration of FSO. Echimovich joined FSO later on.

Each member of this group was responsible for particular projects in his individual capacity. However, the essential orientation of our work was a result of our agreed upon programme. The resulting modernization of statistics in Yugoslavia was thus basically the product of the joint action of the whole group.

Our main concern from the very beginning was to make a break through in the understanding of what statistics is.

It was not a simple task. Any success along that line had to lead to a recognition of mathematical statistics. However, this aim was in conflict with the official attitude of statistical agencies in the USSR and all the communist countries in Eastern Europe including Yugoslavia. In the ruling ideology of the communist parties, mathematical statistics was presented as a bourgeois tool designed to divert the masses from class struggle. It deals with abstract numbers while the reality consists of an international fight by workers for liberation and socialism. This fight is based on principles of historic materialism that guide the masses to the realization of their political aims. Therefore, the only acceptable statistics has the character of class science. In other words, any promotion of mathematical statistics is a service to capitalism in its action against the proletariat. The promotion of mathematical statistics within a socialist country deserves prison and any other form of persecution used in case of the enemies of socialism.

We were aware that we took a dangerous course of action. In order to secure some success there was no point in referring to the achievements of statistics in the US. In fact, the US was an enemy and had to be hated together with everything that was going on there. This was probably the reason why none of the holders of higher positions in the office ever asked me a question about statistics in the US. Nor did they ever propose that I talk to the staff about the achievements that I had a chance to see in the US.

Only now, years after these events were taking place, I realize how naive was my attitude at that time. The following illustration might be of interest. Before I left the US, I wanted to secure for us sources of information about developments in US statistics. Among other matters, I thought that I should do something to make available in Yugoslavia the *Journal of the American Statistical Association*. In order to do that I was advised to register as a member of American Statistical Association and pay, from my poor fellowships, dues for several years. However, I abandoned that idea as I expected that copies of the *Journal* would disappear before they reached my address in Belgrade. As a result, I decided to register Dolfe Vogelnik, director of SSO as a member of ASA. I thought it would be a useful step for the subsequent development of statistics in Yugoslavia. However, later on I learned that I offended Vogelnik by registering him, without his authorization, in the membership of a bourgeois association. This was a sin that brought me later on to trial.

In that situation we realized that no amount of abstract discussion would help us. Instead, we decided to wait for an opportunity to engage in some practical problem that would give us a chance to work and use the results of that work as an illustration of the potentialities of the new statistics. Luckily, opportunities soon appeared. In 1948 the government was interested in an expenditures and food consumption survey. The old statistics was helpless. We offered a scientific survey, an objective estimation procedure, and a possibility to use the results of the established relationships among the variables in subsequent studies of problems in this field. The related survey was carried out in 1949 under Echimovich's guidance and it had a sensational effect. All the top officers of several ministries were enthusiastic about this achievement. They all became our supporters and requested our services in connection with other problems. All these supporters were members of the party. However, they did not care for the ideology. Respect for an efficient tool of work prevailed.

In the same year another opportunity arose. The government wanted to issue legislation providing financial assistance to families with many children. However, there was no information about a frequency distribution of mothers by the number of living children that could help the government to make a decision as to the financial effect of the legislation.

After all the consulted institutions declared their inability to solve the problem and all the statisticians recognized by the party kept quiet, the issue came to us. Echimovich carried out the related survey, organized the field work, trained the staff for the purpose and talked, wherever a chance arose, about modern statistics, the role of mathematics, which studies should be followed by those who want to qualify in modern statistics, etc. In this way the statistical personnel all over the country was involved in the application of modern statistics while, at the same time, the representatives of statistics as class science were shooting their guns against the use of mathematical statistics. We interpreted these events as a great victory of mathematical statistics and decided to strengthen our determination to involve ourselves in the work wherever a suitable chance arose.

While these developments were going on, we decided to attack the problem of statistical education. Krashovec was fully aware of the situation and he agreed to provide us with the necessary official support. As a result, in 1949 a letter was sent to Department of Economics of the University of Belgrade proposing the establishment of a statistical section that would offer students a course of modern statistics and its application. The proposal included an appropriate curriculum and announced the readiness of FSO to carry out the lecturing programme.

The offer was a bombshell. The Department of Economics was a stronghold of the old type of statisticians. Their curriculum consisted of verbal statistics that had dominated the European continent in the last century. In line with the corresponding practice in the USSR, their curriculum culminated in the presentation of averages. None of the teachers of the Department ever followed a course of modern statistics or read a book that dealt with modern approaches in statistics. They took our offer as an attack on their positions.

In fact, they were not aware that our ambitions went much further than that.

At that time the leading personalities of the Department of Economics were Uvalich and Grdjich. They consulted other official representatives of the old line, viz. Vogelnik, Novak, and Macura, the head of the Statistical Office of the Republic of Serbia. They rejected our offer and did not hesitate to qualify it as an attempt of the enemies of socialism to introduce confusion among the young generations. Fortunately, Krashovec was convinced that we made a good move. Our success in the applications and the appreciation of these achievements by some top politicians gave him the courage to persist. We, therefore, decided to stage a major attack on old statistics. For that purpose a meeting was convened in Belgrade, in 1949, of all the leading statisticians in the country with the aim of taking a stand regarding a number of fundamental issues, such as the nature of statistics, the needs of the country in terms of statistical services, modern statistical education, qualifications the teachers are expected to have, etc.

The meeting was attended by a large number of leading statisticians from statistical services and universities. This author presented an introductory statement that pointed out the needs of the country, the achievements of modern statistics within SSO in meeting these needs, and the necessity to modernize the statistical education at all the levels in order to prepare the staff to cope with new requirements.

The meeting was a great success from our point of view. The participants endorsed our views and requested major changes in statistical education. Those who were not able to follow the recommendations because of their inadequate education - had no courage to defend the old line. Novak was one of those who opposed the line of the meeting by referring to his theory that statistics had no role to play in socialism in view of the predominant importance of recording. Grdjich also recommended the need to go slowly and take into account the fact that the country had no qualified staff to meet the requirements of the meeting.

86

After the meeting we concluded that it had to be considered a cornerstone in the history of statistics in Yugoslavia. There was no confusion any more as to the meaning of statistics and the curricula of statistical education. The participants of the meeting went home with a clear idea of the need to carry out a major change in the course of statistics. This was nicely reflected in the article by Grdjich "On statistical personnel and their professional improvement" (in Serbo-Croatian), *Statistical Review,* Vol. I, 1951. As a representative of the old course he admitted that, after this meeting, it has become clear that the basis of statistical education in the future should be mathematical statistics.

Encouraged by this meeting we thought that we should go a step further and secure the implementation of the recommendations of the meeting. We took into account the rejection of our proposal to establish a statistical section at the Department of Economics. However, the spirit of the meeting was considered a strong argument in favor of another attempt in the form of a proposal to establish an independent Statistics Department that would provide a modern curriculum and take into account the improvements of statistical education in other countries. Our aim was to go beyond pure theory. In our view, the department of statistics should be in close contact with applications and see to it that the country gets qualified statisticians who would be equipped with the ability to assist the government agencies in the implementation of their respective statistical programmes.

We proposed a curriculum of four years of studies that included a course of mathematics, a modest programme of mathematical statistics, and the applications, such as theory of sampling, methods of data collection, statistical surveys, designing statistical experiments, statistical quality control, data processing, demography, etc. The department was supposed to be a part of the University of Belgrade with a strong support to its budget by FSO. The beginning of work was announced to a large public and students were invited to register.

However, some days before the beginning of the lectures, a storm blew up the project. We were informed that the project was discontinued. At variance with his usual attitude, Krashovec came to the office with a worried face. He closed himself in his room and did not drop by my office for a normal review of developments. Up to that moment I was his favorite staff member and he would never let a day go without talking to me on some of our issues. After that day our relations became cool and he diverted official discussions toward Echimovich.

The puzzle of that change in Krashovec's behavior was solved only by pure chance. This was at the moment when FSO was moving from Indjia to Belgrade. It so happened that the Director's confidential file was left on a desk waiting to be taken to the new office. I saw it while passing by. On top of it was a letter by Krashovec to some party committee. I do not remember any more what the name of the committee was. In this letter Krashovec presented his "autocriticism" and declared himself guilty regarding the way in which he handled the issue of the Statistics Department. When I saw the subject I went through the attachments. There I found that a group of "distinguished scientists", such as Dolfe Vogelnik, Uvalich, Novak, Milos Macura, etc. sent a confidential petition to the party on the eve of the beginning of lectures at the new Department of Statistics and requested intervention of the party to stop the implementation of the project. The first argument in support was of a general and already known type.

Namely, the Department of Statistics means a recognition of mathematical statistics that is, in fact, a tool of capitalism. The next argument is an illustration of maneuvering behind the screen. It says that the whole project was designed by agents of the enemy with a view to confusing and poisoning our youth who were anxious to study. In other words, it was a recommendation to the party to forward the whole matter to the police and thus protect socialism and the socialist achievements from an open assault by the enemy.

In his reply Krashovec presented a two page apology. He accepted the idea of the enemy all around and confirmed the need for extreme care. However, in order to minimize his own responsibility and thus make it possible for himself to continue as a good party member who should be equally trusted as before, he put the whole blame on his "employee Zarkovich". He said at the end of the letter: "My responsibility in the matter is reduced to my unjustified trust in the work of my staff member Zarkovich. He designed the project and carried it out. He also wrote all the correspondence on the subject and gave it to me for signature. I trusted him and I used to sign everything that he would ask me to sign. I now realize that I should not have done so".

It is true that I carried out the preparations for establishment of the Statistics Department. However, I did it after systematic discussions with him and upon his approval of my action. I did that work as I was convinced that it was useful for the statistical development of our country. Moreover, I am of the same opinion today. I shall also die convinced that I did my duty.

There is another comment to make after so many years. I understand Krashovec's concern to remain a spotless member of the communist party. Had he asked me to accept the blame for what happened, I would have accepted it and would have authorized him to write his apology in the same way. I could have done it for him in a better way than he did it himself. In this case he would have achieved his aim and would have saved his honor. In this case he would also be able to talk to me without uneasiness. However, he failed to do so. I do not want to elaborate on the impact of his act on the subsequent evaluation of his standing. Let me just say that I added later on to his suffering by treating him with generosity in situations where he depended upon my help.

As for the signatories of the petition let them live in the hope that nobody knows what they have done or at least in the hope that nobody will ever be able to point out publicly their contribution to the "defense of socialism".

We took this defeat as one of the unavoidable events in any effort to change the established order. It was obviously a bitter experience. However, it was bound to be that way. The consequences of our project were far-reaching. They implied a departure of a generation of statisticians on the ground of lack of qualifications. No wonder that they established a common front to defend their position. This is why we moved quietly to another and more important project.

FSO was the government agency responsible for statistical work. FSO was thus a representative of the statistical profession. In that capacity it got a request from the government to work out a programme of exams that all the statisticians had to pass in their career before they could get final confirmation of the appointment to the post they occupy. In other words, FSO had to specify what knowledge of statistics all the statisticians were expected to have if they wanted to pass the obligatory exam for a career in statistics.

We took the task as the implementation of recommendations of the 1949 meeting. We were aware that this task had a decisive importance for the future development of statistics in Yugoslavia. If the programme is spelled out in accordance with the modern state of statistics in the world, thousands of young people who are planning to work in statistics will require an adequate education. In order to get that education they will pressure universities and lower schools of statistics to adjust their curricula to the requirements of the service and thus help them to facilitate their statistical career.

The result of our involvement is the pamphlet *"Programme of Professional Exams in Statistics"* ("Program stručnih ispita za zvanje u statističkoj struci"), that was published by FSO in 1951. The pamphlet was distributed immediately all over the country and was obligatory at any exams in statistics no matter where they were held.

Needless to say, the preparation of such a document was a cooperative undertaking. Without cooperation with experts for different fields it would not have been be possible to work it out. However, the spirit of the document and its basic orientations were worked out by our group.

The pamphlet contains programmes for three different levels of employees in statistics, viz. a) statistical clerks, b) statistical assistants, and c) statisticians. The first level refers to candidates with high school education, the second to graduates from lower-level professional schools of statisticians, and the third level to university graduates.

The first characteristic of the document is the introduction of mathematics at all levels. Therefore, no statistics without mathematics. Needless to say, at the lowest level the requirements in mathematics correspond to high school programmes. The second feature of the programme is the division of statisticians at the highest level into three groups, viz. demographers, economic statisticians, and mathematical statisticians. The first two groups have existed for quite some time. Mathematical statistician was a newborn category that recognized the necessity to have mathematicians in the statistical profession. This is how the doors of statistics were open to graduates from mathematics departments.

The next important feature is a modernization of requirements in "General Statistics". At the level of statistical assistants it included history of statistics, organization of statistical surveys, methods of data collection, summarization of data and statistical tables, graphic presentation, frequency distributions, averages, relative numbers, measures of variations, theory of correlation, theory of sample surveys, and time series. At the level of university graduates the same programme was used. The difference was in the amount of theory. At the level of assistants the emphasis was on conceptual understanding. The professionals had to be familiar with more theoretical approaches.

Statistics required for mathematical statisticians included a mathematical approach to descriptive statistics, probabilities, statistical inference, theory of sampling, survey techniques, uses of sampling, design of experiments, non-sampling errors, etc.

This was the obligatory programme in 1951. Not many countries in the world had gotten that far at that time.

No other publication has had an impact on the development of statistics in Yugoslavia that could be compared to the effects of this programme. As a matter of fact, *"The Programme"* marks the final victory of the new orientation in statistics, the beginning of a new era.

Needless to say, the course of these developments was unusual. Instead of the leadership of universities in the development of new ideas and their applications, our universities were lagging behind the level of statistics in the world. They were, in fact, a bastion of opposition and with this attitude they retarded the rate of subsequent developments.

After *"The Programme"* was published, a huge demand appeared all over the country for sources of new ideas. There were no textbooks that would help meet the needs. There were no courses at universities that would be useful to all those who needed help. In that situation we were obliged to proceed with emergency measures. The network of statistical offices organized a large number of courses all over the country for the staff with varying degrees of education. Most of these courses were of short duration, four to six weeks. However, the participants were government employees who were spared exclusively for studies. In this way the achievements were quite satisfactory. Other courses were more ambitious as they had a long duration and were mostly reserved for university graduates from mathematics departments of different universities.[10]

Various measures were also taken to obtain the textbooks and reading materials. In 1951, Echimovich published his book *"Foundations of Sampling Methods"* (*"Osnovi statističke reprezentativne metode"*) that included an introduction to the general theory of statistics. This book greatly helped overcome difficulties. I translated the book *Some Theory of Sampling* by W.E. Deming, which appeared in print in 1952. My lectures on sampling were published by the Statistical Office of Serbia in 1954 under the title *Methods of Sampling*. Echimovich also translated from Russian the booklet *Uses of Statistics in Experimental Work* by Romanowsky. That book was useful in the promotion of design of experiments. The original was in Russian and it was useful to clear the way.

Similar developments had taken place in Slovenia. Blejec left the statistical office of Slovenia and took a professorship at the the University of Ljubljana, where he developed a modern curriculum and prepared adequate textbooks. As a result of his involvement the University of Ljubljana was very quick in the modernization of its statistical education.

Many other measures were also taken to facilitate the promotion of the new course, remove some misunderstandings, develop an interest in uses of statistics in new areas of work, etc. Let me mention along that line my articles *"Teaching Statistics"*, *Statistical Review*, Vol. II, 1952, *"How to solve the problem of professional improvement of statisticians?" Statistician*, 1953, *"Textbooks of sampling methods", Statistical*

---

10 Cfr. Zarkovich, S.S.: Course of mathematical statistics, *Statistical Review*, Vol. 5, 1955.

Review, Vol. 3, 1953, "Statistical education at departments of economics", *Economist,* Vol. 7, 1954, etc.

This action had a great impact on university teaching. Quite a number of old type of professors either left or changed their involvement in favor of demography, sociology, economic analysis, etc. Some of them took the trouble to learn modern statistics. However, the most important improvement came from the recruitment by universities of young staff with a more adequate education and willingness to look around, observe the state of statistics in the world, and make an effort to catch up with the world.

The goal of modernization was thus greatly achieved.

X The achievements (continued)

We were also engaged in a number of specific areas of work. One of them was the promotion of survey techniques. In fact, this was considered to be our essential activity as a result of our understanding that the most efficient way of contributing to the development of statistics would be to help solve problems arising in the current government programmes.

Along that line two surveys guided by Echimovich were already mentioned. In addition to that, Echimovich's favorite area of work was agricultural statistics. He translated into Serbo-Croatian Mahalanobis's paper "On large-scale sample surveys", 1946 and distributed copies to people in positions that might be important in the stimulation of interest in the introduction of objective methods in agricultural statistics. In fact, such an interest already existed. In the governmental setup of that time, there were several agencies responsible for some aspects of agriculture. The Planning Commission wanted to know the fulfillment of the plan of planting and harvesting. The Ministry of Supply was interested in the production and expected deliveries. The Ministry of Agriculture had an additional interest in varieties of crops, seeds used, prices of agricultural products, fertilizers, agricultural machinery, etc. The Statistical Office operated other field machinery for the collection of data on crop areas and crop yields. Thus, each of these agencies had a separate network of sources of information. The results obtained that way varied widely. Therefore, they all welcomed the idea of a scientific and objective method of getting data.

In this favorable climate, Echimovich designed a survey of the rate of yield of wheat in Voyvodina, the main agricultural region of Yugoslavia. The survey was based on crop cutting from a sample of areas of one square meter each selected at random. The harvested crop was put in separate small sacks to estimate the components of the variance. The field work was carried out under difficult conditions, such as heat, very simple equipment, no transportation facilities, etc. The complexity of this kind of surveys was thus fully experienced. In the analysis of results a great amount of useful information was obtained for the improvement of subsequent surveys. Much was also learned about the impact of non-sampling errors.

Some results of this work were presented in Echimovich's pamphlet *"The work on the improvement of statistics of areas and yields in the Autonomous Province of Voy-*

vodina" (in Serbo-Croatian), Belgrade 1952 and some of his other papers on this subject.

Similar experiments were carried out in other parts of the country.

Attempts were also made to find out suitable segments of area that could be used in area surveys. However, that work was not carried out sufficiently far. A national survey was thus missing. In fact, different parts of the country had quite different mapping material available which made it necessary to combine several approaches.

In the promotion of sample surveys we wrote a number of papers and gave many lectures on sampling problems in statistical offices, universities, and other places where it was expected to be useful in the promotional campaign.

After Echimovich already established broad recognition of sampling all over the country, Blejec and myself joined in. Blejec designed a number of very appreciated surveys in Slovenia while I was in charge of a survey of the consumption of fuel in villages, a study of line sampling for the estimation of areas in agricultural statistics, the first livestock survey, etc. However, the climax of our involvement in sampling was the 1953 Census of Population. With the help of Morris Hansen, we got a number of documents about uses of sampling in censuses from the US Bureau of the Census. Our ambition was to examine how far we can go along that line and what the suitable approaches would be. As a result, we used sampling for the preparation of advanced estimates of census results. We did it in Belgrade for Yugoslavia as a whole, while Blejec did it in Ljubljana for Slovenia with the help of a larger sample and a more elaborated procedure (Cfr. his paper "Preliminary sample results of the Census of Population of 31 March 1953 in PR Slovenia", *Statistical Review"*, Vol. 4, 1954). Completeness of enumeration was also checked and some slight overenumeration was found that was attributed to housing rationing. Namely, housing rationing created a tendency to overstate the number of persons living in households. Another study referred to response errors that proved to be a difficult task. The ambition to estimate the response biases took us to a complicated search for information about people living at different places. However, the experienced difficulties provided a valuable guidance for subsequent studies. The accuracy of data on some characteristics was studied separately. An illustration is literacy. For that purpose a special test was developed to check reading ability. The test was administered later on in the field to a sample of persons.

Quite an amount of literature is available about the uses of sampling in the 1953 Census of Population. The following items will serve as an illustration: Zarkovich, S.S.: *Population Census Errors*, FSO, 1954; Sampling methods in the Yugoslav 1953 Census of Population, *Journal of the American Statistical Association*, Vol. 50, 1955; - Sampling Control of Literacy Data, *Journal of the American Statistical Association*, Vol. 49, 1954; - Some remarks on coverage checks in population censuses, *Population Studies*, Vol. 9, 1956, etc.

Many young colleagues participated in this work and thus added practical experiences to what they had learned at various courses. In this way the number of qualified survey statisticians increased considerably. Some of them were V.Balaban, D.Nikolich, B.Babich, M.Obradovich, M.Pirochanac, J.Lilich, Bedenich, F.Raknich, etc. Most of them joined statistical agencies in the republics and strengthened the ability of the country to broaden the programme of survey work.

Another line of our work was the statistical quality control. Much effort was put in the promotion of this area of work that was hardly known at that time on the European continent. However, the results achieved should in the best case be called modest. We probably started too early, before the conditions were mature.

When I was in the US, I was impressed by the developments in the statistical quality control and I thought that it was my duty to see to it that my country made use of these techniques. Industrialization was an obsession, a political slogan that one could hear about everywhere. I took these slogans seriously and expected that the authorities would appreciate a small contribution from statistics.

There was another motivation as well. From the literature that was coming to us from the USSR, I realized that prospects for modernization of our statistics through the agencies responsible for the government programme of data collection would be negligible. The system of work was imposed on us that was presented above. It had a solution for all the fields of data collection. Chances to add something to that or introduce changes, let alone new approaches, were extremely small. On the other hand, quality control seemed to be more promising. Its introduction into industrial production would bring us in contact with engineers who were not so much interested in the ideology provided the techniques offered solve their problems.

My next argument concerned the Soviet literature on quality control. I had a chance to glance at a number of publications on this subject that treated problems in the same way as Western literature. Moreover, one of these books contained a great deal of mathematical statistics as a prerequisite for quality control. Therefore, by doing the quality control we could use the Soviet literature as justification. Our efforts along that line would be the use of the achievements of a socialist country. In this case nobody could oppose quality control on ideological grounds. In this way, mathematical statistics would go through. Expansion in other fields would then be less difficult.

This was our expectation. I rushed with several attempts as soon as I came back from the US. I approached some people in the engineering circles and I told them what statistical control was and what had been achieved abroad. Most of them liked new ideas and I got their support. This was particularly true of Stjepan Hahn who was a highly regarded personality in the engineering disciplines. Hahn was ready to help. He asked me to prepare a promotional programme. He finally decided to organize, as a first step, a public lecture on quality control at the Association of Engineers. It was in 1947. He must have done a very good job in the promotion of the gathering as my lecture was attended by a big crowd.

The participants asked for many explanations in the course of the lecture. I got the impression that it could be the beginning of a large-scale use of quality control. However, during further discussion my attempt turned out to be a failure. In fact, the lecture helped me to learn something about quality control that I had overlooked before. Namely, quality control has no meaning to a hungry market that absorbs any product no matter how poor the quality might be. An engineer summarized the situation by saying: "I cannot produce the rubbish that I would not be able to sell months in advance of production. Your methods assume competition for the market. We do not care for quality under our present conditions".

94

I did not give up in spite of the defeat. I asked Stjepan Hahn to find a factory of mass production where I could try to introduce statistical quality control of the process of production. He found for me a match factory Drava, in Osijek. At that time matches were a symbol of poor quality. A good percentage of them would not lihht. In other cases, the wood would break in the hand and the match had to be thrown away. In still another percentage, the matches would blow up. They were dangerous for eyes and skin. In short, there was a broad interest in quality. The job seemed challenging.

I organized the work. Control charts were all around in the factory. The outcome was again a series of failures. In the study of the percentage of broken matches, I found at one moment that the process ran out of control. I informed the management and they told me: "We knew it without your charts. Yesterday we started using a poor kind of wood. We were aware in advance of its impact on quality".

Similar results were obtained in the study of the percentage of nonstriking matches. I signaled that the process was out of control. The answer was: "We did not get all the chemicals to make the striking head. Yesterday we started the production without two ingredients and we knew what would happen".

In another study, we found out that more than fifty percent of the matches could not be used. The whole business was unfair to consumers. The management said: "The Ministry of Industry is informed. We are selling different products than declared on each box. However, we have the order to continue. There is no other factory".

It was also discovered that one machine was producing significantly more waste than the other machines. The chief engineer was informed. He said: "The operator of that machine has asked permission to change his job. We could not agree as we have no replacement. He is thus doing a kind of forced labor. As a result, he could not care less".

In other words, control charts are useful if the management is able to influence the production process and remove the causes of deterioration. If the conditions of work are beyond the reach of the management, there is little justification for quality control.

In order to learn this lesson, I had to spend many sleepless nights at the factory and spoil my clothes with the oil. My experiment ruined me financially. As a prize I had another failure.

While hoping to be able to introduce quality control in our industry, I wrote three books aimed at the promotion of the uses of statistics among engineering personnel. My particular aim was to establish an appreciation of quality control. In spite of the difficulties that I encountered in the effort to arrange with factories the establishment of projects of actual application, I was convinced that statistical quality control must be recognized and used as in other countries. Industrial production is the same in all the countries in the world. The products of Yugoslav industry will have no access to world markets unless the conditions of work are normalized and management gets an opportunity to influence the factors of production. My books were *Statistical Methods in Industrial Research,* published in 1949, *Quality Control of Products,* published in 1949, and *Quality Control of the Process of Production,* published in 1951. The first of them dealt with general principles of statistics, the second with acceptance sampling, and the third with control charts and their application with illustrations from the production of matches.

The conditions under which these books were published deserve to be mentioned.

The application of recording has created huge problems in industry. The industrial establishments were required to send to the higher authorities more reports than other units of work. As a result, the Ministry of Heavy Industry was overloaded with reports. Mountains of paper were in all the corridors and the Ministry did not know what to do. The issue was a source of headaches even to the Minister of Heavy Industry, who was one of the leading personalities of the YCP. The minister asked around if anybody was available who could advise on what to do with these reports. In the resulting search for a person holding the keys to the puzzle, I was summoned to the office of the Assistant Minister who had attended my lecture on quality control. He asked me if methods were available to analyze data they had at the ministry. I gave him an affirmative answer. He then asked me if any book was ever written about these matters in our language. In the ensuing discussion, my own work was touched upon somehow. I had in my mind the above books. "Why don't you publish these books"? he said. I told him that I had been to different publishers and there was no interest in matters that "nobody would read". He then told me that the Ministry operated a publishing house of books related to industry and offered to publish my "material". Their publisher was "The Industrial Book". I had nothing against the idea. He rang up the director of the publishing house and the deal was made.

My books were published after some time. However, nobody has ever asked me anything about the subject of these books. I gave up further insisting. I cannot blame myself for the lack of initiative. It seems, however, that it was too early for that subject. I abandoned the quality control as I had more promising duties in other areas.

In addition to engineering circles, I also established contacts with a number of people in the Ministry of Internal Trade with a view to inquiring if they would be interested in statistics and its use. I picked up the problem of the estimation of stocks in retail stores. It was an important issue. Many people were concerned about it. It was frequently discussed in Soviet literature. Therefore, one could deal with it without the risk of being called an "enemy". Stocktaking also meant counting physical objects. The subject would thus not be a case of a bourgeois abstract theory.

Lists of retail shops were available by administrative units. Supplementary information was also available about the kind of products sold, volume of sales, number of employees, etc. I, therefore, proposed that stocks be economically estimated with the help of an inspection of a sample of stratified shops. All the advantages were calculated and presented. However, there was no interest in either a deviation from the rules established or the savings that would arise following the use of sampling. A shopkeeper told me in this connection:

"Why do you bother me with changes in our practice? The easiest way for me to live is to carry on the existing orders".

The idea of simplifications and savings was not a sufficiently attractive subject for the bureaucracy of the Ministry of Internal Trade to get excited and start thinking about.

Soviet books on trade statistics prescribe stocktaking for everybody. Therefore, do it that way and have a good time.

Blejec was also involved in quality control in Slovenia. That republic had a rather advanced textile industry. The managers of that industry received information about quality control in other countries and they decided to make use of it. This is how they got in touch with Blejec. Blejec was very successful. The industry absorbed the results of his work. The industry was happy with the achievements and insisted on the continuation of cooperation with Bjelec. The cooperation ended with a real contribution to quality control of the production. Some years later, the textile industry invited Tippet, an international authority on quality control in the textile industry, to visit the factories in Slovenia and make an appraisal of the system of quality control. Tippet said: "I accept the work and have nothing to propose to improve on it".

As to the impact of that work it does not seem that much has remained from these early efforts. A new crisis of statistical development was on the way. Most achievements reported here were either eradicated or reduced to vegetation. No initiative for the application of statistics in industry was coming from statisticians. They could not do much even in other areas of fundamental importance for the statistical profession.

However, the industry itself woke up after a number of years and arranged for a revival of statistics. Different branches of industry developed cooperation with their counterparts in the world. In this way, they learned about uses of statistics. As a result, the engineers took the matter in their hands and reestablished uses of statistics. However, this time it was done independently of the official statistical line and the official representatives of the profession.

The quality of the resulting work suffered. A great part of the applications introduced in industry that way consisted primarily of a mechanical transfer of the ready-made procedures. The knowledge of the underlying theory was missing. The ability of the part of industry to adapt the techniques in circulation to its own conditions was also missing. However, some improvements followed in time. The engineers started studying statistics and introducing statistical lectures at schools of engineering. It appeared that another and independent start took place that was likely to be more promising as it was done by the industry itself.

In addition to these developments, some other events took place in this period. The first of the issues to mention is the publication of data.

In Western civilization, statistics grew up from the need of the society for information. In the early stages, the society meant primarily the government. The governments supported the establishment of data collection agencies and contributed greatly to the development of statistics. However, the interest in statistics went far beyond governments. The industry needed data to know the location and the amount of resources, the distribution of the population, prices, transport, etc. The same was true of business in general and many other activities. The way to meet this broad interest was the publication of available data. The publication of data was the way to offer the information to whoever might be interested; it was the way to improve the efficiency of the society:

A part of that process is the improvement of the education. Statistics provides facts and makes it possible for different types of schools to familiarize students with the knowledge of the facts in the area of their studies. Equipped with that knowledge they are able to carry out their work in a more efficient way.

Needless to say, the condition for this improvement of the educational process is the wide circulation of statistical data. Teachers are thus able to absorb the facts and involve their students in the related studies. In other words, dissemination of data is an essential contribution to the improvement of education.

In connection with this the following illustration might be appreciated. An author's colleague, who was professor of foreign trade at the Department of Economics of the University of Belgrade, was asked to address a meeting of economists. The title of the talk was "The present state of Yugoslav foreign trade". His reaction was: "I talk to students about foreign trade by using general principles from foreign literature. I know nothing about Yugoslav foreign Trade. If you want facts you better approach one of the leading political personalities of the Ministry of Foreign Trade. They are the only people who know facts and what facts can be disclosed".

It should also be pointed out that the amount of available statistical information, the state of data collection skills, and the ability to analyze data also depend upon the dissemination of data. Development of statistics as a science was growing in the past from the contacts of research workers with data and their efforts to make data more meaningful.

This is why the publication of data was introduced at an early stage of statistical development. This is what we used to do in Yugoslavia before the last war. However, after the last war, the YCP, as soon as it took power, imposed an absolute blackout on any type of statistical information. Statistical data became top secret. A disclosure of data was made equivalent to a crime, a spy activity. Summarization of data, the preparation of tables and calculations were strictly controlled to make it impossible for the enemy to get hold of any bit of information. After office hours, control teams would go through the offices to check if any piece of paper was left on the desk. The rolls of paper in calculating machines were checked to make sure that no data remained on them. All the working tables had to be put in separate sacks and burned in the presence of persons of confidence. The tables that were the result of statistical work were prepared in a small number of copies only and distributed exclusively to the top political leadership.

Needless to say, it was a barbarous act against the society, its future, and its civilization. After a very short time, it showed disastrous consequences. Articles in newspapers became void of content and reduced to an endless repetition of political slogans. They became boring and neglected by readers. Articles in scientific periodicals followed the same line. Substance was absent everywhere. A new type of author appeared who was able to talk at length without conveying any idea worthy of attention. Economic and sociological research disappeared entirely. Literary production in many fields of work was reduced to a repetition of various political documents.

After the conflict between the YCP and its counterpart in the USSR, the ban on the publication of data was lifted.

In the beginning of the new era, the publication programme was rather modest.

The responsible people were probably careful. They wanted to see how the new system would work. After it was realized that there were no reactions that might develop into trouble, the programme was broadened and developed later on into a standard system of publications.

The measure taken by the YCP to re-establish the publication of data was presented subsequently as a wise and courageous decision that should be glorified by the public at large. This was, however, taken by people as an attempt on the part of the YCP to wash off part of the responsibility for a decision with disastrous consequences.

Another event that took place in this period was the establishment of the periodical *Statistical Review* (Statistička Revija). Its publication started in 1951. The responsibility for both the establishment and the publication of the *Review* was with FSO. The aim of the *Review* was to publish papers and news of interest. The *Review* filled a gap in the publication of statistical material. The activities reported above resulted in many papers that had to be published and preserved for all those who might wish to consult documents related to the past work.

Statistical Review has continued its publication till today.

In this period The Yugoslav Statistical Society was also established. After several years of preparation, the *Society* was formally established in 1953. Its membership included all the statisticians with recognized seniority.

The *Society* accepted the publication of the *Review* as its organ. The main activity of the *Society* was the organization of biennial meetings. For each meeting a number of topics was included in the programme and the members were invited to present their contributions for discussion.

Later on, the *Society* was organized by republics. Each republic has its own *Statistical Society*. The old *Yugoslav Statistical Society* has become the *Association of Statistical Societies*. The office of the President is rotated by republics no matter how many members there are from each republic and what their professional standing is.

Another important achievement of this period is the spirit of search, the favorable atmosphere for the development of science. It was somehow recognized that science is impossible without an efficient system of communication. We felt the need to follow the developments in the world. This was the way to know what was going on, what problems were on the agenda of the others, what methods the others were using, what results were obtained, etc. We established contacts with the most important centers of statistical work. FSO was on the mailing list of many institutions in the world and we were able to keep up with the state of the profession. We were receiving a huge amount of publications, including material for internal discussion. It also worked in the outward direction. Our work was noticed in other countries as we used to send our material to others. As a result, our work was a part of the statistical production in the world.

This system of communications was not imposed on us as a result of some policy decision by the authorities. It developed spontaneously from the requirements of our work. We moved in that direction freely, without any restrictions. We had no secrets.

A part of the new atmosphere was the development of a critical attitude with respect to the available know-how in statistical methodology. We learned at a very early stage that the performance of different techniques depended upon circumstances. This was a great stimulus to our involvement in research. Before attempting to solve the problems on our agenda, an attitude developed of an obligatory search for information from similar studies by others. The next step was to appraise the available experiences in the light of our circumstances. The resulting outlines of solutions were examined with the help of old data, pretesting, etc. At the end of such a long process, decisions were made regarding the approach to adopt.

This is just the opposite of the accusations addressed to us that we deal with abstract formulas and neglect reality. In fact, it was only in this period that a systematic study of our specific conditions became a fundamental requirement of work.

The development of a scientific approach to work had a great impact on all our activities. The staff had become aware of the limitations of the methodology they were using. They were aware that a long journey was needed on the way toward improved performance. And they wanted to participate in that journey. They started reporting problems arising in the field and suggesting improvements. Quite many of them started a collection and analysis of experiences. Much of that work was transformed into reports, proposals, papers, and other forms of literary production. The staff felt responsible for the quality of work they were doing. In the discharge of that responsibility, they were willing to engage even in those types of work that required great sacrifices, such as the participation in field experiments under a shortage of transport, food, hotels, etc. A field machinery was established that was able to carry out the most demanding tasks. That field machinery was fit for the future.

XI Disillusionment

The YCP played out its main political trumps in a very short time. On its way to power it announced the rule of socialist ideals for everybody. Among these ideals the argument of freedom was mentioned more frequently than anything else. The YCP claimed to be the promoter of a wave of freedom that the country had never seen before. However, instead of that, it introduced totalitarianism and imposed an absolute ban on the expression of any views different from its own politics.

The YCP also claimed to be a bearer of an ideology based on a scientific theory of the society. That ideology gives a chance to the communist movement to establish a society of happiness. The means available for the purpose are social and economic planning on one hand, and recording as a source of factual information for decision making on the other. However, instead of becoming a society of happiness, the country developed into a collection of failures that can hardly be compared to any other case. The big trumps were thus transformed into illusions. A disillusionment process developed rapidly. A nice sketch of the history was unable to stand the test of practice.

Each totalitarian regime claims absolute support from the population. The proofs are: participation of people in voting for government candidates with 99.9 per cent of persons listed with voting rights, requests by the sick persons in hospitals to be taken to voting places to express their satisfaction with the proposed candidates, manifestations of enthusiasm in connection with government decisions, massive participation at political rallies, applauding during political speeches, etc.

This effect is achieved with the help of a tested programme of measures that starts with the dance of terror. In this period of lawlessness, people realize that complete surrender to the power is the only way to survive. They give up unconditionally. Their attitude is governed by the awareness of helplessness. They accept to live in the hands of the power; they behave according to the wishes of the power; their obedience is complete. In order to maintain that state of mind steps follow such as jail, discrimination at employment and promotions, discrimination in the choice of candidates for higher positions, discrimination in the distribution of housing, etc.

However, after strict control is established in all aspects of life, the issue arises of the price to pay for totalitarian achievements. The price consists of apathy and paralysis.

101

The people have learned to behave according to the wishes of the power. The people are requested to follow the party. They do so and keep quiet. Any initiative might put them in trouble. They are not asked to open their eyes, search for solutions to problems of the society and propose improvements of work. They behave as machines. The result is a crippled society.

All the totalitarian governments, no matter whether they are of communist or anticommunist type, develop very fast a state of shortage of almost all kinds of consumer goods. If it is not always the shortage in an absolute sense, it means at least a poor quality of products. The choice does not exist. Esthetics is entirely neglected. If alternatives are available, they are reduced to different names of equally poor products.

There is nothing surprising about that. This is the only possible course of totalitarianism. So far there has been no single case of a totalitarian regime that had a sound economy. Totalitarian governments divert a considerable part of the national resources toward aims, such as a strong army, the military industry, military glory, a strong police, tight control of borders, an elaborate propagandistic machinery, maintenance of various channels of repression, organized mass manifestations of joy and happiness, etc. Needless to say, the only way to carry out this programme is to put the burden on the population.

The poverty of the population is one of the strongest means that totalitarian regimes use in keeping power. No totalitarianism can tolerate the economic independence of its citizens. Economic independence means a possibility to neglect the prescribed forms of behavior without any consequence. It also implies a neglect of participation at manifestations of enthusiasm, reduced size of crowds at political gatherings, reduced percentage of votes, etc. Thus, economic independence generates a behavior that is contrary to fundamental claims of totalitarian regimes.

Symptoms of a paralyzed society became evident at an early stage of the new Yugoslav state. The YCP did not have the means in its ideology to channel the developments toward an efficient economy. Young people without experience and knowledge were appointed to key positions with a mandate of absolute power. Most of these people never did any work. Foreign experiences were not mobilized. Nobody thought of a programme of studies that would follow the main lines of the planning exercise. Various groups were pulling the economy in different direction. Strong personalities started interfering with planning by introducing their own projects. Most of them wanted to leave behind some visible monument of their leadership. The others insisted on certain modifications of the already accepted plans. The outcome was a complete lack of a coherent system of work. At the beginning of our First Five Year Plan, I was in the office for a control of the fulfillment of federal investment plan. It was one of the most important parts of the total plan. I found many discrepancies between the plan on my desk and the activities reported from the field. I went to see the Vice President of the Planning Commission to ask him for guidance regarding these discrepancies. He told me: "Forget about your plan and take as the plan the items included in the reports coming from the field".

The advice was obviously inadequate. It was an admission of the dubious value of our approaches.

The stage was thus reached very early of a lack of confidence in the ongoing experiment. It was not only true of common people in streets who had no say in big social changes. It was equally true of the top leadership of the YCP. In the office for a follow up of the investment plan, we had to prepare a report of the fulfillment of the plan for a period of six months. For that purpose we issued a table showing that the investment plan for the country as a whole was fulfilled with 37 per cent. Later on some trouble was reported about the adding machine. We repeated the summarization and the new version of the table showed 12 per cent only. I went home to sleep on it and see what best we could do. The next morning I went to see the Vice President of the Planning Commission who was responsible for the investment plan. I told him the story with maximum excitement and almost unable to breath. I expected him to be furious. However, he smiled and said: "Don't you worry. It is not a serious matter. I do not trust your data anyway. I have a better source of information. My driver takes me around and after I have travelled for a couple of days, I know much better than your recording what the fulfillment of the plan is".

This is how the life destroyed confidence in the ability of communist ideology to steer a rational direction of the national economy. Huge preparations were made to fulfill all the prerequisites of the ideology for success. Private property was abolished and the party appointed to all the key positions persons of confidence. The enemy was thus ruled out. The YCP was in absolute control of everything.

In order to complete the preparations for the historic achievement, a huge network of recording was established. Much has already been said about the size of this enterprise. Novak[11] has pointed out the case of a ministry that requested from individual establishments a monthly report containing 13,000 (thirteen thousand) indicators. In a study of the state of recording in the establishments, it was found that an establishment had to answer 609 questionnaires out of which 26 referred to daily reports. The same study also showed an enormous amount of duplication. It was found that the same information was asked up to 60 times.

In some cases, the size of the recording machinery took enormous proportions. The case was mentioned of a garage on the Yugoslav seacost to service cars of foreign tourists. It was a new two-floor building. The ground floor was reserved for cars in servicing while the top floor was used for administrative employees. The whole available space was full of desks and a large group of employees was doing the recording. For a much larger output a garage in Western countries would not have more than a couple of employees.

At that time, the country was already in a deep apathy and tired of experimentation. Under these conditions data were hardly a way to better management. The society was already suffering from a shortage of everything and the instability of everything. If raw materials were available today, it did not mean that they would be available tomorrow under similar conditions. It was pointed out in the case of matches that the production was continuously facing the danger of the appearance of unexpected factors, such as unknown quality of wood, lack of essential chemicals, turnover of labor, damage to machinery, lack of spare parts, lack of foreign currencies for imports, etc. The man-

---

11 *Rekord Keeping*, Vol. I, 1950.

agement was thus obliged to apply improvisations. It was a kind of catch-as-catch-can production in which statistics was not able to help find the way out.

In this situation the economy turned to non-economic measures as a source of solutions to its problems. It primarily meant an orientation of the economy toward politics. Cultivation of contacts with political personalities was a road to success. The presentation of business problems at political meetings was a way to involve the party machinery in a supporting action, such as the pressure on other establishments and institutions to provide facilities, agree to a transfer of labor, secure transport, accept commitments regarding the availability and timing of facilities, etc. Needless to say, the economy had to pay back for the services rendered. It became necessary for the management of establishments to participate at political gatherings, support sporting activities, finance cultural programmes, contribute to the establishment of nurseries, sporting grounds, etc. Publicity was more important than the internal matters of efficiency.

Although the exaggerations of recording were broadly known and transformed into many jokes, people had no courage to open their mouths and raise the related problems. The pressure continued on all the units of work to introduce and maintain good recording. Good recording was a part of good behavior. This is why recording was transformed fast into a bureaucratic activity, a routine. Attention was focussed on issues such as: "Do the reporting units send in their current reports on time"?, "Have they filled in all the entries in their questionnaires"?, "Do the entries in individual cells tally with column totals"?, etc. If units of work were caught guilty with respect to these formal criteria, they were publically exposed for their conduct. They ran the risk of being mentioned in the press and at political meetings. The directors of such establishments were accused of negligence with all the related dangers for their career.

A friend of mine was responsible for the economics department of a big company. Recording was a part of the office under his control. After several articles were published in the press about the neglect of recording and delays in the submission of reports, the director of the company told him: "I do not want headaches because of recording. I do not know how you should do it. Do whatever you want. However, do it on time".

The following case is another illustration. A colleague of mine was a chief statistician with a big construction company. He was not a statistician. However, he was put on the job in the hope that the company would not be blamed any more for failures in recording and reporting. At the occasion of 1st May celebrations, which include prizes for good work in the previous year, he got a prize and his name was in the newspapers. The citation was: "High quality recording and reporting". The prize surprised me as he was most of the time with his friends in the street and coffee shops. When I saw him, I asked for an explanation of his achievement. He said: "Other people send in incomplete reports that are also full of errors. Their figures never add up to the respective totals nor do the marginal totals tally with the grand total. I reverse the process and start with an acceptable grand total that I break down afterwards into marginal totals, etc. In my tables there are no errors and my boss is happy with my achievement".

"How about your construction sites? Do you ever go there to get data"?, I added. He just smiled.

This is how recording developed into an exercise which had to be carried out because of the pressure of the power although those who were involved in it had doubts as to its use.

Difficulties with planning were also widely known. One source of headaches was the lack of meaningful indicators for both the formulation and the follow-up of plans. A shoe factory had a plan expressed in pairs of shoes without a distinction of shoes for males, females, children, sandals, etc. As a result, in order to realize the target of the production, the factories moved in the direction of the simplest items. From the recording point of view everything was all right. However, disastrous consequences appeared in the market. In fact, on the basis of recording we were unable to know what was going on in the production. Similarly, in the metallic sector the plan was broken down into categories of products expressed in tons. Nails, screws, and similar products were planned in tons. As a result, the market was flooded with long nails while smaller categories disappeared.

It should also be mentioned that the quality of products was entirely beyond the reach of our recording. Our indicators were of a quantitative nature. A pair of shoes might be a high quality product or rubbish that could be sold exclusively in a situation of extreme shortage. From the recording point of view all the shoes are alike.

In this situation, operational decisions in the economy by central authorities were faced with many complications. The construction of a new factory was stopped as 30 tons of iron were missing for the concrete. After various interventions, the case came to the Economic Council for consideration. The first step taken by the Council was to get information about the quantities of each profile of iron needed. Then a search started of the places where the iron could be obtained. The production figures speak of quantities produced in tons without additional details. Telephone calls followed to identify places where products needed could be found. After the calls to producers were completed it was found out that some profiles were not available. It was suggested to get in touch with some companies that might have stocks. Again a round of calls. It was thus concluded that the whole request could be met by taking parts of the iron from three different places. These places were informed of the Council's decision. However, the Economic Council was informed that the order could not be carried out as the shipment of the same iron was already on the way to other companies. The Economic Council accepted complaints from one of these places and issued its final order to the others. A new series of calls was needed to locate the missing part of the iron.

However, this is not the end of the story. The construction company got the needed iron at the expense of other companies that had ordered and paid for the iron some time before. The Economic Council insisted on priority reasons. However, other companies considered the judgement arbitrary and presented many arguments in favor of their case, such as political, social, and economic consequences of the decision to assign a lower priority to some activities without a thorough examination of problems created to others.

Interventions of this kind impose on top of the economy a layer of bureaucratic activities that make the economy dependent upon a mechanism that is external to the economy itself. The mechanism consists of federal agencies, the agencies of republic, and the local authorities. In addition, it includes the party and other organizations of more or less political character.

The impact of that bureaucratic machinery on the economy had a paralyzing effect. It increased the cost of operations. Next is the system of delays that the administrative machinery introduced in economic decisions. The problems had to be reported through the existing hierarchy. This was a slow process as the information to higher levels was to be accompanied by comments from lower levels. Additional time was needed to work out solutions. The travel of decisions back to the originator of problems was equally complicated as all the outlets of the bureaucracy had to be informed to get a chance to comment.

The existence of this machinery was considered as a source of headaches by those who concentrate on work and make an effort to do it properly. These were the establishments that look ahead, carry out early preparations for the future, make contracts with other companies and specify the services needed, etc. The system of interventions made it possible that their staff be transferred to others, their shipments of raw material be stopped, etc. It thus happened that the work of good establishments was disturbed by action taken in favor of more important ones who might have been careless in the discharge of their responsibilities.

The system of interventions was thus killing responsibility for one's own work. It created the feeling that the outcome of work was not within the reach of one's own forces. It stimulated interest in contacts, friends, and political interventions rather than the work. It also demoralized good workers because poor work was sometime supported at the expense of the good one.

These are the experiences that pushed the YCP to the courageous idea of abandoning the involvement of the federal government in operational issues of the economy.

The solution opted for was decentralization, transfer of the authority for economic decisions to the economy itself or, in other terms, to the business and local authorities. Instead of operational matters the federal government would follow the developments in the economy and see to it that the events were channeled toward the agreed upon aims. As a result, the federal government had to be reorganized accordingly, together with governments of republics and local authorities as well. A part of the reorganization affected the recording as well. The Directorate of Recording was abolished as well as the Federal Statistical Office. Instead, a new agency was established in 1951 under the name of Federal Institute of Statistics and Recording with Vojin Guzina as its director. The Institute had two sectors of work, one concerned with statistics and the other with recording. However, the name of the new agency did not correspond to the facts. Recording of the earlier type was not continued. In the new organization, statistical reporting was reduced to monthly reports of industrial establishments. However, it was done for statistical purposes. The recording sector included economic statistics that was based on a system of current reporting while the statistical sector included primarily social statistics.

In the new organization, Novak was the head of economic statistics and Krashovec the head of social statistics.

In 1953 a new change in the organization of data collection took place. The Federal Institute of Statistics and Recording was abolished and the Federal Institute of Statistics was created instead. From that moment on "recording" disappeared from the scene. New generations of statisticians do even not know what it was.

Needless to say, the ill fate of Yugoslav recording does not mean that recording was eliminated as a tool. It was a useful tool before the Yugoslavs used it and it will remain to be so in the future. However, it will only be useful if established as a tool of management after a very careful consideration of its cost and benefits. It needs to be a part of the organization of work and it is to be continuously kept under control with a view to examining its adequacy under changing conditions.

Novak neglected such a rational approach. Recording was introduced by the party top as a political achievement of the socialist state that should be based on the available experience in the USSR. All its essential parts were thus ready and not a subject for study. It was accepted in advance, before the process of gradual expansion had a chance to offer suggestions as to how far the exercise should be allowed to go. Novak wanted politics, recording that should be based on "self-initiative of struggling masses and their leaderships, on conscientiousness guided by marxist theory, experience of the October Revolution, practice of the USSR, the Spanish Civil War, and the necessities of the particular moment of development of fighting and revolution".[12]

It is very questionable whether on this ground anything could have been done different than what he did. The task that he was facing required a staff with scientific education and experience, people with sharp critical minds and ready to accept lessons from facts and experience. However, Novak did not want that. His requirements of the staff did not go beyond young age and membership in the YCP.

This was certainly not the road to success. Yugoslav recording will remain in history as a misuse of national resources. It was an illustration of the tragedy that arises when people are not allowed to open their mouths about matters that concern the whole nation.

---

12 Novak, A.: Statistics and Recording, *Thirty Years of Statistics in SFR Yugoslavia*, FIS, Belgrade, 1974. p. 20.

XII Some sad matters

History frequently gives a chance to various persons to activate their passions, drive, and intelligence in the effort to build the world of their dreams. History also gives chances to people to destroy the achievements built by somebody else. However, cases are rare of persons who have involved their passions in building something and have used afterwards the same passions to destroy the own results.

Novak was one of those who had that exceptional destiny. When he was involved in building up the recording, he was convinced that he was making a contribution to the solution of a fundamental problem of human society. He never hesitated to use any means to break obstacles on the way toward a society dominated by recording. Those who did not follow his line were "enemies of socialism", "ignorants", "people unaware of marxist theory", "followers of anti-marxist views", etc. After he started dismantling the whole organization of recording, he was doing it in great excitement with a view to removing from the Yugoslav society all the remainders of the past.

Novak mobilized the same passions against statistics. Statistics was the discipline that he was never able to tolerate. However, it took him some time to implement his mission against statistics. He waited for an opportunity. When it arose he did not hesitate to implement his vision of data collection.

In fact, Novak announced his intentions quite early, as early as 1949. However, we discarded his messages. He told us what the position of statistics was. Statistics was a means of capitalist domination. In addition, this means was dangerous as it was being pushed forward in the name of science. Fortunately, the masses were aware of the trap. Therefore, they would see to it that this "science" was swept away together with all other tricks that capitalism used to continue its domination.

This was it. Novak kept repeating his song whenever he got a chance. We listened to his preaching with the sympathy of parents who listen to first lessons they get from their angry children. However, we disregarded his words. Somebody said: "The boy has got temperament".

In course of time, Novak's song about statistics was played frequently through public channels. After some time, it came to me in one of the unpleasant versions. When

108

we were moving from Indija to Belgrade, an old lady, who was chief of the registry office, told me that she did not get instructions as to what to do with the confidential files. She came to the idea of distributing them to the persons concerned. In this way, the poor lady committed a terrible mistake. I am referring to it because she died soon after that mistake.

The confidential files included all the correspondence that might offer guidance to the authorities about political orientations of persons concerned. That information goes to the central file of all the citizens in the Ministry of Interior and to any other place in case of need. A part of that file is the document called "characteristic". This is what the bosses or the personnel officers have to say about each of their employees. Naturally, the central point of each "characteristic" deals with the attitude of persons concerned toward the regime. "Characteristic" involves any piece of information that might be indicative of that attitude.

I went through the most recent "characteristic" that was written about me by Krashovec. Krashovec said: "He does not care for what I tell him to do. However, he works hard. I never saw him away from his desk". However, the earlier "characteristics" were very bad. One of them said: "He is unable to get rid of his non-scientific views of statistics although his attention was called to the consequences of that attitude. Arch-reactionary". "Non-scientific views" are thus sufficient to be included in the category of people who are recommended to the police as "arch-reactionaries". Novak was obviously not alone in his desire to protect the nation from "non-scientific views".

Krashovec was aware of the content of these official "characteristics" and he had to be careful in controlling the expressions of our "non-scientific views". Novak was also keeping an eye on our work. Krashovec was sure that Novak would not fail to attack all of us should we take any step that could be used against us.

In this way our work became very complicated. In addition to the difficulties to achieve some progress under serious limitations in any respect, we also had to keep thinking of how best we could continue working without being attacked. An illustration is our work on the improvement of statistical education. Krashovac was aware of our views as we had discussed them many times and he was convinced that we were on the right track. In order to strengthen our action he asked me to write a paper about statistical education in developed countries. As a result of that request, I wrote the article "Teaching Statistics". This was in 1950. I gave my manuscript to Krashovec and he kept it for several months without saying a word to me. Later on, I learned that my paper was sent to party authorities for consideration. After a year and a half upon the submission of the manuscript, Krashovec told me that the paper would be published in *Statistical Review*. Rodoljub Cholakovich, a member of the Politburo of the YCP, who was frequently the top judge in matters of science and culture, was requested to read my article and advise on the action to take. He apparently told Krashovec: "I read that article carefully and I do not see what are you, comrades, afraid of". In other words, several comrades were afraid of. After they got Cholakovich's *placet* a part of their fear was gone. However, a part only. You never know what might happen tomorrow. Therefore, precautionary measures were never superfluous. My paper was published in 1952 in *Statistical Review*. It was composed of small characters used for various news and other less important matters. It was the only paper published that way.

Krashovec was obviously aware of the content of my paper. This was the rationale of our action to modernize statistical education. However, he needed help to break Novak's opposition. It was not a negligible point to get a member of the Politburo on one's side.

In this period another event took place that greatly damaged my interest in the continuation of the work that we started.

At that time I was living in a room that was a part of a relatively large apartment. The room was located on the ground floor and it was possible to see from outside what was going on in the room. One night, at about 2 AM, somebody knocked at my window. I got up and saw two persons in civilian clothing. When I opened the window one of them told me: "Open the house. We are from the police".

I do not know how my wife survived that shock. I was also shocked. However, I have put quite a lot of time in thinking about the era we lived in. The idea of being exterminated for some reason was frequently on my mind. At that moment, I thought that my turn had come and I accepted my destiny without too much excitement.

My thoughts were concentrated on the fact of the night visit. If the police want an investigation, some information, or a statement, they could send me a message and the business would be done during the day. Therefore, the night visit was used in case they wanted to take away somebody without being seen by other people who would talk about it afterwards. Night visits were thus reserved for people who were taken away and who never came back.

When I opened the door, they came in and presented their documents that I did not look at. They stayed in the middle of the room and looked around. They kept quiet. Minutes were centuries long. Eventually one of them said: "We would like to have a word with you. Come tomorrow at 6 PM to such and such address. It is not an office. It is a private apartment". Later on, I passed by that house on several occasions. This was in the present street 29 November No. 39. I did not climb up to check if my hosts were still there.

The visitors left. The rest of the night we were not able to close eyes. We were less excited than at the beginning. If they had wanted to kill me (or us) they would have taken me (or us) with them. What did they want? We frequently repeated that question. We were unable to eat. The excitement killed our appetite. However, we had one coffee after another.

During the fixed appointment, they asked me many questions about the people in the office. They asked me for my opinion about quite a few persons. The idea came to my mind that they wanted indications of points that could be used as a basis for further conversation. If I do not like somebody or *vice versa* that could be useful. They could start building on that basis. This is why I said that I did not know most of the people mentioned by them. Those whom I did know I presented in the best possible way. The impression left at the end of the meeting was that I did not know much. They told me they would inform me of the time and place of the next meeting.

This is how a long series of my meetings with the police started. By the time of the next meeting I had worked out my attitude. No matter what might happen, I decided to play the role of a man without acquaintances, not interested in people, and particularly a man with a modest intelligence and poor curiosity.

After some meetings they offered to me to become their agent. To make it attractive, they told me that prewar politicians work for them and keep them informed about the old ruling class. Then, they said that the most beautiful girls work for them so that they can easily pull in a trap any man. They also told me that I was their choice in the statistical office because nobody would ever think of the possibility of my being an agent. They also told me that they wanted somebody to keep contacts with foreigners.

The next time they asked me for my agreement. I said I was a poor man without an apartment, on the edge of misery and, to show my cooperative mood, I indicated Krashovec as a good candidate for the job. I said that he could easily afford to go to restaurants with people without running the risk of financial disaster. They told me that my economic position would be entirely changed and I would live in their service at a higher level.

I did not say "No" to the offer. However, I insisted on my lack of ability. I said I would spoil everything and they would have trouble with me. At that point they started shouting at me and threatening me with the guns that they kept on the table. They told me that my life was in serious danger. At the end they asked me to prepare a detailed report about a colleague of mine whom I knew although not very well.

An interesting thing is that they never told me the time and place of the next meeting in advance. In this way they probably intended to increase the tension and speed up the approach of a nervous breakdown on the part of their candidates.

For the next meeting I decided to stick to the role of a fool. I told them I had had coffee with the (she) comrade whom they were interested in and spoke about ten minutes on problems that she referred to. Suddenly one of them jumped up and said: "You are crazy. Why are you talking about her? We are interested in a man with that name. How can it be that a person is that confused"? ˜

The meeting continued like that for some more time. I was firm with my decision to play a fool no matter what happened. In addition, whenever I was able to do so, I advised them to get in touch with Krashovec as he was the man who knew everybody.

At my great surprise they abandoned me after that meeting.

After these methods of torture, I was half-finished. I did not sleep and I lost my appetite. I lost the taste for living. I frequently wished they would kill me and thus end my miserable existence.

Even today, after so many years, I ask myself what it was? Was it associated with the purges in 1948? Was it connected with the petition to the party to intervene and block the enemies who wanted to establish a department of statistics? Was it part of an action against "arch-reactionaries" with non-scientific views? It might also be that it was an independent effort on the part of the police to pick their agents from a group of people beyond suspicion?

111

It was a real disgusting experience. It made me frequently fall into apathy. On so many occasions I wished that they had finished me off so that I would not go in my thoughts over an analysis of the details of those events.

However, I was not an isolated case of misery. I realized that Echimovich was also losing his nerves. He was talking frequently of his wish to change his job. This was certainly a difficult decision taking into account the contributions that he had made to the statistics of Yugoslavia. He did his best to push the Yugoslav statistics toward world standards and he rightly expected to get some recognition for that in the form of an appointment to a leading post where he could influence subsequent developments. However, he never got anything. He was disappointed. He probably interpreted his case as an obvious political discrimination. He applied on two occasions for the job of lecturer at the University of Belgrade and he was turned down although he was a distinguished candidate. Those who were responsible for the decision did not like the idea of having a colleague who was so much above regular university standards.

Echimovich had a character that was incompatible with the standards of his environment. He did not care for politics. He thought it was a useless activity and he frequently expressed that view. The only quality that he appreciated was hard work and the resulting contributions. However, this was not the basis for any recognition.

As he was nice to colleagues and willing to help people in their studies, Echimovich became quite popular. At the peek of that popularity, the party tested him in political matters. They "elected" him president of the labor organization in statistics. However, he finished the testing at the first meeting of members. He opened the meeting and said: "Don't be afraid. I am not going to make a political speech. I don't like stupidities".

He realized that his character was not suitable for career and recognition. This is why the idea appeared in his mind of quitting everything and going back to Zagreb where he could give up and spend the rest of his life quietly. Novak strengthened his wish to go away from statistics. Novak's malicious remarks regarding our work spoiled Echimovich's interest in the continuation of his statistical experiences. I remember a protest that came from Montenegro about a sample that we had selected for that republic.The meeting of the directors of statistical offices decided to have the same precision of estimates in all the republics. As a result, the size of the sample needed was about the same in all the republics. However, Montenegro expressed the size of the sample in precentages of the total number of households and protested against such a large percentage in the case of a small and poor republic while Serbia was favored with a small sample.

The argument of an equal absolute number of units for the same precision in different republics was not appreciated. Novak took it as a provocative attitude on the part of mathematical statistics. He fired on us all his hatred. He said something equivalent to this: in this country all the political bodies take into account differences between republics. However, our samplers do not care for politics of the country. They want to be above the society, etc., etc.

The attack was made at a public meeting.

112

On another occasion, we had to oppose a growing practice of the authorities in republics and communes to change the sample selected by us. Cases were reported to us that the authorities added some units which they liked or dropped the ones that caused trouble to the field staff. We insisted on the need to respect the sample as it was selected. Novak took our attitude as an illustration of scandalous behavior. Parliaments of republics and the associated agencies had a constitutionally recognized right to take decisions on any issues in their respective territories. However, mathematical statistics wanted to be above parliaments, etc.

Echimovich told me that his stomach was unable to digest this type of experience. He rushed with his preparations and left for Zagreb in 1952.

In Zagreb his activities declined sharply. He worked in a provincial statistical office that was afraid of any initiative or any development that was not previously recommended by headquarters. This is why he concentrated on his own studies. One of them was his Ph.D. in mathematics from Zagreb University.

As he could not stay idle, Echimovich joined FAO in 1952 and disappeared from Yugoslav statistics for ever. This is how politics eliminated a man of great caliber.

After several years he came back to see if conditions improved so that he might reconsider his earlier decision. Somebody asked him to give a talk to the staff about Indonesia, where he was working at that time. He spoke romantically about many people in Indonesian villages who lay down in the shade and eat bananas that grow by themselves and do not require any work. Novak was present at the talk. He asked for the floor and attacked the lecturer for his blindness and lack of understanding of social issues. In fact, no people can be happy before they make a revolution, confiscate property, socialize the means of production, etc., etc.

Echimovich never appeared again. I hope, however, that somebody will be able to remove the dust accumulated over the past and write an account of Echimovich's contributions to statistics of Yugoslavia. If his work is seen in the context of the state of statistics in the world of that epoch, it will be clear how much the country has lost as a result of political discrimination.

Novak's attacks on statistics continued in the new setup when he and Krashovec became Assistant Directors for economic and social statistics respectively. The office of economic statistics had always negative comments about the work in social statistics. The conflict took disagreeable proportions and badly damaged the authority of statistics.

It seems that V. Guzina, the director of statistics, was disgusted by the animosity between Novak and Krashovec. Guzina was a specimen of communist according to our prewar standards, viz. when the communist party was in opposition. He was intelligent, very modest, straightforward, willing to listen to others, and a great reader of books on a large variety of topics, such as social sciences, philosophy, and primarily economics. In fact, he was an economist. This was his main line of interest. However, his outstanding feature was in his moral principles. As I remember him, he hated any form of showing off, any flattery, pressing for career, selfpraising, and, in general, any form of cheap behavior.

Being a prewar communist, he did not need to start his career at a low level, as the commoners did. His starting position, according to the vocabulary in Western countries, was at the level of under-secretary. He thus kept various positions at that level in economic fields. However, his career was not an easy one. With his character, he could not expect to have an easy life. The government matters were in the hands of a few strong politicians who did not like opposition on the part of their junior officers. This is how Guzina entered into conflicts on several occasions. He was particularly disliked by Kardelj. That was sufficient for difficulties in a career. Guzina developed the reputation of a man who has an opinion after his superior has already expressed a different opinion. This is sufficient to start a career decline. He was transferred to the position of director of statistical office.

Guzina was not interested in statistics. Nor did he care for its problems. He was physically present in the office on rare occasions. His interest was in economics and he was requested to keep attending the meetings in spite of the shocks in his career. It may, therefore, be that he was not aware of what was going on in the office. It may also be that the members of the party, knowing his character, had no courage to inform him about matters that he certainly considered as below any serious standard. He thus behaved in the office as a foreigner who got the statistical job by chance, as a kind of misunderstanding. Some colleagues thought of him as an "extra-terrestrial". He did not fit the environment of the statistical office.

In 1953 Guzina was transferred to another job and we were all convinced that it was the right step. Another part of the same package was Krashovec's transfer to Ljubljana. Novak remained alone, victorious. In fact, he succeeded Guzina as director of the Federal Institute of Statistics, viz. the highest post in Yugoslav statistics.

Several months before these appointments were made, it was clear to all of us that the fight for succession would enter a critical phase. In line with his usual behavior, Novak was using every opportunity to put blame on the work, attitudes, and approaches in social statistics. He was aware that personal attacks on Krashovec would not be appreciated by his superiors. He was, therefore, attacking the work. The future of the country was at stake. Novak was aware that his success in these attacks would hit the right target, viz. Krashovec.

Krashovec was also aware of the situation. He needed support. Needless to say, we were ready to give him all our support. However, that had no weight. Our political standing was zero. Therefore, we could not contribute. In that situation, Krashovec counted much on the support by his friend Macura, the director of the Statistical Office of Serbia. While Krashovec was director of FSO, he was Macura's close friend. This friendship was useful to both of them. Krashovec involved Macura in everything that he was doing. This greatly contributed to Macura's reputation among the directors of the republican statistical offices. In this way Macura became the editor of *Statistical Review* that was started under the authority of FSO.

However, Krashovec overlooked the fact that friendships frequently have a conditional character. The following is an illustration. Macura was transferred to statistics from the government office for prices. Some time after he came to statistics, Macura succeeded to appoint as his Deputy his friend Radovanovich. It so happened that the police arrested Radovanovich on charges of sympathy for the USSR. Macura immediately convened a meeting of all the staff. In his speech he praised the police, blamed his deputy, and expressed happiness about the fact that the police was able to demask an enemy who had infiltrated the ranks of sincere and devoted patriots. After some time the police released Radovanovich as not guilty. However, Macura never wanted to see him again. Suspicion is obviously a sufficient sin.

Later on Miljenko Ban, one of the best statisticians in Macura's office, was expelled from the YCP. The poor man entered the party as crowds of other people did at that time to buy peace, career, salary, etc. In doing so, Ban probably omitted to disclose some of his past sympathies or contacts with anti-communist groups. He was caught and fired. The next day, Macura convened a meeting of the staff to denounce publicly Ban's moral profile. He did not admit any of Ban's achievements in statistics. Ban became a nobody.

Krashovec rightly concluded that a man of Macura's type could be useful. However, to what extent? Krashovec was able to point out to many achievements of his office that were widely recognized. In professional circles he had the reputation of a man who created a favorable atmosphere for work. Novak had nothing comparable and he was jealous. However, Novak claimed ideological purity. According to him, Krashovec was using anti-marxist approaches in his office. His "achievements" were a danger for the fruits of revolution. By attacking Krashovec he assumed the position of defender of revolution.

This conflict took very sharp forms in the second half of 1952 and the beginning of 1953, viz. during the preparations for the 1953 Census of Population within the office headed by Krashovec. The newspapers were writing about the census and the top political leadership was involved in decisions regarding some census issues. Krashovec had had plenty of opportunities to appear in public. Novak had nothing to show in terms of work. On the contrary. He was still fresh from an unpleasant defeat in his battle for recording. He had no idea what his future was going to be. No wander that he put so much emphasis on political interpretation of the situation.

Macura was aware of the situation. He was Krashovec's friend. However, Novak was fire. The one who would oppose him had to be ready to experience the consequences.

In that situation, Krashovec played a strong trump. He convened a meeting of all the senior statisticians of Yugoslavia to request their opinion about the methodology of the forthcoming census and the related issues. Should the meeting support the work done, Krashovec would be able to ignore Novak. The statistical profession of the country would be on his side.

Novak was present at the meeting although the matter was outside his official concern. After some time he asked for the floor and staged a violent attack on Krashovec personally. His excitement was beyond any control and we were afraid that he would attack Krashovec physically. Novak fired on Krashovec the worst offenses that are available in the communist jargon, such as "anti-marxist", "enemy of the revolution", etc. He wanted to impose the conclusion: if you want to save the revolution you have to destroy into pieces all the work done in Krashovec's office.

This was the first time that I saw Krashovec excited. The movements of his lips showed that he was at the edge. He asked for the floor and attacked Novak with the same vocabulary. He also referred to ignorance which was Novak's weak point. He eventually proposed arbitration by Macura, who had a chance to participate in the preparation of the census. Novak agreed to the proposal. He welcomed the idea of Macura's participation. We were all shocked knowing the ties between Krashovec and Macura. As the chair called on Macura, the conference hall became dead quiet. We all knew Macura as a man who would never have an opinion in a situation of this type. We all looked at Macura and nobody believed that he would have the courage to open his mouth. However, Macura stood up and moved toward the rostrum. The participants could not believe their eyes. Macura approached the rostrum, climbed up, paused for a while, looked at the audience and said: "Comrades, I am very happy to have this chance to present my opinion on important issues that were raised here". Then he made a pause, looked at his wrist watch, and said: "Oh, damn it, I have almost forgotten. I have a meeting with the "Blue".[13] I am already late. I am very sorry". He ran away and left the hall.

Macura was true to himself. We admired the excuse that he concocted. In a moment he decided to abandon his friend, the census, the preparations for the census, and the modernization of census methodology. After all, what is the meaning of all these matters as compared to one's own career. Macura remained in statistics and made his subsequent career in Novak's shadow while his friend Krashovec disappeared from statistics for good.

After Krashovec left and Novak took over, Macura was aware that a very visible change was needed in his behavior. Novak would certainly stay in the office for years. It was obvious to Macura that friendly terms with Novak were needed. In order to convince Novak of his good intentions, Macura decided to switch to a hard line attitude. He started talking more frequently about the role of the party. He was doing it even in situations when it was awkward to do it. Novak understood Macura's hints. He was aware that Macura was ready to accept his authority and leadership. As a result, Novak arranged for Macura's transfer to the Federal Institute of Statistics in the capacity of Deputy Director. The deal between Novak and Macura became quite clear. In recognition for his acceptance of Novak as supreme boss, Macura got a free hand in all the international matters of Yugoslav statistics. In other words, Novak was the Prime Minister and Macura was the minister of foreign affairs. Foreign matters was the area that Novak did not like. He did not know foreign languages. In addition, his manners were not suitable for international contacts. As for Macura, he channeled his career in the right direction. He was certainly the only one who had clear ideas as to what he wanted.

In this period I had a chance to experience the consequences of Macura's adherance to a hard line. One day he asked me to be at a meeting hall at a particular time. He came along. We were alone. He told me that "comrades" were concerned about my contacts and my cooperation with the "enemy", viz. the statisticians in US. He pointed out that letters were coming to my address from the US. The same was true of books

---

13 The nickname of the Vice President of the Federal Government.

and other publications. "How can it be that the enemy is contacting just you"? He also mentioned that I offended Vogelnik by registering him as a member of the American Statistical Association.

From what he said it was obvious that my case was discussed at internal party circles. They had probably picked Macura to talk to me and remind me of my sins. Some record must have been kept at some place about my behavior as he would not know otherwise the story about Vogelnik's membership in ASA. Macura was not on friendly terms with Vogelnik. Therefore, Vogelnik could not have talked to him about this case.

It was not clear to me what Macura wanted. I guess that Novak wanted him to get involved in the execution of the tough line and break with his old friends. I interpreted that our meeting ended in a kind of warning.

On another occasion, Macura was much tougher. He was probably interested in showing his support for the hard line. We had another meeting to investigate my behavior. This time he was more direct. His language was more specific. The accusation was again the cooperation with the enemy. The proof was an article of mine in the *Journal of the American Statistical Association* about uses of sampling in the Yugoslav 1953 Census of Population. He also expressed surprise at the lack of standards in my behaviour. "No other citizen of the New Yugoslavia would fall that low and accept cooperation with the enemy". He also mentioned that steps might be taken against me. However, nothing visible happened. Some notes were probably added to the confidential file kept under my name in the personnel office.

Later on we again had a word about my sins. At that time, the Bureau of the Census had published *The Population of Yugoslavia* by Paul F.Meyers and Arthur A.Campbell as part of the series "International Population Statistics Reports". To Macura, this publication was an intelligence document. It was based on many pieces of information collected through a network of spies. He did not tell me what evidence was available about my involvement in spying. However, this conclusion followed from the context. Paul Meyers was presented as an agent involved in studies of Yugoslavia. Meyers also collaborated in the *Journal* of ASA. He thus concluded that my cooperation with the Bureau of the Census and the *Journal* left no doubt as to the kind of circles that I belong to.

I told him that estimates of the population of a country can easily be made if data are available from earlier censuses. He was surprised to hear that any demographer can do that without spies. He appreciated the idea of "population laws" and seemed to have understood how stupid it was to keep data confidential. I also told him that I had no contacts with the *Journal* of ASA nor was there any need for that. Whoever has anything to publish he can easily do so if good substance is presented. He probably wanted to test this information. He wrote a review of *The Population of Yugoslavia* that was published later on in the *Journal* of ASA (Vol.50, 1955, p. 1409-1411). Before his review was sent to the *Journal* he asked me again for the name of my contact in the *Journal*.

Even today I do not know if he was ever able to understand that there are so many matters in the world that are free from spies.

In the beginning of Novak's directorship we expected that Macura would use his position to advise Novak to go slowly, keep intact the essential services in the old Krashovec's sector, and continue methodological studies that we had started in 1948. However, Macura failed to do so. We therefore felt at Novak's mercy.

The results of that position were evident. For us, there was no work any more. The use of sampling in 1953 Census of Population was the last project. For some time after that we kept ourselves busy with the publication of results obtained and the analysis of experiences. That was the end.

In that period we suffered another loss. This time it was Blejec.

In the Statistical Office in Ljubljana Blejec had responsibility for statistical methodology. In 1948 he was promoted to the office of Assistant Director in that Office. This was during the period of Debevec's influence on statistics and the related hopes for the future. However, Debevec's tragic end had impressed Blejec. He thought that the best thing to do would be to join the university and abandon the work for the government. He moved in that direction and contributed largely to the modernization of statistical education at Ljubljana University and in Slovenia in general. However, he kept contacts with applications. His cooperation with various agencies was appreciated. However, he started cooling off after he realized from personal experience how strong Novak's pressure was against statistics. He also had a chance to follow the Novak-Krashovec conflict. Blejec was a very quiet person and he could not tolerate such attacks and tensions. He was less and less willing to mix with the developments outside the university. As a result, in this period of Novak's domination in statistics, Blejec withdrew almost entirely. He was lost for data collection.

Blejec's case is a measure of Yugoslav tragedy. Blejec was a sincere, honest, and hard working man who was always ready to go far in sacrificing his own interest in favor of the statistical profession. He also had a charming personality. It was always a great pleasure for friends to see him. However, he was unable to appreciate politics. He thought that it was a waste of time. Nor did he ever try to feint any kind of interest in any aspect of politics. This is why party circles never cared for him. In line with his character, he never did anything to show that he would wish better treatment. He accepted his position as the only possible solution under the circumstances. As a result, the government statistics lost the benefit of the huge working capacity of a man who had marvelous ability to use theory in the efforts to solve problems of practice.

It should also be added that other colleagues who matured after 1948 and specialized in data collection problems left the survey work in this period. Some of them went to other government offices or to industry. Others took jobs in branches of statistics that were not affected by personality conflicts. Some others went to the US to teach mathematics at various universities. In this way our strong group of survey statisticians was eliminated.

My position was not any better. However, I did probably more than the others to build substitutes for the lost ground in survey work. In this period I published a great part of material that I kept accumulated from earlier yers. I also tried to move in some new directions. An illustration is sociological research. I got an invitation to write a paper about sociological research. I did it with an emphasis on empirical studies, use of statistics, studies of survey techniques at universities, etc. However, it was considered a hot issue again. It caused concern as I presented the subject in a way different from the views of social sciences in classical books of marxist philosophy. My paper went again on a long trip to different party personalities. The editor of *Our Reality* (Naša Stvarnost) was authorized to publish my paper after a year of various controls. According to what I was told in this connection, the party censorship did not see anything in the paper that might develop into a danger for the achievements of the revolution. The paper appeared in 1955.

With the accumulation of this kind of experience I realized that I had to reconsider the matter of my future.

In this connection I thought that I should have a word with Macura. I was aware of the recent change in his behavior. However, I expected that he would give me some hints as to what to do. I was wrong. He cut me off by saying that Novak was responsible for long-term developments. He told me to see Novak.

After considerable hesitation, I decided to ask for an appointment with Novak. I told him how I felt about our position. He did not try to convince me that matters were not so bad. Instead, he told me bluntly: "I am not going to dismiss you. You will keep getting your salary. However, keep quiet. Do not open your mouth and do not propose anything. We shall never accept anything from you".

In this situation I realized that I had to quit. In 1953 I took steps to get a teaching job at the University of Belgrade. The year after that I left FIS although I continued going there almost daily to work in the library. I also wanted to make it clear that I was available at any moment for a new period of cooperation should there be any interest in it.

I had resisted the temptation to leave as long as some hope existed for work. However, the atmosphere in the office became very difficult. It was particularly difficult for those who had definite views and self-respect. The way to survive was to keep quiet, be ready to compromise with one's own conscience and, above all, be ready to find the way to agree with the supreme chief.

In a communist regime, a federal agency is the best place to work. They normally have the best resources. If nothing can be done there hopes for the change to better hardly exist. This was confirmed after I moved to the university. There were no calculating machines, no resources for practical work, and no funds for staff to get involved in research projects. I was thus squeezed to lecturing. However, I could not attract students if they had to be separated from facilities in the applied statistical work. In fact, some resources were available for research. However, nobody knew anything about that money. The matter was never raised publicly as the money was used to pay the employees who worked for two strong persons who alternated as deans of the School. Some money was also available for travel. However, it was again reserved for the same two persons. One of them went on a four-week tour of France at the expense of the university. After he came back, he reported to the Council meeting that his trip was very successful: he succeeded in establishing contacts with the School of Law in Paris. Needless to say, nobody was able to understand the meaning of that success. Wasn't a letter sufficient to establish contact? However, everybody kept quiet. The participants of the meeting were aware that the price for any question might be too high.

This is how I gradually came to the conclusion that my commitment to work for my own country under any circumstances made no sense any more. My commitment had some sense as long as we had access to work. In this case one might say: "I shall keep working no matter how little this work is recognized". However, if one is physically separated from the work and labelled as a part of citizens whose contributions are rejected in advance, the commitments have no meaning any more. In this case, the problem arises of professional and physical survival. In an applied field of work, a professional disappears from the scene if separated from work. The same is true of physical existence. If one is used to work and lives for the work, this line of life becomes his own identity. One cannot live in a different way without changing the identity. I went to see Echimovich many years after he left the statistical battlefield. He had bought himself a personal computer. His wife told me that he was sitting at that computer day and night. When I saw him later on he told me that he was involved in an analysis of fictitious surveys. "I am programming the analysis that was beyond the courage of my thoughts in 1950. Now I keep refining my approaches. I am very happy when I discover some improvements". Echimovich from 1949/50 was obviously destroyed. Under that name the existence continued of quite a different person.

I thought that the reasons of professional and physical survival obliged me to go away and thus revive the dream of another chance for the continuation of efforts to modernize statistics in Yugoslavia.

XIII A farewell to hopes

The continuation of events was consistent with the developments already presented.

Novak was very happy with his position as director of statistical services. He interpreted his appointment as a recognition by both the party and the government of his views, his opinions, and his earlier action. In his own interpretation, his appointment was also a slap in the face of those whom he opposed.

Although Novak's interpretation of the situation was probably far from the truth, he certainly enjoyed the support of the party for his unconditional acceptance of any aspect of party politics. At variance with other people with a standard self-respect in professional matters, Novak accepted to militate vehemently for the establishment of a "scientific management" of social and economic life with the help of record keeping. Soon after that the party made a decision to destroy the achievements of the modernization of statistics. In this way, the party engaged in a declaration of war on modern state of the profession. Novak carried the banner of that action. A new era thus started that could be called a farewell to hopes.

Novak's rule in statistics extended from 1953 to 1963. He thus had plenty of time to carry out his mission.

In his fight against the modernization of statistics and the introduction of science in current statistical work Novak was consistent. He was aware of the implications of modernization. He grasped quickly that modernization implied studies, follow up of developments in the world, collection of literature about experiences of other countries, and studies of foreign languages. He was aware that he had nothing to offer along that line. A recognition of the need for the promotion of science in the improvement of work would imply the end of his authority. Recognition of science meant for him his personal defeat and a need for his transfer to some other job with a reputation of a man who was not successful in the work assigned to him.

Novak was aware that he would never score any victory on the basis of science and a rational consideration of issues. Therefore, he transformed the argument of statistics into politics: statistics is against socialism, against revolution, against the

121

"achievements of proletarians in our country". Therefore, Novak rang the bell of alert. A mobilization was requested of all the progressive elements to prevent the enemies of socialism, etc.

This was the old song. By repeating it, Novak pretended the role of champion in the fight for the protection of socialism. He also influenced the attitude of the staff in his office. As they were all members of the YCP, the opposition to new ideas in statistics became a part of the policy of the members of the party. Condemnation of the new statistics was imposed as part of the obligatory ideological programme.

Novak exploited the fact that we had no single member of the party in our group. However, it was not because we did not want them. In fact, we were anxious to get some. The fact is that we did not succeed in convincing party members to accept the hardship of studies, lack of recognition, work after office hours, low salary, and all other matters reserved for those who had sympathy for the new statistics. We were interested in people who would take the course toward studies no matter what the price would be. However, there was no single person in Novak's office who was ready to accept that. None of his staff ever opened a book of modern statistics to see what it was about. It was much easier to accept Novak's exhortations against statistics. This attitude was easy, more profitable, and more promising.

Novak thus made a very bad service to the YCP. It so happened that Novak's personal views became the party line in statistical matters. To be more precise, the party did not oppose these views. The YCP was identified with a very questionable development tendency. In fact, the party became a promoter of backwardness. Although I do not believe that a corresponding stand was taken by any responsible party body, the fact is that the YCP never did anything to disassociate itself publicly from theories advocated by Novak. It was so easy to transfer Novak to some other job.

This is how the YCP encouraged a neglect of studies of scientific developments in the world. As a result, ignorance was a feature of members of the YCP. No single paper was published by any party member that would show familiarity with science and new approaches. Party members had no knowledge of foreign languages nor did they show any interest in learning. Young people who wanted to study and build their life on the basis of achievements and quality of their results, realized immediately that they had nothing to do with the party. The party lost the authority. Young people did not see any point in filling their time by attending meetings, talking, reading useless propaganda literature, etc. The party became entirely unattractive to all those who opted for hard work and use of recognized standards of science.

Outside of our group there were other people as well who did not like Novak's intransigence and aggressiveness in the attempts at imposing his own views. However, in earlier years Novak was not much concerned about it as he occupied the top position in statistics and was able to count on the support of party circles. Later on the events took the course toward decentralization. Thus, Novak was obliged to take into account the views and attitudes of other people and particularly those who were at top positions in the republics.

Needless to say, these people were also members of the party. Their appointments were not based on any knowledge of statistics. In fact, none of them was a technician.

They were staff with some amount of recognition by the party for their political attitude. The party counted on their services and they counted on the party for a good job. This is how they came to statistics. It was a matter of chance. Had other jobs been vacant at the time when these people had to get a new job, they would have gone somewhere else, outside statistics.

The primary concern of these people was a consistent demonstration of faithfulness and party discipline. They were not excited, as Novak was, about any issue in statistics. Their position was quiet service and no involvement in any risky event. This primarily meant a continuation of the inherited state of business. Nobody can be blamed for what was inherited from predecessors. Similarly, any fight for new ideas, new approaches or changes is risky. Nobody knows what might come out. The condemned views might get support in the future. In other words, the alliance with views of the present ruler might develop later on into a headache.

These people were not happy with Novak. They were afraid that Novak might pull them into unpleasant fights with unforseeable consequences for their career. This is how they started raising their voice. They did it carefully but they did it. Novak was aware of this rising tide of opposition in which a prominent role was played by Macura.

In that situation Novak made an efficient move. He decided to use Macura as his pawn to break the opposition of statistical circles in republics and strengthen, at the same time, the striking force of his personal policies.

Novak had little respect for Macura. In front of his staff he expressed that view about Macura on several occasions. While talking about Macura, he would lift up his left hand with the palm up and would blow the air afterwards over his palm indicating in this way that Macura had no weight and could easily be pushed in any direction by any wind.

Other leading party appointees in statistics had similar views. However, this was primarily a matter of jealousy. Macura had qualities that they did not have. While they were all involved in various fights for socialism and the improvement of society, Macura was more modest. His line was his own career. In pursuit of this aim he developed the ability to keep quiet, respect the power, stay in good terms with influential people, be kind to everybody provided it does not affect one's own career, consider all the friendships conditional upon the interest of the career, etc. Among all the directors of statistics Macura was the only one who was at any moment aware of what he wanted. Therefore, he had no difficulty in taking his decisions and defining his line of action. All those who laughed some time ago at his personal characteristics envied him later on.

Some of Macura's typical steps were already mentioned. He started his public appearance in statistics with his signature on the petition to the party to protect the achievements of socialism against the enemies working under the shield of modernization of statistics. Needless to say, he never read a book of modern statistics. Therefore, he had no idea of what he was doing. However, he could possibly not miss the chance to join the strong ones.

The rest of his career was a repetition of this recipe. When Krashovec, as director of federal statistics, started backing the modernization of statistics, Macura gave him full

123

support. In this way Macura strengthened his friendship with the top statistical officer. The benefits followed. Macura was sent to attend some international meetings where he played the role of government spoksman in statistical matters. When Krashovec decided to publish the periodical *Statistical Review,* he picked up Macura as the editor. However, at the 1949 meeting on statistical education, Macura played no role. It was too risky. Similarly, when he was asked to take a public stand in the dispute Krashovec - Novak at the meeting for the preparation of the 1953 Census of Population, he ran away from the rostrum. He abandoned his friend Krashovec who counted on the continuation of an old friendship. However, Krashovec failed to appreciate that Macura couldn't possibly take a clear stand in an open fight. As soon as Krashovec was kicked out, Macura's choice was easy. He adopted a victorious hard line and made it clear to all of us that he was hardly able to recognize our faces. Therefore, no hope for his benevolent attitude in any discussion of measures against those who wanted modernization.

Credit goes to Macura for being the first among the party people in statistics to guess that qualifications - or something that looks like qualifications from formal point of view - might become in the future an element of a career. As a result, he started building up his curriculum. Thus, at variance with usual standards, he agreed to be the editor of a number of periodicals dealing with different topics. As the editor of *Statistical Review* he published his own paper "Contribution to the consideration of socio-economic characteristics in demographic statistics" (Vol. I, 1951) which is a presentation of international recommendations as compared to programmes of past national censuses of population. This paper might be used for information of students at a seminar. However, this was a fertile line. Macura continued with such a presentation of international documents from meetings that he had attended. A collection of such papers was published as a book under the title *Contributions to the Theory and Policy of Population* (Belgrade, 1974) which has a pretentious title and a generally known content. Macura also developed taste for statistical theory and philosophy. In 1951, viz. at a time when our modernization of statistics reached the level of the developed countries in many matters, Macura published his own paper "Preparation of statistical research" *(Statistical Review,* 1951) that introduced terminological confusion in addition to being about a century late from the point of view of its content. A sample of his philosophical writing is "The impact of statistics on the development of social sciences" *(Thirty Years of Statistics in FR Yugoslavia,* Belgrade 1974) which has a challenging title and the content that leaves the readers embarrassed. However, the approach was useful. After repeated presentations of his own candidature, he became an "academician".

Novak offered to Macura the position of Deputy Director at the Federal Institute of Statistics with the responsibility for international matters of Yugoslav statistics. Macura jumped in at once. He was fully aware of what he was doing. The offer meant a switch of his life and his career to the international scene. It offered a possibility to forget about domestic fights, unpleasant situations, sudden changes of the line, abandonment of friends and aquaintences, etc. In return, he would earn the authority of a government delegate, develop friendships with other delegates and directors of statistics, and, above all, open an enormous number of paths to his future career that a delegate from a communist country is authorized to expect in exchange for a friendly face and a readiness to cooperate with everybody in everything. Besides, there would be a hundred of meetings to attend, hundreds of papers to read, a chance to reproduce them at home in the own language and thus make a substantial contribution to his own professional standing.

Novak was aware that Macura would take the offer. Novak took it for granted that Macura would forget about his past action and attitudes that were not quite compatible with the line implied in this offer. However, the challange was exciting. Macura's dreams worked out his decision. His subsequent career was a consequence of this decision.

Novak was happy. He needed the domestic front for himself. He wanted to carry out to its completion his victory over the attempts at modernization of statistics. He needed a consolidation of the victory. For that purpose Macura's support to his line was essential.

When he got Macura on his side, Novak quickly quieted the statistical leaderships in the republics. Deprived of Macura's support, the "republicans" lost the courage to open their mouths. A complete silence was thus introduced in the presumed consultations between statisticians. The attitude developed of attending meetings as a way of getting instructions and orders. Statistical machinery lost the taste for thinking or asking questions. Obedience became the supreme quality.

The staff reacted accordingly. Most people gave up and squeezed out of their mind any interest in the developments in the profession. A reduced number of books and periodicals were coming to our library. However, there was nobody to read them. Nobody wanted to see his own name on the list of potential allies of the enemy. As a result, an unbelievable apathy extended over statistics. It paralyzed interest, killed curiosity, and reduced the whole profession to a routinized repetition of yesterday. The resulting silence extended up to the present day. Novak and Macura could be happy. They secured a long-lasting victory over the human mind.

In that situation it became clear that going out of statistics was the only alternative. However, this idea brought me to despair. Days and nights I lived with this idea and, after each new review of the situation, I always came to the same conclusion. Any continuation of the miserable life that we had without work and without any hope for change was equivalent to a lack of air. Sooner or later despair would come up and disintegrate gradually the physical existence. Deadly atmosphere was all around. I went to see a couple of colleagues who had already left. Their faces were motionless; they witnessed the internal tragedy. They did not talk. Only one of them collected his energy to say: "Go".

However, the idea of going was painful.

"Where do I go from the place where I was born? What will happen to my emotional ties to the place of my youth? Shall I be able to stand the separation from my roots? What consequences will appear in my behavior? Shall I be able to continue without major damage to my stability?"

I carried these questions in my mind wherever I went. They would appear, as in a movie, one after the other. I had no answer. I became a question-asking machine. However, it was always the same type of questions that were already asked in a million different forms: "Shall I be able to live without so many small things that impressed themselves very firmly on my mind, such as my creek, my oak, my walnut tree, and the vast meadows that were full of small flowers with an incredibly pleasant smell"?

At one of these moments of outbreak of memories I packed and rushed to the place of my origin. The train was very crowded and the trip was very fatiguing. I arrived before sunset. Everything was deadly quiet, as before, when I was a child. I went to see all of them, the creek, the bridge, the oak, the walnut tree, and then I ran over the meadows to absorb as much of them as possible and oblige the ground under my feet to feel my presence and remember that we can never be separated. At that point, however, I fell down. I discovered that I could not stand up. I felt I was attached to the ground by some invisible and strong ties. I was crying.

After some time, I jumped up. I felt I was all right. I was strong again. I was calm and a voice told me: "You will go. Surely you will go. This is our destiny".

On my way back, I could not find a seat in the train. For hours I stood in the corridor on one single foot. However, I was happy. I had an impression that, while laying down in the meadow, I sucked the substance of life that made me strong and able to stand all the hardships of the idea of going away from the place of my mysterious attachment to innumerable small things.

When I came home I wrote a number of letters to colleagues in different countries and expressed my interest in some suitable assignment. Some offers came quickly. One of them was from P.V. Sukhatme, a distinguished Indian statistician who was in charge of statistical work in FAO. At that time, an office was established in FAO for the promotion of the development of agricultural statistics. The work primarily referred to less developed countries. The improvement of their know-how was the main concern.

I have always considered myself lucky for the chance to get involved in that work. This was more or less what I wanted to do at home. However, my work at home was not successful. All our efforts to help the country absorb the benefits of the rapid progress of statistics in the world broke against a thick wall of politics that was continuously pushing slogans and had no interest in real work. My failure was instructive though. I learned a great deal about obstacles to development. I was thus convinced that I was equipped with a useful experience for the promotion of statistical development in countries where the political conditions would be more favorable.

The prospects of a large-scale involvement in the improvement of statistics helped me considerably to solve my personal problems that arose in connection with the idea of leaving my country and going to work in other countries. After an analysis of the possibilities with FAO, I found that my position was more convenient than I thought it was when the idea of departure first arose. I realized that I would be doing what I was not able to do at home. I was sure that, in the course of that work, I would broaden my experiences and become more fit to continue at home after conditions improved. In other words, my going away shall improve my output after I return home. The departure would thus help me to realize better my original intentions.

No less important was the political interpretation of the proposed work. It was work for the United Nations. For many people there is nothing in it that one should be proud of. The name of United Nations was frequently associated with big bureaucracy, inefficiency, a lot of paper work, etc. However, I kept these stories far from the idea behind the United Nations. In fact, the United Nations meant for me hope for many people, abolishment of colonies, recognition of human rights, a chance for small nations to take the floor at big international meetings and present their problems, mobilization of good will to assist the less lucky ones, and so many other activities that were kept in the list of dreams in the course of human history. In this sense the United Nations was the highest achievement made so far. It seemed to me special luck if somebody had a chance to participate in UN work and the realization of its great ideals. And it was particularly so in the work proposed to me. It was not a bread and butter involvement in the administration but a participation in a design to make the know-how available and thus help the less developed countries to secure real meaning to their political independence.

There was another aspect of that issue. Namely, I considered the foreign policy of the Government of Yugoslavia as an implementation of the great principles of the United Nations in the area of foreign relations of a small country. I appreciated greatly the Yugoslav participation in the efforts to establish strong ties between less developed countries. It was the only way for them to raise their voice and insist on recognition of their interest.

Now I felt that I would be able to contribute to this politics. Needless to say, I was not involved in any form of diplomatic activities. These activities are carried out through the established government channels by people chosen for that purpose. In these activities there was no place for a non-party person who had the ambition to keep for himself the responsibility for his own action. In spite of that, I saw for myself a way to participate in the foreign policy of the Yugoslav government. For that purpose, I thought I had to engage in service to LDC, assist them to whatever extent possible in their development efforts, and thus contribute to their political independence and the affirmation of principles of the UN. Needless to say, my involvement was independent of national institutions. I was a part of UN machinery. However, I always felt that I was in line with the developments in my own country. I was not able to contribute to the improvement of our domestic work but I had a feeling that I would have more luck in matters belonging to other countries.

After a long period of consideration of the pros and cons concerning my departure I left for Rome in 1955. I left behind the tragedy of Yugoslav statistics. It does not mean that it had closed down. Novak was anxious to do what he was able to do. He bought printing facilities, managed to convince the government to get him money to buy a computer, improved the publication of data, etc. However, he locked all doors to any form of science that had become even more necessary after the arrival of the computer. Statistical methods were thus in a deplorable shape. It helped me greatly to stabilize abroad. However, I felt that the day of my return would not be far off.

It might also be appropriate to say that I felt I was forced to get out of Yugoslav statistics. It is true that Novak told me that I would not be dismissed. I accept that. However, pressure can take very refined forms. One of them is to make life hopeless, stupid, not worth living.

Later on, some time after I had already left, my wife saw Macura at a party. He told her: "I am surprised at what your husband did. We all had a better opinion of him.

None of us ever expected that he would jump at the first bone that fell from a capitalist table".

Some years later Macura himself took an assignment abroad that couldn't have been more than a very tiny piece of bone. My wife saw him before he left for that assignment. She said: "Some years ago my husband took an assignment abroad and you said that it was a step below his dignity. How about yourself"? He said that he had to sacrifice himself in favor of poor countries. "Comrades have insisted that I should sacrifice myself".

In this respect Novak was much more consistent. He asked my wife: "What the is man doing who abandoned the work on the establishment of socialism in his own country and ran away to another country for better pay'"?

XIV New political developments

The Soviet political, social, and economic system offers guidance in tackling many issues that arise in building a socialist society. It is, therefore, understandable that countries where the interest in socialism arose looked for guidance from the Soviet Union. A new and independent attempt would require considerable sacrifice. Major failures are also not excluded. The Soviet model makes it possible to bypass bitter experiences.

However, the use of the Soviet model as an inspiration in building socialism is limited. The Soviet system has a world-wide reputation of inefficiency, clumsiness of the administrative machinery, slowness, carelessness on the part of workers, reluctance on the part of people to use their own judgment, etc. This is why the Soviet system is not considered in countries that have already achieved higher standards of efficiency.

The next difficulty with the Soviet system arises from its excessive use of coercion. The Soviets operate a huge police apparatus for collecting and piling up of information on the behavior of all their citizens. The police files are fed by an extremely elaborate network of informants located at each place of work and in houses where people live or go to spend some time. Deviations from prescribed standards of behavior are thus known. Those who dare to deviate easily develop conflicts with the authorities and run the risk of concentration camps, jails, dismissal from work, withdrawal of residence permit, and other threats. As a result, people accept any conditions of work. They give up their personality and carry out the imposed pattern of life. Under these conditions, dynamism and initiative do not grow. Such a society is at variance with the essence of Western civilization.

For these reasons the use of the Soviet model was restricted so far to countries under the Soviet political and military domination. Yugoslavia was in this category. The Soviet troops chased the defeated German army out of Yugoslav territory and left behind the YCP to organize power according to the Soviet model.

In this rise to power, the YCP contributed its share. During the war the YCP developed recognition of its role in underground activities. At the end of the war it operated an organized political block that easily managed to fill the vacuum created by the fall of the German machinery. As the YCP from its beginning adopted the ideology of the Soviet type of socialism, communism in Yugoslavia had much stronger roots than elsewhere.

Now the game of history started. The whole world considered Yugoslavia a leading dependent of the Soviet Union. At that very moment, the YCP was excommunicated from the brotherhood of communist countries. As a result, Soviet arms were rattling at Yugoslav borders and the Soviet propaganda machinery was spreading hatred and disdain at the address of the YCP. The response of the YCP was similar. Any sign of appreciation of the Soviet Union was brutally scrapped off. Yugoslav authorities circulated stories about rapatious exploitation of the country through the mixed Yugo-Soviet companies. It was also made public that Soviet agents infiltrated the Yugoslav police, the army, and all other sectors in order to be able to control all areas of life and influence decisions. As a result, any expression of sympathy for the Soviet Union or any hint that could be interpreted that way was treated as treason, association with the enemy, attack on national independence. The police intensified its vigilence in large-scale witch hunting against all those who might have a nice word for the Soviet Union. Those who were caught as suspicious were deported to concentration camps and bestially tortured. Many of them have disappeared forever.

This is how the process of self-destruction of the communist movement started on a world-wide scale. Needless to say, only the future will be able to evaluate the consequences of the Yugoslav rebellion. However, one might say that it hurt the striking power of communism in a way that exceeded by far everything that bourgeois propaganda could do. The bourgeois voice always had a limited impact. It speaks from a "parti pris" position. Now revelations about communism were coming from the mouth of a communist party with a widely recognized reputation. This mouth revealed that the Soviet Union was at the mercy of bureaucrats who recklessly ruled over millions of slaves. Their socialism implied a system of privileges that were rapidly increasing on the way to the political top while the rest of the people were kept at poverty level and deprived of any right to raise their voice. Soviet relations with other socialist countries were based on exploitation. At variance with bourgeois statements of the same type, a huge amount of evidence was now offered to the world to sustain the revelations. References were offered of names, dates, companies involved, steps taken, etc. No doubt was left as to the tragic reality disclosed.

The disclosed reality pointed out the difference between dreams about socialism and communist practice. Socialist dreams imply freedom for everybody, a society dominated by moral principles, respect for law, elimination of poverty, etc. As against that, the Soviet society means a large-scale revival of the vices of bourgeois society including moral corruption of all kinds, privileges for political supporters, paradise for flatterers, replacement of appreciation for work and merit by political favoritism, etc. In other words, those who want to become members of the communist party have to examine their conscience and understand the moral implications of the contemplated step.

The impact of the situation created was incredible. Opposition against communism became particularly strong among young people who did not like compromising in moral matters.

The communist movement was thus stripped of its moral authority. It lost attractiveness in the eyes of those who were guided by moral principles. It could not claim idealism and sacrifice for the benefit of the society. Instead, it became a profitable business. All the high salary positions were reserved for members of the party. The same was true of the positions of honor and prestige and the distribution of opportunities and roles in any form of public life. The membership card of the communist party was the condition to be a journalist whose name appeared in newspapers, to get a leading role in opera or theater, to become chief of a department at universities, etc. There was nothing more efficient that a person could do for the promotion of his own interest than membership in the ruling communist party.

This was the beginning of moral disintegration of communism in Yugoslavia. The process started in this epoch and increased in intensity in subsequent years. Disillusionment rapidly took on catastrophic proportions. There was hardly any member of the party left who was not fully aware of the dangers of the decline in moral standards. In fact, the events announced a transformation of the party into an organization for power control.

The disillusionment process immediately hit the party fanatics, viz the people who were ready to sacrifice themselves for the realization of communist goals. During the last war the fanatics carried out many heroic acts in situations without any hope for survival. However, dangers did not stop their action. Before they were shot dead, so many of them looked at the German guns crying: "Long live communism" or "Long live Stalin".

The same zealots were now told that Stalin was a criminal while his rule was one of the darkest pages of history. The Soviet socialism was said to be a lie. The fighters were requested to spit on their past lives, their wounds, and the days they spent in jails. They were told that nothing of their past preaching was true. Their sacrificing was in vain. They committed treason. Wives were asked to divorce their husbands on this ground, while mothers were requested to refuse contact with their children if they maintained any sympathy for the Soviet Union. The treatment reserved for Soviet friends was cruel. There was no regard for their personality. Most of them lost the ground under their feet. They looked around to inquire what happened and what wrong they did in their lives. However, before they had time to understand the events, they were put in jails and tortured.

This is how a large fraction of fanatics of the YCP was destroyed. In fact, their personality was destroyed. They lost both dignity and integrity; they were humiliated and discarded; they lost the courage to look at other people; they withdrew from all activities in the society except sleeping and eating. There was no role for them. They disappeared for good.

However, together with its fanatics, the party lost its spearhead. The events eliminated the hard core of those who succeeded in overcoming the hardships and continued keeping high the party flag. If such a thing happened to a communist party in opposition, such a party would have disappeared for many years without hope that the damage would be repaired. However, the YCP kept power in its hands and this is what helped it to survive. If nothing else, the party in power has the prestige resulting from the authority to distribute positions, power, recognition, privileges, fortune, etc. This is sufficient to keep it going. The YCP thus survived a very difficult period. It passed through a stage of critical weakness. In fact, it was a party without muscles.

As a result of these developments, the party entered an ideological vacuum. After all these events took place it was easy to say what the YCP did not want. However, these are negative statements of policy principles. In case of a party in opposition, they might be sufficient to provide substance for current activities. However, a party with absolute power in its hands had to be able to say more about itself, its programme, and the aims that it is striving for. The party needed an identity. It is true that the party kept the adjective "communist". However, it had to say what makes it different from the analogous party in the USSR that also claimed to be a communist party. If there was no socialism in the USSR, what was the socialism that was the aim of the YCP? An urgent answer to these questions was needed. Everybody expected an orientation, an answer to such questions as: "What does this country represent"?, "Where do we go"?, "What do we want"?, etc.

At that moment, the YCP missed a chance that history does not frequently offer. The party had the support of the population regarding its attitude toward the USSR. The people did not expect positive results from socialism of the Soviet type. It was thus an ideal opportunity for the YCP to get people behind it, become a champion of freedom and assume the world leadership in the establishment of socialism that would be based on a recognition of socialist ideals.

It is difficult to understand how the historic opportunities are sometimes easily dropped. In the eyes of the Yugoslav population, freedom was by far the most important issue. The people were ready to stand any hardship or other difficulties in exchange for freedom. Therefore, an orientation of the YCP toward socialist ideals with freedom in the center would have solved the problem of the ideological vacuum and made it clear to all the world that Yugoslavia raised the fundamental issues of modern history.

In fact, this was the same situation that the USSR faced at the end of the last war when her troops, on their way toward the West, started crossing the borders. Many people expected at that time that the USSR would keep their regime for themselves and would understand that chances were negligible of any serious impact in the Western world without freedom. Accordingly, the expectation was that the USSR would enter Western countries with a banner of freedom and start a large-scale drive for freedom and the beginning of a new era of history. However, the USSR disregarded the opportunity. Instead, it entered the Western world with police, spies, and a package of steps that made it impossible to count on impact in the world.

Yugoslavia followd the Soviet example. As soon as the YCP took power, it established a rough totalitarianism. Now, after the break with the USSR, the YCP had no courage to open the freedom file. In fact, the YCP tightened further the controls and reached a level of oppression that could have nicely served as a source of inspiration to any totalitarian regime. The network of police officers, spies, and informants that was built with the aim to eliminate the Soviet impact on the members of the YCP was strengthened.

However, mere power was not sufficient in that situation. The self-destruction process was moving fast. Disillusionment took unexpected proportions. The party badly needed an orientation, a means to capture the lost ground and claim moral authority, leadership, and a missionary role in the socialist movement. Briefly, the party was in need to fill the ideological vacuum.

The YCP expected to accomplish this task with the help of "self-management", the abolishment of "administrative management" of social and economic life, and the decentralization of power. At variance with the Soviet system that emphasizes the role of the central power and leaves a very limited range of responsibilities to lower level units, such as manufacturing establishments and local authorities, Yugoslav socialism - according to new ideology - implied the involvement of people in the decision making process. In each unit of work, self-management bodies were established with the responsibility for decisions for work-related problems. The Federal government lost the authority to issue orders. Instead, it carried the coordinating activities within the limits agreed upon by the delegates of lower level units. The power of the bureaucrats was shaken. According to the new theory, Yugoslav socialism became dependent upon people, their sense of responsibility for the management of their own business and their ability to find out adequate solutions in any given situation.

The decentralization process affected the YCP as well. In the earlier setup, the Central Committee of the YCP had absolute power in any matter of national life including the selection of bearers of important offices while the central committees of the party in republics had the task to implement these decisions. Under the new arrangements, prominence was given to lower level party bodies. As a result, a kind of federation of parties appeared. Party matters were discussed and policy decisions taken eventually by central committees in republics. The decisions taken were obligatory for all the members of central committees of the party in republics who were delegated to the Central Committee of the YCP. The decisions of the latter body are based on a very complex consideration of views of delegates from the republics.

A similar decentralization was also carried out within the republics which were split into communes and cities. Each of them has the own party committee. These committees are responsible for the implementation of party decisions within the respective territories. The autority for the important appointments within the territory is included. The delegates of communes and cities also sit in central commities of the respective republics.

However, this was only the beginning of "democratization" of the country and the involvement of people in the decision making process. For each major branch of activity there was an administrative secretariat (department or ministry) in the federal government that was responsible for the implementation of government policies in the field concerned. An equivalent agency was also established in the government of each republic. The authorities of communes and cities also included offices of that type. Thus, if the federal government wanted to make decisions regarding agricultural issues it had to convene a meeting of all the republics and request their opinion on the basis of the agenda circulated in advance together with the related documents and papers. In the republics the same consultation process was needed with respective communes. In this way, a very complex and time consuming machinery was to be moved as a condition for formal validity of the procedure.

Similar consultations were also carried out horizontally, viz. between different sectors of work. Thus, the Committee of Agriculture of the federal government had to include in its consultation process the representatives of labor organizations, the army, economic chamber, Socialist Union, YCP, etc. However, if these organizations wanted to participate in this work they had to carry out their vertical consultations through contacts with the same organizations in republics, communes, cities, etc. In this way meetings of the federal Committee on Agriculture were attended by representatives of republics and the representatives of different sectors of work. However, before coming to meetings each participant must have carried out corresponding vertical consultations.

In order to be able to carry out these consultations effectively, each of the above mentioned organizations had to adopt essentially the same structure as the federal government. Thus, the army was concerned with all the sectors of life and was obliged to interfere with developments that were sometimes very far from purely military matters. The army was concerned with agriculture, the ability of different regions to feed the people, the improvement of these abilities, measures that could be taken to compensate for losses of various regions in case of war, etc. A way to carry out these studies was to establish an army office for agriculture that was responsible for army interest in agriculture. Similarly, the census of population was of considerable interest to the army as it disclosed many aspects of national military potential by small administrative units. This was why the army might wish to have a census section within its statistical office with a view to formulating the army requirements in any census project.

This is how an enormous structure of employees was gradually built. This machinery immobilized the decision making process at all levels. In addition, the maintenance of that machinery proved to be very costly. It involved reproduction and circulation of documents. The reproduced materials that were circulated to the participants of the meetings frequently amounted to several hundreds of pages. Then came the reading that was unavoidable as the decisions might be taken that could not be approved by all the institutions involved. Also the loss of time on the part of those who attended meetings was included. Then came the cost of consultations. In any attempt to measure the resources involved, one had to take into account that meetings were continuously held at different levels, in different sectors of work, with different agenda, etc.

The inefficiency of the system is obvious.

In addition to consultations, many other issues arose. The system provided for the right of each participant to insist on protection of his own interest. It frequently led to a variety of views that did not make any decision possible. In such a situation the lengthy process of negotiation started aiming at achieving a compromise. In many cases there was no compromise whatsoever. A regulation was passed by the federal government that no business establishments would be allowed to import goods for more than a fraction of the value of exports. As a result, the most important region of the country for agricultural production had no import rights as its products were sold at local markets against the local currency. In order to bypass the difficulty, the authorities of that region decided to request the payment of their agricultural products in foreign currencies. This is how another regulation of the federal government was neglected that makes obligatory the use of local currency in all domestic transactions. However, the issue was not solved. Each partner insisted on the own interest.

The decision making process at the level of the federal government thus became extremely complex if at all possible. Federal institutions lost their authority. The delegates who sat on various bodies would "veto" proposals of higher bodies if not in agreement with local views. The contested issues were postponed for subsequent meetings or dropped altogether.

In this way, procedural matters were put above the interest of the country. An illustration of the priority of form over substance was the procedure for the staffing of the federal government. All the high posts of the federal government were assigned points depending upon the importance of the post. Each power center was then given an equal number of points that they had to surrender in requesting particular positions for their candidates. Needless to say, some posts were of no interest and it was difficult to fill them. On the other hand, the demand for ambassadors and leading economic positions was high. In the resulting negotiations the chances of different candidates depended upon the support they had in the respective centers of power. The qualifications of candidates were hardly ever considered seriously. It thus happened on a number of occasions that several candidates got the job as the head of a branch of work that they had never heard about prior to their appointment.

On the part of lower level units this situation generated an incredible growth of ambition toward independence. In practice, this trend meant the freedom of doing whatever was found useful to make money at the expense of others or getting other forms of benefits with the help of resources that belong to the society.

This tendency toward independence was very pronounced in large establishments where different units of work went as far as having their own self-management bodies, their own bookkeeping, and their own policies that, in some cases, could not be easily coordinated. The transportation department was expected to service the establishment as a whole. Various departments reported their claims for services in transport. However, the priorities depended upon the transportation department. If somebody made an attempt to impose his own needs, it might be interpreted as an attempt to dominate or interfere with somebody else's authority and rights. Such an attempt might have consequences on the priority assigned to subsequent claims.

In a factory a typing pool was established to service all the typing needs of the factory. The transportation department would bring a letter to type. They were told to collect the letter the next afternoon. However, as the letter was urgent, the way to get it done was to bring some chocolates or offer from time to time a ride home to the girls working in the pool. The system of "give and take" which developed is a very unpleasant part of work. However, there was no alternative. Any order from the director general was not considered as it would have irritated both the director and the girls in the pool. Corresponding consequences would follow.

It is obvious that this tendency led to the establishment of a very clumsy machinery in the national economy. The maintenance of that machinery reduced the productivity of work. The cost of non-productive activities increased greatly. Independence led to negotiations, time consuming talk, compromising, the right of partners to change views, and so many other matters that reduce output.

It was not necessary to wait long to see real chaos in some cases. Self-menagement can easily be used (or misused) to find a justification for projects that benefit small groups of individuals at the expense of the national economy. It happened that the assembly of a poor commune made a decision to build a large and modern hotel with the aim of creating a basis for the development of tourism and providing jobs for the local unemployed. The decision was strongly supported by the people concerned. A nice location was also granted to reduce the cost of the project. The construction started. After some time, about twenty per cent of the work was completed and the project was declared bankrupt. The commune had no money to continue. At that point, political pressure was used to find resources to continue. The money needed in such situations was always in some way found. The most common way was a salvage operation by "broader social community", which is a refined name for the government budget. Namely, the arrangements were made for a loan. The work continued and the hotel was completed. An important local personality became the director, another the deputy director, and a whole group of others became chiefs of finance, of the restaurant, the kitchen, supply, washing services, etc. In addition, there were many other permanent workers and part-time staff. Other benefits of the hotel were also secured. It paid taxes to the commune and inflated the communal income. It provided an opportunity to the commune to organize meetings and all sorts of other gatherings. Communal bosses also got a chance to go out in the evening and have dinner in a decent place, etc., etc.

Needless to say, with such a broad expenditure programme, the hotel was unable to cover the cost of operations and pay back the loan. However, this was not so bad for the commune. The "broader social community" was always there. It helped to keep it going.

The best part of this story is that the whole matter was planned from the beginning as a project at the expense of the "broader social community". The bankruptcy, the loan, the political pressure, etc. are all parts of the initial design.

Under these conditions not much imagination is needed to put through any project at somebody else's expense. As a rule, any such design is successful. The following case deserves to be mentioned. Since the last war, Yugoslavia has most of the time been in trouble with coffee imports. Foreign currencies have not been available and the shortage of coffee is sometime absolute and long. During one such period of shortage, a case became known concerning a village in Serbia. The assembly of that village decided to build a factory for roasting coffee. The information was added that the capacity of the existing roasting establishments already exceeded many times the needs of the national market. Yugoslavia was able to supply roasted coffee for several European countries. After a short time the news came from an adjacent village that its assembly also decided to build a roasting factory. The work was soon completed and the question arose of the justification of the use of resources in such projects that are bound to be investment failures. The investigation has shown that both assemblies were convinced that they did a very good job. Namely, the government established the practice of distributing the total imported coffee to roasting establishments in proportion to their capacity. These two villages reported their capacity to the government and secured their share in the coffee business that was very profitable as the shortage of coffee on the market made it possible to get any price. In addition, the calculation of the price authorizes the payments of loans, the interest, the salaries of the staff in the period when there is no coffee for roasting, etc. In other words, the village assemblies did a good job. The factories were paying taxes and providing many other benefits.

In the subsequent discussions somebody raised the question to both factories: "What about your know-how? Do you possess the technology for roasting coffee"? The answer was: "There is no need to worry about the technology. The demand for coffee is so great that you can sell any quantity in advance no matter how poor the quality might be".

The new climate of the economy facilitated the appearance of what is called "economically unjustified projects". This is a refined term for what is called in plain language "abuse of power" or "abuse of the office". Individuals or groups might start a project aiming at gaining prestige that will be used later on in quite a different activity. Another "economically unjustified project" might be started to create the position for somebody with good connections. The director general of a big hotel proposed to his assembly the establishment of a dental office so that patrons could repair their teeth while on vacation. The proposal received all the necessary support. At the next stage, complete equipment was ordered from Germany and paid in foreign currencies. Then a vaccancy announcement was published for the position of director of the office. It so happened that the wife of the director general applied and was chosen by the selection committee. Upon her appointment, she supervised the preparations for the opening of the office. In the meantime, the equipment was placed in the basement of the hotel. After some time, the director general of the hotel was removed from the job because of other "economically unjustified projects" while the equipment for the dental studio is probably still in the basement waiting for its last removal to the rubbish pile.

Not far from that place, and probably under the influence of similar "projects", a new building was constructed for the office of the commune and a local school. However, in the course of the work, the material and the resources were diverted to the construction of a football stadium that was completed before the school building.

Sheer corruption arose, such as appointments based on cash payments, payments to medical staff in hospitals to get hospitalization, payments to dentists in the "society operated" offices to be entered on waiting list, etc.

Much more serious "economically unjustified projects" were those that arose as a result of political pressure from the top. An illustration was a big factory in Macedonia that was constructed with the help of foreign loans, mobilization of local resources, various cooperation arrangements, etc. Upon the completion of the work the factory had to be closed. It was found that the available raw materials did not have the quality that would make possible economic industrial production. The decisions to construct the factory were also based on false reports. The rushed decisions were based on some speculation. The names of a number of top politicians were mentioned in the search for responsibility. However, nothing happened. Dust covered the case. There should be no violation of self-management decisions.

The country was thus forming a very fragile economy. As mushrooms after the rain, cases started popping up of economic decisions that were on the borderline of the incredible. For illustration, the following case was reported by the Yugoslav press. A business company was caught unloading a shipment of washing powder in an Italian port. The same shipment was loaded back on to the same ship by another Yugoslav company that was importing washing powder to the Yugoslav market. The operation was economic nonsense. It is hard to believe that such things were possible. However, similar operations have frequently taken place in Yugoslavia. In this case the export was authorized to the factory of the washing powder to get foreign currencies and purchase

137

the raw material abroad for the continuation of production. The importer was another company that had foreign currencies to purchase the washing powder abroad and make a good profit at local markets as detergent was a scarcity.

Similar developments were frequently reported. Oil refineries were built in each republic. As a result, that industry was put on a track of irreparable inefficiency. The pharmaceutical industry took the same course without any regard to a complete lack of both the know-how and the industrial tradition in some of the regions involved. The established factories neglected domestic cooperation and relied greatly on expensive and out-of-date foreign licences. Independence of centers of power from each other was the primary aim. Economic losses were not sufficient to impose cooperation. Each republic had its own electronic industry, its own production of cosmetic goods, production of spirits, as well as basic industries, such as steel, textile goods, construction work, etc. The same tendency was not given up even in the automobile industry, which is a typical area of concentration of efforts in the world. In Yugoslavia each republic built its own assembly plant of cars made by foreign automobile makers. A small national market was thus split into pieces that made impossible efficient production. To make it worse, each of these plants was strongly supported by the respective centers of power.

Interest in the country as a whole gradually became a very unpopular argument. Very strong suspicions would arise about anybody who would talk about national priorities. The case would be referred to as an attempt at going back to centralization and would provoke rage and hatred on the part of the new centers of power. Nothing should exist in the country that could escape control by these new centers. "Yugoslav" as a designation of nationality was equivalent to "enemy". Each republic maintained its own foreign trade network that operated independently and frequently competed with each other at foreign markets. In their mutual fights they were ready to go below any reasonable price level. Agriculture was considered the future source of strength of the national economy. However, it was entirely decentralized and the services were abolished that exceeded the possibilities of each center separately, such as marketing intelligence and the collection of information about new developments. It was prefered to lag behind the world than have anything in common with each other. This tendency went as far as becoming a conflict with common sense. The national railroad was broken down into independent systems under the control of each region. It resulted in incredible operational difficulties. A ticket sold in one place for a journey crossing the borders of several regions had to be split up into different accounts proportionally to the lenght of the itinerary in each unit. Record keeping of coaches crossing regional borders was also established. At each border new engines would take over. The staff was also changed to avoid the duty "abroad". Income was thus used for the maintenance of complex operations, and resources were not available for repairs and renewals.

In the same way other services were operated, such as telephone and mail.

In such a situation the only way out was to re-establish the state, the order, the respect for law, and, above all, keep the interest of the country high above any kind of group or region. A real revolution was needed that should be much deeper and more far-reaching than the events of the war or the resistance to the Soviet Union after 1948. A very radical transformation of everything was the only hope.

Needless to say, a prerequisite of such a social change is a great deal of courage and moral integrity. The step needed was, in fact, equivalent to starting from scratch.

However, the YCP was not ready to embark upon such a task. Its leading staff had grown old. They had become employees of the political routine. They lost the taste for new ideas. The benefits of the position conquered were attractive. Therefore, the party leadership opted for the easiest line: keep going. In other words, old problems remained and new ones came up as a consequence of unsolved past problems. Inefficiency, arbitrariness, violations of regulations and government decisions, and a reckless orientation toward one's own interest kept growing. The ruling bodies issued appeals on the economy to take into account social and political consequences of negative tendencies. However, there was nobody to listen. Nor did the authors of appeals trust the effectiveness of their action. The federal government lost its orientation. Unable to establish any reasonable programme of recovery, the federal government started taking loans wherever possible. After some time republics moved in the same direction. Their line was continued by individual establishments and local communities. As a result, the already considerable headache increased further. The payment of debts became a new burden. The economy of the country was unable to pay its debts. Dark clouds covered the skies.

XV Polycentric totalitarianism

In a short time the YCP reduced the economy of Yugoslavia to a real mess. It was difficult to find a member of the YCP who would believe in the ability of the YCP to get out of the situation. Under normal circumstances a political party that committed only a small fraction of failures made by the YCP would be obliged to quit and give a chance to other political groups to try to do better. However, this general principle was not applicable to the YCP. The YCP remained at power in spite of its failures.

A standard explanation of this fact is in totalitarianism. A regime that uses all the means in a totalitarian programme is able to continue its rule no matter what the situation is in the country, provided the exercise of the power is based on a sufficient amount of determination and recklessness. In fact, none of the known cases of totalitarianism in the past has lost power as a result of failures in domestic policies.

Such an explanation would not be quite adequate in case of the YCP. The YCP established a totalitarian regime and made it clear that it had no intention to quit no matter what the situation in the country. In that respect, Yugoslav totalitarianism behaved as any other totalitarianism. However, the difference between the totalitarianism of the YCP and other regimes of the same type arises at the moment of consolidation of power and the choice of long-term policy orientations. While the standard type of totalitarianism would rely on force as a primary weapon, credit goes to the YCP for an early understanding that mere physical force cannot be the basis to build upon the rule over a longer period of time. At an early stage, the YCP realized (or was forced to realize) the need to broaden the base of power control over additional layers of members who were unhappy at earlier stages with the concentration of power in the hands of those at the top and little or no power at all on the part of lower ranks of membership.

It is not easy to specify the components of the interest on the part of the YCP in its new political course. The unhappiness of the membership with the excessive power at the top was certainly an important component. This attitude on the part of the membership might have been a result of the poor showing of the political leadership in the centralized management of the economy. The related difficulties were widely known. They generated the opinion on the part of the membership that the course originally taken by the YCP was wrong. If the centralized direction of the economy was not successful, the logical alternative was to give more power to the lower strata of the membership. The thinking in this direction was also strengthened by a normal tendency on the part of the membership to get more authority and increase further their authority and their standing. As a party with absolute control of all the activities of a modern state, the YCP put many members in the position of prestige and high social rank. However, the prestige obtained created an appetite for more prestige and demands for more authority and broader responsibilities. In addition, the ideological vacuum that troubled the YCP also pressed on the leadership to take the inclinations of the membership seriously and build on it the substantive part of claims by the YCP for a new role in international communist circles. Therefore, there were many reasons that worked in favor of new approaches to power control.

As a result, the YCP took the course toward decentralization. Under this banner, the YCP survived the power crisis. In the new situation, many members became quite happy. New centers of power were created and many people in provincial places were promoted to positions of power. The federal government was responsible for coordinating activities while the decision making in most issues was transferred to republics, provinces, communes, and local communities. Many members of the party who were unknown a day before, got overnight enormous power in their hands. They were happy and their happiness gave a new strength to the YCP. The YCP became a party supported by its members.

However, the period of happiness was quite short. The decentralization led to many problems and raised the question of the ability on the part of the YCP to govern the country. New centers of power started moving along lines of their own interest. They developed their own policy principles that were primarily based on local interests as seen and interpreted by new centers of power. The local interest was gradually put above the interest of the country as a whole. In fact, the latter was entirely neglected. The willingness of the new centers of power to compromise in favor of the country as a whole was reduced to very little. This is what created many problems. Once the authority was transferred to local units, it was not possible any more to give them orders and oblige them to follow any policy that they would not accept. The result was a complicated process of coordination of views. However, this process led to long and painstaking deliberations. Needless to say, this process further increased the inefficiency of the decision making. In some cases, the top decision making bodies were entirely immobilized.

As for procedural difficulties that were caused by the accepted legislation, new complications were soon added as a result of a normal tendency on the part of new centers of power to further strengthen their authority and increase their independence. In order to make these tendencies effective the new centers of power did not hesitate to start a dangerous game with the help of sources of trouble in the past, such as different religions, different nationalities, tradition, local rivalries, different script, etc. This was a very useful weapon to mobilize the support of the local population and destroy, at the same time, the bridges with other parts of the country. In some cases, animosity developed between parts of the country to the extent that no generally agreed upon programme was possible any more. Cases were also reported of many crimes commited by groups of youth from different regions in case they had to cross borders of other units. Violance appeared that had never been seen in the past during the rule of capitalist regimes.

This is how the country was heading toward disaster. A major crisis was on the horizon. The picture of that crisis generated an understanding on the part of the leading members of the YCP that a common destiny was at stake. Serious issues were in the air including a question mark against the way in which the YCP used power. The question of the responsibility of the YCP arose for the results of the exercise of power and the direction of national affairs. In that situation the fear of an unknown future helped establish an understanding on the part of the YCP of the need for a joint programme of power protection and the exercise of power as well.

This is how the polycentric totalitarianism was born.

In this device there is nothing new from the ideological point of view. The party keeps absolute power and is not willing to share it with anybody else. It continues with absolute control of all aspects of life with a particular emphasis on matters related to politics. The exercise of power is an application of the known theory of proletarian dictatorship. The difference arises in the implementation of authority. The responsibility for power control is now decentralized. The real power is in the hands of lower level units, viz. republics and communes. However, they carry out their work on the basis of an agreed upon programme which shows what the citizens are allowed to do, what action should be taken in case of a deviation from the accepted behavior, what penalties will be inflicted on culprits for "acts against the people" or for any action that annoys the party.

The maintenance of power was the only national programme that was accepted by the YCP as necessary and applied all over the national territory. The programme was implemented by the Ministry of Interior in each republic. The federal ministry of interior was responsible for supervision of the programme over the whole territory and the coordination of proposals for various adjustments of the agreement that might be needed in various situations.

In this way, continuation of the rule of the YCP was secured.

The outcome of the agreement thus reached was a new form of totalitarianism. The main levers of power control included police, army, and their foreign network under the shield of Foreign Affairs. The police was of course responsible for standard services of any police, such as passport control at borders, criminal investigations, traffic control, etc. However, the emphasis was on political matters. This is why the size of the service was huge. The network of police stations was dense and they were heavily staffed. They maintained lists of all persons living in their territory and kept an eye on developments in the area. They were entitled to stop any person for investigation without any formal authorization. They kept their confidents in all the places of work. They recorded all incoming information. The police also included special services, such as customs. Customs was particularly suitable for inspection of border traffic. Police agents were entitled to open luggage at any point of national territory under the pretext to check if the import tax was paid. Without explanation, they could withdraw passports or refuse to issue new ones. Briefly, there was nothing that remained outside their reach. Perfectionism of police operations was an appreciated goal. The newspaper *Politika* of 25 November, 1985 carried an article about the Institute of Security that consisted physically of a complex of buildings with the job to follow the progress of science in the world and detect the developments that could be used by the Yugoslav police so that it could match the degree of sophistication applied by any kind of enemy.

More drastic forms of defense of power against "aggressors" was the reponsibility of the army. The aggressor was any group of persons operating within or outside the national territory who professed ideas different than the ideology of the power. The army was thus a political weapon; it was a political army. For that purpose, the backbone of the army was the political office that had a commissioner and his assistants in each unit. Their task was to keep an eye on the behavior of all the staff, organize and carry out political indoctrination and cooperate in the fulfillment of that task with civilian services with similar responsibilities. If a person with a poor political reputation joined the army, the political office of the respective unit would be informed. *Vice versa* was also true. Needless to say, the records of the political office served as a basis for the recruitment of military staff, the promotion of soldiers to officers in reserve, for decorations, etc.

The protection of the power from those who live outside the national territory was the responsibility of the diplomatic service that consisted of parallel and independent channels of different lines of interest. They collected information about activities of citizens while abroad and informed of their results the responsible offices at home. The means used in this intelligence work were many. Diplomatic services were entitled to refuse the renewal of visas to suspected persons and cause trouble with local authorities. They recorded addresses and places of work of citizens living abroad. Those who did not cooperate had problems with passports. Embassies also operated a service for issuance of certificates that secured benefits, such as fifty per cent reduction of the cost of travel home with a national airline, free import of goods while going home, etc. Failure to cooperate led to cancellation of benefits. The same treatment was reserved for those who did not participate at political lectures for emigrants, who did not send children to schools established abroad for the purpose of indoctrination, etc.

With such a power protection machinery available, it became possible to abandon the earlier and more aggressive forms of repression and switch instead to legally imposed decisions of self-management bodies. In other words, the party did not rule the country. All the power was with the people, self-management bodies, and the delegates whom people "elected" to represent them at these bodies. Party decisions did not have a legal value. They were not binding. Legal authority was recognized exclusively to decisions of self-management bodies.

The transformation process of party decisions into legally recognized decisions of self management bodies was done in a large number of ways. Generally speaking, all members of self-management bodies were, at the same time, members of the party. They knew what the party line was and they behaved accordingly. Failure to do so would have many unpleasant consequences. As to higher level bodies, there was no difficulty whatsoever in the implementation of party decisions. All these bodies were headed by professional party staff who had at their disposal an infinite number of means to impose adherence to party views. The awareness of the consequences from opposition to the imposition of party views is sufficient for a smooth party rule. However, should somebody represent any source of difficulty, various committees and bodies could easily be changed to drop out the points of resistance and put in the additional support.

With this structure of the decision making machinery there was no danger whatsoever that any document, opinion or proposal could go through that would be considered as a deviation from the established order. Possible mistakes by lower level bodies would immediately be caught and corrected by higher level bodies.

In spite of that, the danger still existed that some "enemies" would raise their voices. It is obvious that such voices might be interpreted as signs of unhappiness. They might generate the opinion that the party was not doing adequately its job. The idea might arise to have somebody else at power who would implement and test alternative forms of exercise of power.

Cases of this type generated a real horror for the YCP. Therefore, any possible steps were needed to prevent the enemy from making recourse to such a "diversion". This is why vigilance was promoted to the highest virtue. Many pairs of eyes and ears searched for cases to get involved, discuss, report, plan some action, observe results, etc. Priests were supervised while they celebrated their masses to check on what they said and who were the people they talked to. Thousands of meetings that were held all over the country each day were attended by informants to make sure that no word was said in excess of the limits considered decent. Whatever groups of people meet, there would be somebody to check if "enemies" were there. No wonder that big excitement arose in the Party if somebody in a group of school children said loudly that students wanted more freedom. Thousands of "political workers" would concentrate on studies of such childish "diversions". Army officers, leaders of labor organizations, delegates to various bodies, party leaders, etc. would all be informed about the "enemy attacks" and would talk about it in their speeches.

If any sign arose of deviation from the established order, a real hysteria would be expressed in all the communication media with a view to "demasking" the enemy. An illustration is the case of Veselin Djuretich who wrote the book "The Allies and the Yugoslav War Drama". The book was accepted for publication by an authorized publisher. It passed the regular censorship. Two reviewers presented their evaluation in writing. However, the book included the opinion that the nationalist movement under Drazha Michaylovich was involved in the promotion of aims of the allied forces in the same way as the YCP although their approach was different. In fact, the YCP captured Drazha Michaylovich after the war and sentenced him to death. The official stand of the YCP was that he collaborated with the Germans.

In its essence, this case is insignificant and would not cause much discussion under normal circumstances. Many historic events have been evaluated in different ways. Should a historian hold views that are in conflict with the facts he would discredit himself and would bury his credibility. However, the matter does not become a case for the mobilization of public opinion.

In Yugoslavia it is not so. The case created a real panic. Party speakers fired vehement comments at the author. They smeared him and his moral and intellectual integrity. The case was presented as the "scandalous" behavior of an "irresponsible" individual. Even children in schools had to listed lectures about "abuses of freedom".

In fact, panic arose because the case showed that the protective arrangements against expressions of opinion different than the official views of the YCP did not work satisfactorily. They made it possible for the "enemy" to slip through. Therefore, the paroxysm of communication media had to generate additional fear and oblige all concerned to carry out their duty in a more desirable way. The publishers got their warning. The authors as well. The institution of "reviewers" had to be strengthened so that it would better respects the aims that it was supposed to serve.

After Djuretich's case arose in public, the book was sold out immediately. As nobody wanted to hear any more about a new edition, the author himself financed the publication of a new edition. However, his intention was revealed and the prosecutor confiscated the book. In the newspaper *Politika* of December 12, 1986 there was a news item about the prosecutor's decision. Namely, he was obliged to take the steps because the opinion expressed in the book was "in disagreement with established historic facts".

Imagine now the state of our culture if the courts were authorized in the past to interfere in matters of truth.

The following is another case of a similar nature. A group of members of the Academy of Sciences in Belgrade worked out a document that was expected to be an analysis of the country's political situation. Somebody passed a draft of the document to ruling bodies of the YCP. As a result, all the communications media, factory assemblies, and all sorts of associations and sporting clubs had meetings to move resolutions against the enemy act of the Academy of Sciences that dared to speak about problems of the party's concern.

In the polycentric power protection, propaganda was also changed. It was not abolished. On the contrary, it was intensified. However, the earlier aggressive methods were replaced by more sophisticated means. For example, nobody would ask people at this stage to join session of collective reading of newspapers. Nor did it seem possible any more to organize collective attendance to political lectures by groups of people living in the same house. The people did not care any more for speeches nor were they willing to attend meetings. Instead, new means were worked out that have a chance of being more efficient under the new circumstances. The awkward political indoctrination of groups in the earlier period was replaced by a circulation of mountains of all sorts of publications that all supported party politics. Thus, the only information available to the public was of an apologetic nature. The party was everywhere. There was no shelter against party propaganda. Various courses were continuously going on. Children of elementary schools were given lectures about communism. Students of high schools had in their curricula an obligatory topic of communist ideology. At the universities, marxism was equally made obligatory together with occasional lectures on selected topics. At each place of work, lecture programme was going on. In order to secure attendance at these lectures, work was interrupted. During the military service, the youngsters were included in an obligatory programme of political indoctrination. Wherever people worked or met in larger numbers, the opportunity was never missed to put aside time for propaganda. To be able to carry out such a huge amount of propagandistic involvement, many schools were operated to prepare people for leading roles in communist propaganda. The graduates of these schools became school teachers and professors of communism at the universities. Political departments were also established at all the universities and their duty was to educate qualified communists for politics and social action in general. The same aim was also assigned to other departments of social sciences. The school of law and the school of economics were supposed to be bastions

145

of communism. The whole country was thus involved in propaganda. Marxism became a part of any type of studies. All the teachers were expected to provide support to communism. The university teaching was supposed to be fully in the hands of communists.

In this way the awkward and aggressive glorification of power was replaced by concentration on the mind of the youth. The adults had their experiences. They had many chances to realize the weight of the burdens of life. They were aware that a good part of the related problems was due to circumstances imposed by the power. On the other hand, the mind of the youth is open. The youth accept nice words. This is particularly so if the words come from their teachers, viz. those who are expected to prepare them for life.

Indoctrination of the youth was carried out systematically with no regard to cost and the impact of propaganda on the rest of the scholastic programme. For purposes of propaganda, the whole national history was re-interpreted. Parts of the history before the YCP was established were abridged and presented as a kind of introduction to the great achievements of the YCP. In earlier periods everything was bad. The people used to suffer and protest. After the establishment of the YCP the rays of hope appeared. The YCP came on the scene equipped with a scientific theory of history and politics. It had the necessary determination to start the fight for the future happiness of everybody. In fact, it sacrificed its best members for the benefit of the nation. A large-scale glorification was introduced of the important events of the YCP. Children were told stories about meetings, decisions, battles, etc. The amount of the detail in the curriculum grew with age. The same things were repeated on many occasions. Later on more abstract issues were touched upon. High school children got lectures about marxism, dialectical materialism, philosophy, the established social and economic order in the country, etc. In the presentation of that material there were no doubts or problems. The YCP has always been able to solve all the problems. It never committed mistakes.

Needless to say, propaganda is a huge waste of resources. Thousands of textbooks had to be written and re-written. Many working groups worked on the establishment of adequate educational aides. The time devoted to propaganda was enormous.

What for? Most of the material presented to children was not absorbed. In order to pass the exams, children were obliged to learn by heart many passages from their textbooks without understanding the meaning of the material. After exams were over, they forget everything. When they entered the life and started carrying their burden, they faced a reality that had nothing to do with the world of dreams in their school days.

Needless to say, the propaganda among children was an activity for domestic consumption. It was an "internal matter" that was very much used and very little spoken about. For the adults and particularly for the world beyond the national borders, the YCP prepared a project that could be called "democracy".

As a result of the Campaign for Human Rights, the agreements in Helsinki, the establishment of national committees in some countries for the supervision of the implementation of Helsinki agreements, and the growing intervention in favor of freedom that were addressed to the YCP in the course of contacts of Yugoslav authorities with foreign financial circles, the Yugoslavs were frequently reminded of the need to respect the freedom of the own citizens and thus secure the basis for both the revitalization of the economy and the establishment of conditions for new loans. Yugoslavia was not in a position to disregard the requests for freedom.

In the same direction went the requests by Yugoslavs themselves. The government was obliged to let people emigrate to Western countries as it was unable to give them jobs. It was also an economically sound step as the emigrants started sending money to their relatives at home. This money was an important source of foreign currencies for the government. As a result, the government took steps to convince the emmigrants to keep sending more money or deposit their savings in Yugoslav banks. However, hesitation followed. Many people had the courage to say that it was because of the lack of security in Yugoslavia. They were afraid that national matters were governed in an arbitrary manner so that the danger existed for their property to be confiscated.

The credibility of the country was thus put in question. The YCP was obliged to do something. However, the only choice left to the YCP was to establish the appearance of democracy. All of a sudden articles started appearing in the press with content that was critical of various government proposals and measures. The television news frequently carried discussions of failures in government planning, inadequate selection of procedures to deal with social and economic issues, cases of the abuse of power or corruption, problems that were arising in almost all the fields of work, concern of the population about the level of living, poor prospects for the future, and the like. In other words, everything looked to a foreigner as a democratic approach in matters of public interest. The YCP did its best to create impression that the situation in Yugoslavia was the same as in other countries with a widely recognized respect for democratic principles.

However, it was an appearance. Some time ago, the authorities gave themselves an answer to the puzzle. In a television programme that was normally open to the public to raise questions, a sharp criticism was presented of provincial political magnates with respect to a worker who did not find any protection of his rights. He left the country and went to work in Switzerland. However, the listeners were advised not to call for interventions as the picture was made several months ago. A relative of mine told me that during this time the picture was studied by several commitees and became eventually a properly tailored "democracy" with a strict choice of each word. It had to be sharp but not too much; it had to be criticism within limits; it had to hurt the subordinates but not the principles.

Needless to say, the feature of this "democracy" was the strict control of the YCP over all the communication channels. Only those differences of opinion were allowed to appear that were previously agreed upon by the respective party organs. Only the party was allowed to criticize itself. An absolute blackout was imposed on independent communications. There was no single communication channel that would stay outside the party control. Even a literary or philosophical magazine could not be published without a *placed* by the respective party body and the appointed editorial board. The right to participate in these expressions of critical views was limited to adequately tested persons. Reliable contributors sometimes said more than it would be said in a real democratic discussion. However, the sharpness of criticism was tailored to fit particular purposes.

The euphoria caused by these cosmetic changes was considerable. The sale of magazines and the appearance of new ones went up sharply. However, after some time, people realized the meaning of the gesture. In the eyes of those who would be able to say something in a discussion of far reaching issues there was no change. The YCP itself created ample support to various reservations against its "democracy". Parallel to the implementation of the project "democracy", steps were taken in an opposite direction. A case has become popular of a young man who wrote a paper about the policy principles of the YCP. The paper was in a draft form and was captured before it reached the stage suitable for circulation. The author was sentenced to 18 months in prison. Similarly, a group of persons circulated the first issue of a literary periodical in mimeographed form. The police intervened and destroyed everything.

The proletarian dictatorship thus continues. This is why people have given up hope for being human creatures. And hope is everything. Hope makes the human being what he is at his best. Hope is the source of creative drive. Hope gives sense to one's life. Hope is the hard work, perseverance, initiative, achievement, optimism, happiness, the life itself. Similarly, broken hope is despair, lethargy, apathy, paralysis of action, torpor, and death. The period of history dominated by broken hopes were always void of content. However, there is more than that in a society of broken hopes. It becomes an easy prey of the underground world. Dark forces of the underground encounter no obstacle and the society gets invaded by lack of moral criteria, aggressiveness, rapaciousness, recklessness, and other related qualities.

Another part of the picture comes from the living conditions. Young employees live two or three in the same room. They have no privacy nor are they able to organize their life. The bulk of their income goes to food expenditures. An extra income has become a must. For this purpose, people work in the afternoon, after office hours or during the night. They have no time for anything else. Others use their regular work hours to do other work on the sly for pay. Their productivity is low. Some others steal materials from the place of work, use them in the afternoon, and charge for both the work and the material.

Corruption is an indispensable outcome of these circumstances. To have an application processed or to shorten delays for issuance of any document, one has to leave a gift for the responsible officer. Those who need hospitalization or tooth repair have to find a way to pay for it although they are entitled to get free service.

Needless to say, under these circumstances, the society is reduced to physiology.

Another part of time is to be reserved for the fulfillment of the requirements of what could be called "certificate society". The authorities do not trust citizens. As a result, certificates are frequently needed to justify rights or status. Thus, the identify cards are changed from time to time as some enemies may have entered the country illegally. They might have gotten the documents somehow. A change of identity cards is a means to catch them. In order to change the identity card, a number of documents is to be appended to the application. In order to get them, people have to leave work and go around to various offices, present their requests and return to pick up the final documents. The absence from work is justified as the change of identity cards was imposed by authorities. Needless to say, many people abuse the situation. Once they get out they do not come back on the same day. To make it worse, the procedures to follow to get the documents change frequently. Therefore, one goes once to inquire about the procedure. The next time the application is placed. The third time one has to go in person to get the document. On top of that is the fact that the officers dealing with visitors are also running around for the same documents. It does happen that one has to repeat the same visit and hope to find the officer concerned at the counter. I applied for a reduction of the airline fare. It so happened that I went 14 times to various places and eventually gave up.

The certificate issue is a small part of the complexity of daily life. The other part is the shortage of goods. Before you go to work in the morning you will need to do some shopping. In the house there is no place for a weekly supply. Nor do you have adequately large refrigerators. So you do your shopping each day. The first day there will be no bread. You will come again or go to another place. The next day there will be no milk. You might have children. So you go around till you get it. You go home happy that you succeeded. However, the elevator does not work. You walk up to the sixth floor. By the time you are set for work you are already tired. The only thing that you worry about is a nap.

This is how it goes all the time. There is always something unpredictable that causes worry. This is why the following joke was composed. Persons A and B talk:

A: As a rich man you will certainly go to hell after you die. Do you prefer to go to communist hell or the capitalist hell?

B: I prefer the capitalist hell.

A: You are mistaken, my dear. You better go to communist hell. Before they put you on fire for boiling there will be many delays. The first day there will be no wood to make the fire. The next day the matches will be missing. The third day there will be no water. The fourth day there will be no container to put you in. And it will continue like that. Eventually they will get tired and you will be forgotten.

However, the YCP concentrated its attention on power protection programme. In this way it confirmed the standard shortsightedness of all totalitarian regimes. The maintenance of the power protection structure was costly. No economy can afford such a burden of unproductive expenditures without an impact on the level of living. In addition, the concentration of attention on power protection shifts the emphasis from creative work to flattery, servility, and obedience. The result is the unhappiness of the population with the living conditions and the regime that is responsible for the situation. The question of an alternative road to the future thus arises.

Decentralized power control is particularly dangerous in this kind of situation. Being afraid of consequences that might develop from the unhappiness of the population, the authorities of lower level units seek support through a compromise with the local population. This is how local YCP circles get ready to tolerate attitudes and activities that are frequently in sheer conflict with official ideology. This is how the phantoms of the past enter the political scene, such as animosities on grounds of nationality, religion, script, tradition, etc.

The fear of the consequences of these new tendencies in the policies of the YCP

149

has become a big national issue at the moment of writing. Suspicion has arisen in almost all the lower level units regarding the intentions of other units. A state developed that most units have lost confidence in the intentions of other units. Soon after that this suspicion was transformed into open attacks on each other. Various units identified the "enemy" in other units. This was followed by accusations and a real "verbal war". In some cases the tension has become worrisome.

This state of political matters had its consequences. In order to be able to get facts about the attitude and intentions of other units the main centers of power supported the maintenance of an intelligence service with the task of keeping an eye on policies of other centers of power and thus enable themselves to stage a counterattack as soon as "offensive" steps are noticed. The maintenance of this system of observations and the corresponding preparation of the "war of words" further increased the expenditures on unproductive purposes and contributed to a further rise of unhappiness and apathy on the part of population. It also had an impact on moral aspects of the power protection campaign. Participation in propaganda carried on by various centers of power was not an activity that could claim much respect. This is why people with recognized moral and intellectual authority refused to participate in it. As a result, the power centers were obliged to depend upon the support of people who were willing to serve any power in exchange for high salary, privileges, and various forms of public recognition.

In this way the spiral of deterioratiomg events took Yugoslavia in its course. Needless to say, nobody knows what the outcome of this situation will be. However, judging by the dark clouds that cover the skies, the storm might easily develop into a major catastrophe.

XVI A puzzle

The developments presented in the earlier chapters are quite confusing. Some of the steps taken are shocking. One finds it difficult to accept them as possible. This is particularly true of the attitude on the part of the authorities in situations where one would expect a mobilization of brains to assist in a consideration of far-reaching decisions that had to be taken. At these crossroads of development the usual practice is to carry out large-scale consultations in order to get as much advice as possible and thus prevent skipping over some relevant facts. At variance with this, Yugoslav statistics ran at these moments into measures that one is unable to understand. Even more peculiar was the ease with which these decisions were made. In fact, some of the fundamental decisions were made as if they were routine matters under the authority of the junior staff.

For illustration the reader is reminded of the problem of reconstruction of prewar data that was dealt with in Chapter IV: "New Statistics". Prewar data according to the new administrative division of the country were needed as a source of information for the formulation of plans and for the purpose of measuring the achievements of the socialist society by referring current data to 1939, i.e. the base year.

However, the accomplishment of this task ran into difficulties. The first of them was due to the modest state of statistics in the prewar period. The available data were far from satisfactory for an ambitious activity such as planning. The country had a census of population in 1931. However, it never had a census of industry or a census of agriculture. Current agricultural statistics was reduced to administrative guesses by agricultural extension work personnel. Only in some fields, such as foreign trade, education, etc. were more data available. Therefore, a reconstructed picture for 1939 could not offer data for sound planning.

The limited value of the supply of data for 1939 was further reduced by changes that took place in the country during the war. There were considerable shifts of population. It may not be an exaggeration to say that more than one fifth of the population were killed or changed residence. The infrastructure was equally affected. Therefore, the statistical picture of the country for 1939 that was obtained from prewar data had a restricted value. It did not show the state of the national problems at the initial stage of socialism nor was it adequate for a measurement of changes and achievements in the postwar period.

Needless to say, the government had better options available and it was not difficult to work them out. This was the period of the rapid rise of statistical theory and of survey techniques in particular. The introduction of science in data collection offered a number of tools of primary importance for a solution of outstanding problems. Therefore, the step needed was to open all the doors to new ideas coming from different parts of the world and absorb the achievements. A part of the step to take was the establishment of a strong data collection agency that would take a number of censuses and surveys and thus build a fresh statistical picture of the country in the postwar years. First of all, this picture would provide a broad spectrum of data for the formulation of plans. It could also serve as a basis for measurement of changes taking place as a result of postwar developments. In addition, other surveys could be established on a current basis to provide additional measurements of changes in any area considered important.

Instead of such an approach, a line was taken that had far-reaching negative consequences on the quality of planning in Yugoslavia. The country was deprived of a sufficiently broad range of data for planning purposes. In addition, the available data were of an unknown accuracy. As a result, the planning went in the direction of what could be called catch-as-catch-can work, i.e. use of guesses and various assumptions rather than facts.

Nor was the information to the public about the achievements sufficiently reliable.

Consequences on statistics were no less serious. Instead of joining the course of events in more developed countries and thus establishing the ground work for a modernization of national statistics, an orientation was taken toward forgotten approaches of the past. Yugoslav statistics opted for a century old methodology and disregarded modern achievements. In this way it fell in to primitivism that it was not able to get rid of later on.

Why was such a course of developments needed?

The same question arises in connection with the decision of the Yugoslav authorities to introduce recording. In fact, recording is the real topic of this chapter.

The purposes of recording in Yugoslav data collection were presented in Chapter IV: "New Statistics". Difficulties arising in the application of recording were discussed in Chapter VIII: "The New Setup".

As soon as recording was introduced in Yugoslavia its restricted value as a source of information became obvious. Namely, recording is primarily useful for a simple type of planning purposes as in the case of production that can easily be expressed in quantitative units, such as the production of bricks. In this case, production is planned in the number of bricks. The result of the production can easily be counted. The number of bricks in a specified period is also a measure of the fulfillment of the plan.

Similar cases of simple recording refer to area planted, area harvested, the number of livestock, etc. However, these cases include a small part of the information needed in planning. The majority of the characteristics in data collection cannot be dealt with with the help of recording. This is primarily true of characteristics of individuals, such as those arising in censuses of population, current population surveys, labor force surveys, health surveys, expenditure surveys, food consumption surveys, transportation surveys, etc. This is equally true of surveys that refer to large populations and the resulting need to work with samples of units, such as area surveys, yield surveys, livestock surveys, fruit surveys, farm surveys, surveys of prices, etc. In other words, a large sector of data collection is outside the application of recording.

One cannot blame the Yugoslav authorities for a lack of understanding of this fact. This is seen from an early decision to establish two agencies for data collection. One of them depended primarily on surveys and the other on recording. The problem arises in the amount of support to these two lines of work. Recording was a favorite of the political leadership. It was attached to the most powerful agencies of the government and was located in the center of Belgrade. The statistical part was located in a far-off small place.

However, the fundamental mistake of the epoch was the adoption of the view that proclaimed the theory of statistics as a capitalist tool. Any interest in statistical theory was a political sin. The theory was squeezed out of the university curricula. Any reference to theory in the government data collection was a way to become an "enemy".

The consequences of the imposition of this attitude were far-reaching. The authorities were not able to disregard the need for statistical surveys and censuses. As a result, various surveys remained in the programme of work. However, the theory was missing to build an adequate methodology and orientate data collection toward modern standards. In other words, animosity against the theory of statistics deprived the country of an aspect of modern developments. The quality of data collection was kept below the available standards.

Another point is the impact of the ban on the level of general scientific development of the country. Statistical theory is a part of the methodology of modern science. Statistical theory is essential in agriculture, medecine, psychology, economics, sociology, etc. The ban on the theory of statistics and its cultivation at universities and research centers has become an obstacle to the development of science.

This is how the Yugoslav science started lagging behind the state of science in more developed countries. It is sufficient to glance at the Yugoslav periodicals in the last thirty years to notice the gap between the state of science in the world on the one hand and our own standards on the other. The difference arises in both the choice of topics and the methodology used. Statistics is taught at many departments of all the universities in the country. However, contributions are missing in the recognized periodicals. More than any amount of words, this fact shows what price the nation had to pay for the neglect of an important line of scientific development.

Nor was recording a satisfactory source of information in areas where it was introduced. An illustration is the labor force statistics. Following the practices of the USSR, Yugoslavia has never established labor force surveys. The information about the labor force is obtained from current reports of all the units of work. They report the total number of employees, their classification by degree of qualifications, the number of hours worked, etc. If the units of work are classified by branch of industry and territorially, the resulting information is the labor force statistics. The same is true of unemployment data. They follow from current reports of employment offices that show the registered unemployed by age, sex, degree of education, qualifications, etc.

Such a picture of the labor force would hardly be acceptable at present. Regarding the unemployment, the reports of registered cases have an unknown value. Registration provides some benefits, such as the inclusion of the period of unemployment in years of service, priority in the choice of jobs offered, participation of unemployed persons in the national health insurance scheme, etc. It might thus be that the number of registered cases in much above the number of persons seeking jobs. The coverage of data about employment varies also by the number of registration points. Persons living far out may not be registered. Also, the labor force in agriculture in the private sector is out of the system.

The labor force surveys aim at an assessment of the total labor input in a specified period of time by a variety of classifications. However, the information about persons registered does not provide any information about the work done in the course of the registered unemployment. Most unemployed persons do some work for pay while waiting for an official offer of a job. The registered unemployed persons certainly contribute to labor input. The same problem arises in case of data about employment. A high percentage of employed persons has secondary employment. Information about that cannot be obtained from current reports from places of work. In other words, a picture of the labor input that follows from recording might represent a serious under-estimation of the work actually done. In the calculation of productivity of work, the biased picture of labor input might lead to considerable distortions.

Needless to say, there are other deficiencies that arise in labor force statistics based on recording. For example, in recording there is no information about length of travel and means used to go to work. They also say nothing about the opinion of employed persons about the job they have and their possible intention to find another job. This is why most countries in the world seek a broader range of information that can only be obtained from statistical surveys of individuals.

The next issue is the value of recording as a tool of management.

When recording was introduced in Yugoslavia, we were told that units of work are privately owned in capitalism. Therefore, the managers are free to do their business in any way they consider adequate. On the other hand, in socialism private property is abolished. The society is the owner of everything. The purpose of the management is to secure an efficient method of use of resources so that the work provides a maximum benefit to society. Recording is a tool to achieve this aim. It is expected to provide essential facts that guide the decision making process.

As it was already pointed out, it does not seem that there is any system of data recording that can secure by itself adequate management. Nor does good management necessarily require a system of recording. Management decisions are taken in the light of a broad context of facts that might be related to a large variety of factors of work. A statistical report saying that in an establishment five employees did not come to work on a particular day would hardly be of any use to management. At an airport five absent employees might refer to staff engaged in cleaning operations as well as to flight control officers. In both cases the statistical report is the same. Five persons are missing.

However, in the case of cleaning personnel there would be little concern about the issue. In the case of the five flight control officers it might mean closing down that particular airport.

In other words, if any use should be made of statistical data it is to refer them to a broad context of facts about the unit of work concerned to ascertain the meaning of the information in the light of other facts. Statistical information by itself is generally not sufficient to guide decisions. Nor would any management make decisions on the basis of statistical data alone.

In the illustrations presented the management would probably not be interested in any statistics. If they start their day with a report by the manager of the shift, they would get a picture of all the problems, suggestions for action to take, an assessment of possible consequences of various problems, etc. Such a report might represent all that is needed in an adequate management. Any form of recording might be disregarded.

However, there are also cases when a numerical report of the work done in a period of time will be all that is needed for decision. For example, a report of the quantity of a product manufactured is all the information needed for sales and shipment departments to organize their subsequent action.

There are also cases where the manager will consider the establishment of any recording system as a waste of resources and time. In a manufacturing establishment with fifty employees, the manager is continuously present in the workshop. He knows all the workers, he is aware of their involvement in work, absence from work, their skills, the quality of their products, etc. With the help of his senses, he will get all the information needed for his decisions. Therefore, any attempt at introducing any kind of recording will be for him an addition to the cost of operation without a sufficient gain in the productivity of his establishment.

In other words, management consists of a series of decisions that have to be taken on the spot, in the light of a broad context of facts that reflect specific circumstances of each particular unit of work. The meaning of any numerical information about any aspect of work is very relative. It will vary from case to case starting, on the one hand, with situations where no recording is able to contribute to the adequacy of decisions, to cases, on the other hand, where some recording might be useful for some purposes. In other words, if the recording has a character of a useful tool of management it can only be so if it is organized on the spot in a way that fits the specific circumstances of work.

This is why recording is excluded in Western countries from the government sponsored system of data collection and left to all the units of work to decide on their own if they are interested in it, for what purpose, to what extent, in how long intervals of time, etc. In other words, the recording becomes a part of the organization of work in each unit; it represents an internal matter.

In spite of these restrictions, recording was introduced in Yugoslavia in all the units of work. The reasons that led to the acceptance of such a system are not quite clear. Why the choice was made to accept a system of data collection that does not deserve the attention reserved for it?

155

An answer to this question will be attempted in the continuation. Some points will be presented here that, individually or in combination, might help explain the origin of recording.

The first point refers to circumstances in which the system was conceived.

After the revolution, the Soviets badly needed some system of data collection. Property was nationalized and an entirely new group of people were put at decision making positions. Their skills and experiences in the management of work were modest. However, they had to make decisions. For that purpose they needed some help and guidance. Some kind of statistics appeared to be a key to success. As a result, some solution to the problem of data collection had to be found.

As to the characteristics of the solution needed, the political power in the USSR imposed the requirement to work out a system that would generate data by small territorial units. The country was divided into a number of republics. Within each republic there was a hierarchy of other smaller units. All these units were involved in planning and some kind of participation in the direction of the social and economic life within its own territory. Some statistical picture was thus indispensable at all the levels of the hierarchy of units.

In a search for a satisfactory solution, the Soviets did not have the option of the present survey methodology. Although the Russian statisticians were on top of developments in survey methodology before the First World War,[14] this was the period when only the first steps were made toward the present survey methodology. Knowledge of the theory and experience in its application were quite far from the level needed to successfully operate a statistical undertaking of vast proportions. Had the Soviets chosen to rely on the available abilities of tzarist machinery, they would have run the risk of postponing the achievements that they urgently needed without being sure that the alternative approach would provide a satisfactory solution even after quite a few years.

There was also another element in the game. With the alternative of relying on old services in statistics and the application of statistical theory, the Soviets would need to accept the leading role of the available technicians. In other words, their essential political programme would be dependent upon scientists and people who read books, cooperate with other countries, and make any effort to absorb the progress in the world no matter where it takes place.

No communist party would agree to make itself dependent upon outsiders. This is so at present and it was even more so in the USSR of that period. After the interventions of foreign troops to push the new power out of control and create various difficulties to the new regime on the way to stability, the excitement against the enemy reached a climax. The communist party saw itself encircled by enemies. The enemy was everywhere. Extreme vigilance was thus required everywhere and by everybody. As the enemy was a genius of evil, it was particularly necessary to stay away from anything that was not absolutely clear and within the understanding of the party's rank and file.

---

14 Cfr. Seneta, E.: A sketch of the history of survey sampling in Russia, *Journal of the Royal Statistical Society*, Series A, Vol. 148, 1985.

Question marks were also raised about the whole area of sciences. Statistics was a part of the suspected source of danger. It was particularly true of mathematically oriented statistics. It was a part of the developments in the world. It was cultivated in Western countries. *Ipso facto* it was a disguised enemy that was making attempts to penetrate the USSR and search for an overthrow of the new power. Therefore, Soviet statistical system had to be straightforward. It could not incorporate anything that was beyond the reach of the ordinary party membership. It needed a means fully controllable by the party.

The result was the system of recording.

Soviet recording is a great achievement that will retain its place in the history of statistics. Credit goes to all those who invented the system and worked out its details in specific fields of statistical work. Recording helped meet the needs of the USSR for data. On the part of the USSR population recording contributed largely to the appreciation of facts. With all its defects, recording contributed to the maturation of the society. One could go as far as saying that it was an important achievement under the conditions of the moment.

The merit of the system is in its straightforwardness. Recording does not require any theory. Nor does it require any particular education as a prerequisite to be involved successfully in recording in any field. Plain common sense is sufficient to learn everything in a couple of hours that is needed to keep things going. Recording was thus suitable as a large-scale data collection in a society that started with a modest number of people with higher degrees of qualifications.

However, after the system of recording was established in the USSR, the statistical development of the world did not stop. On the contrary, it was moving ahead rather fast. As a result, new requirements on data appeared in modern societies. The tools were also developed to meet new needs. The progress of technology added its support to further developments in the requirements for data. Parallel to that Soviet recording was rapidly becoming an old-fashioned approach to data collection. The further the developments in the world went the less satisfactory was the tool of recording. In more recent years it has become an inacceptable solution to the problem of data collection in a country that pretended a guiding role in the attempts to shape the future of the modern society.

A great problem of recording is in the fact that Soviet society failed to build a mechanism that would enable the country to follow the statistical developments in the world and thus keep the achievements of recording within useful limits. It was pointed out above that recording helped solve some problems and kept open some other issues. Research was the way to understand the shortcomings of the invented tool and limit its uses to justified cases. Instead of that, the Soviet practice overemphasized the usefulness of recording. Recording was given attention that it did not deserve. It has thus become *the* socialist tool. As a result, the whole system petrified in the course of time to eventually become a part of a rigid bureaucracy. It was going on as it was. It had the merit of existing. Recording has become an achievement beyond doubts and discussions.

The issue takes us to the role of the party in both the establishment of the system of recording and its subsequent transformation into a rigid data collection system.

Regarding this point much has already been said about the related approaches of a communist party at power. An outline of the respective party attitude was formulated in the early version of ideology of the communist movement. The party is the avant-garde. It consists of people who have become aware of the injustice of capitalist society and are willing to engage in the fight to overthrow the rule of capitalism and establish a society of justice and equality. This fight requires sacrifice. Capitalism will use all the available means to keep the conquered positions. Therefore, on the way to the conquest of power the members of the party have to be ready to stage strikes, lose jobs, go to jails, and even sacrifice their life.

After the power is taken, the task of the party is not ended. Capitalism will again use all possible means to recapture the power. For this reason the party is obliged to continue the same militant attitude. This task is no less demanding in terms of courage and determination. The fight continues for the establishment of new institutions, against hidden agents of capitalism, and the lack of interest in the future on the part of all those who primarily want a quiet life. This is why party members have to take a leading role in all the aspects of life and thus prevent any relaxation of fights. Everything is to be in hands of the party. The party has control of everything; it directs all the developments toward communist goals.

The leading role of the party in all the units of work means in practice opposition on the part of the party to any approaches to work that are beyond the understanding of party members. Everything that is beyond the level of party members is dangerous, risky, doubtful. Even more, it might be a trick of the enemy to create trouble. Therefore, the professional level of party blessed approaches is low. Any attempt to introduce procedures that require abilities above the level of party membership is opposed. In other words, the party plays a reactionary role; it prefers to move along the known approaches than to agree to experiments and new ideas.

This is how the party behaved at the moment of the establishment of the system of recording. It was unable to accept that some scientists come to meetings of the party and tell the members what to do and how to do it. In its attitude, the party was systematically on the side of old-fashioned views. In the interpretation of events by the party, the important achievements were always in line with old-fashioned approaches. This is what it always celebrated; this is what it recognized in its official publications. Recording had a wholehearted support of party members. It was clear and simple. It offered all the chances to the party to engage in initiatives and decisions. The party did not insist on critical approaches. It just kept the system as an adequate socialist achievement.

Another contribution to the petrification of the system of recording comes from the organization of political activities in communist societies. In order to provide a short title that would point out features of politics in a communist country, a journalist defined communism as a "discussion society". In fact, an endless amount of discussion of the same issues is going on permanently. However, these discussions hardly ever end in binding decisions. Everybody has the right to raise any issue. However, the institution concerned with the issues will continue the line chosen as it has other discussion bodies that also keep the right to continue discussions. For these reasons the discussions continue.

This is obviously the inefficiency of the Soviet system in practice. Its roots are also in the ideology. After the society has become the owner of the means of production, the management is transferred to the "people". The people know what they are interested in. As a result, they will direct the economy toward the agreed upon goals. For that purpose they will formulate the aims to be achieved and the decisions that should best lead to a realization of the accepted goals. However, involvement in these discussions is not limited to the staff of the unit of work concerned. Since everything is owned by the society and the events in various fields are interconnected, it means in practice that everybody is entitled to get involved in a discussion of any issue or the business of any unit of work.

Consequences of this situation are presented in Chapters XIV and XV.

The citizens have their organizations, such as government machinery, party, labor union, Socialist Union, army, veterans union, etc. Each of these organizations has its vertical structure arranged according to levels of hierarchy. All these organizations are involved in discussions of current issues. Items for discussion might be included in the agenda at each level. However, before a stand is formulated the issue is to be discussed vertically and horizontally.

Needless to say, this mechanism of discussions is used fully in more important issues. There are many issues that will remain at some lower level. Discussions of a decline of production of bricks in an establishment located in some village will be restricted to local organizations.

The manipulation of that discussion machinery is in the hands of the party. The party is the originator of items that appear on the agenda all the way through. This is particularly so in matters where the party wants a general mobilization of population behind its projects. An illustration is the "memorandum" of the Serbian Academy of Sciences. The document was critical of the state of matters in Yugoslav society. The party reacted violently. It can't tolerate statements that any business under its authority could be anything but very good. In the preparation of action against the "memorandum", the party needed an expression of disagreement of all the population with the attitude of the academy. As a result, meetings of all sorts of bodies were convened on this subject all over the country. The newspapers carried many articles expressing criticism of the academy by local bodies in remote villages.

In these discussions, statistics plays an important role. Namely, a practice developed to have documents prepared on any issue that is to appear on the agenda. This is how thousands of documents are permanently in circulation. In the preparation of these documents, statistical data are frequently used in the presentation of problems. Statistics is thus a way to provide facts and channel discussions to specific problems that arise from these facts.

As these discussions appear at all levels of hierarchy statistical data also have to be available at all the levels. In other words, the system of recording is the basis on which current operations of the political structure are built.

These uses of statistical data have damaged the reputation of statistics in the eyes of the population. The management of an establishment for the production of bricks

159

will probably not need any recording beyond the registration of labor present for purposes of the payroll. However, in order to meet the requirements of discussion machinery, the establishment is obliged to carry out the prescribed volume of recording and make available its results. As an activity that does not contribute visibly to the success of the operation, recording will be interpreted as a bureaucratic activity. From the point of view of the establishment it is imposed without valid justification.

A similar attitude will appear on the part of participants of various bodies that find the brick establishment on the agenda of their meeting. They are aware that their discussion will not add much to facts already known to the establishment itself. Nor will they see better what the right analysis of the situation of the establishment should be. They will consider statistical data as a contribution to the maintenance of a jargon of documents. Statistics thus refers to the form rather than the essence.

This is how the system of recording went into uses of doubtful value. However, the system of recording continues along the line established. Proposals for a modernization of the system not appear. The whole matter is covered by silence.

This strange phenomenon seems to be a result of a combination of socialist theory with tzarist tradition in the relationships between the power and the population. Socialist theory is a product of Western civilization. It implies a continuous search for new ideas, new solutions, and improvements of the available achievements. Creative forces flourish. They generate dynamism that does not recognize limitations. It expanded over all the fields of life including the society as well. It quickly resulted in a sharp criticism of the society and the attempts at an outline of a better shape of the society. One of these results is socialism. The idea was developed in a variety of versions that reflect their authors and circumstances of different societies. However, socialism is a continuous involvement in a search for new experiences and studies of impact of technological and scientific development. There is nothing that is solved and final. The only permanent line is the process of search.

At variance with this is the view of power in the tzarist tradition. The power is a devine order. It is personalized in the tzar who acts through his machinery. The individual is an object of that power. The power has all the qualities at their best. The power has the intelligence to know what is to be done. In order to follow the path to the supreme aims as reflected in the acts of the power, the individual has to offer obedience. The power will never fail to do what is needed. The individual is thus a follower. His duty is to accept the order as established. Any doubt as to the righteousness of the established order is a sin. Changes, adjustments, and improvements make up a part of responsibilities of the power. The individual is a servant of the established order.

These two opposing attitudes are combined in Leninism. Western socialism offers appealing arguments for success of the action to overthrow the capitalist order. However, the power established after the revolution becomes a divine order. The new power has all the attributes of the tzarist power. It knows everything and it will take all the steps needed for the promotion of welfare for everybody. Therefore, the citizens are expected to follow the path designed by the power.

Nor will the power care for the opinion of individuals. When the Yugoslav authorities realized that centralized operational decisions led to an inefficient economy, they decided to abolish the authority of the federal government in operational matters and transfer that authority to economy itself, viz. the business establishments.

In this situation, the role of statistics had to be drastically changed. Separation of operational decisions from the government administration meant giving up operational uses of data. In other words, there was no need for daily and weekly reports. The administration was not able to make any use of them. If daily and other short-term reports are needed, this is exclusively at the level of the establishments themselves. This type of data represent an internal matter of each unit of work. They have to organize the related work in their own way and to the extent considered appropriate.

On the other hand, the interest of the government administration switched to the information about tendencies, various indicators that show characteristics of the global behavior of economy and the society in general. In other words, the interest is concentrated on data collected at longer intervals, such as a month or longer. In addition, the interest arises in a reduced volume of data collection. Long questionnaires are not needed any more as the government and the related users of data are not interested in such an amount of data. The needs of the administration would be adequately met with the help of a modest number of properly selected figures.

In the statistical terminology, it means the reduction of government needs to occasional surveys for the estimation of totals, averages, proportions, etc. In other words, Yugoslavia was in the situation to do the same thing that most other countries were doing.

A rational attitude in that situation was to mobilize the existing know-how to solve the statistical problems of the country in a way that would correspond to post-war achievements of the theory and the accumulated experiences in its application as well. The step needed was equivalent to what other countries were doing. It was necessary to carry out consultations with technicians and foreign experts, encourage research, collect information about developments in the world, improve statistical education and thus establish a basis for the continued use of progress in statistics.

Instead of that, tragic approaches were used. In his article in *Thirty Years of Statistics,* Novak provided information about what happened. He proudly pointed out that he and Krashovec, viz. the heads of two separate agencies for the government data collection, sat together over a cup of coffee and worked out the future of Yugoslav statistics. After they designed the future of statistics, they went together to see the responsible minister who enthusiastically approved their design. That was all. The rest was the implementation of the agreement.

According to this design the methodology of data collection remained the same. The universality of reporting was continued. In other words, all the establishments would keep reporting in the same way as before.

Two persons thus decided what the future of Yugoslav statistics would be. Their decision is still valid. Up to the present time it has never been questioned or changed. And these two persons were not statisticians. They have never studied statistics. The state of statistics and the world experiences were unknown to them. They were political appointees. Their familiarity with statistics amounted to what one is able to learn in a couple of years as director of statistical services. Nor did they care to consult anybody in the group of available technicians. Similarly, they did not care for the well-established statistical approaches consisting of studies, experiments, and research in general.

The analogy with the past goes a step further. For all those who might have failed to accept the power, the tzar established an institution called Siberia. Long lines of people used to travel to Siberia. Similarly, for the same category of people, the USSR established labor camps, the difference being that more people travelled to these camps than their fathers did to Siberia.

The result is the widely known sleepiness and apathy of the Soviet society. No initiative, no interest in changes or improvements. The progress of the world is coming up and passing by without causing much reaction on the part of the Soviet citizens. They accept the order imposed and carry out the duties prescribed. However, nothing more than that. They keep quiet.

I had a long discussion in Moscow with an elderly Soviet colleague who made excellent contributions to the development of statistical methodology in the early period of new statistical ideas. He told me how much he suffered because of his involvement in "bourgeois theories". At the end I asked him: "Why don't you continue your early work and add the results of your subsequent thinking to it? He told me: "Don't you think that I had enough"?

Yugoslav statistics is in the same situation. A terrible carelessness about the progress in the world dominates all the sectors of work. There is no interest in what is going on in the world; there is no interest even in the improvements that are at hand and easy to carry out. Lethargy rules across the board.

How long will it be like that?

Obviously, statistics is a part of the society. It can hardly be different than the rest of the society. The drowsiness is a general state of the country. The disease is spread over the communist world as a whole. Statistics is thus a part of a big package of issues that is called the future of the communist world.

The issue of the future of the communist world is also connected with the future of the world as a whole. Should communism not be able to solve the issue of its inefficiency, desastrous consequences might easily affect the whole globe. This is why many eyes from all over the world are looking at communist countries with anxiety to discover symptoms that could be interpreted as a move toward improvement.

The stakes of the desired change are enormous. They imply freedom for everybody, the abolishment of the ambitions of the party to run the country, the abolishment of discrimination between the members of the party and the commoners, replacement of the present political favoritism by recognition of work, achievements, and skills, freedom of speech and writing, abolisment of propaganda, and a return to the responsibility of individuals for the discharge of their duties. And this is only a small part of what is to be done. The task is thus so big that skepticism arises in the face of its proportions. Should communism do this, what would remain of it?

Let us wait and see.

XVII From a distance

I left Yugoslavia in 1955. In FAO I got involved with my new responsibilities. The work conditions were excellent. The colleagues in the office were nice. I was happy with what I was doing. I was convinced that my work was in line with the needs of less developed countries. I thus had all the satisfaction that one could wish.

And yet there was still one issue that bothered me. This was the state of statistics in Yugoslavia.

I am touching again on this issue as it worried me considerably. Before I left Yugoslavia, my concern was the following: "Should I abandon the promotion of statistics in Yugoslavia and go to work somewhere else"? After I left, the new version of the same issue became: "Was my decision to leave the country correct?

I admired the respective positions of colleagues from developed countries. To my knowledge none of them has ever suffered from this type of question. It would be foolish and very pretentious should an American say: "I cannot take an overseas assignment because I am afraid that my departure might have a negative effect on subsequent developments in US statistics". There are so many Americans and so many institutions in US who are concerned about the future of statistics. The individuals, no matter who they might be, are, therefore, fully free to base their decisions on consideration of personal interest. Better prospects for career or better salary are normally their main arguments. Once the decision to go away is made the question of what would happen at home does not arise. I have never seen a colleague from DC raise the matter of moral responsibilities in connection with the decision to go abroad.

In this respect the situation is quite different in LDC. The difference is due to the scarcity of qualified personnel. In LDC each qualified staff member is practically alone in a given field of work. If he is adequately involved in the work, he can practically feel his achievements under his fingers. The development of the country depends immensurably upon individuals. Should such a staff member go away to work in some other country, there will be nobody to attend to the work with equal success. Therefore, the development of the country would suffer a setback. In such a situation, it becomes difficult to push forward one's personal interest and disregard the country and its future.

163

To the extent of my ability to judge, most colleagues from LDC are inclined to give serious weight to such an interpretation of their responsibility.

I was happy to notice this state of affairs. This is an important asset in the hands of LDC. However, in spite of that attitude, technicians from LDC frequently do go to work abroad. This is primarily because of some form of discrimination at home. The discrimination is based on reasons of political affiliation, religion, race or other issues. The people discriminated against are not given an adequate chance to cooperate and contribute their share. For reasons that have nothing to do with work they are cut off from positions of influence; their achievements are artificially reduced; they do not get the necessary satisfaction from their work; they are essentially losing time and accumulating worries. This is how they are obliged to accept the best alternative, viz. go abroad and secure the benefits from life in a society with less discrimination.

Regarding our group, the discrimination was sharp and offensive. We never got a chance to put forward alternative ideas and reasons. We were excluded *a priori*. Our future held the gradual decline of technical knowledge, apathy, and disintegration of personality. In that situation, departure from the country was an attractive alternative to retain both human dignity and hope for the improvement of one's own technical abilities.

In that respect I had no doubt whatsoever. I had lived for quite some time in conflict between my desire to be useful to my own country and the growing mass of proof that nothing appreciable could be done as long as the work was governed by irrational criteria, preconceived views, and discrimination against all those who do not share the views of the power. I have been examining this conflict for years. When I was out of the country I had a strong and definite feeling that there was no single fact that would call for a reconsideration of my reasons for departure. I was convinced that I did what I was forced to do in order to avoid complete destruction. Even today, after so many ears, I am of the same opinion.

However, the situation was not as simple as I expected it to be. After I settled in at FAO, the idea of responsibility for the promotion of statistics in my country reappeared and began preying on my mind with a considerable intensity. However, this new appearance of an old issue did not involve a reexamination of my earlier decision to go away. Instead, the issue appeared in the form of what could I do from abroad to contribute to the improvement of statistics in Yugoslavia?

The reappearance of the issue of the promotion of statistics in Yugoslavia included a strong emotional component. Those who in the past kept the mandate to shape the statistics of Yugoslavia have never cared for our desire to be useful nor have they ever taken any step to examine with us our reasons and our views. Because of that, failures followed one after the other. However, the failures never led to a revision of past attitudes or to attempts at learning from past experience. Why should it now be different? Nothing happened that could be interpreted as a sign of change.

However, the emotions worked. How many times should parents be expected to help their erring child? Seven times? I remember the answer: seventy seven times. The country and the people living in it stay above the regime and politics. The contributions made to improve conditions and promotion of development have a lasting value and

164

are independent of the temporariness of politics. For the sake of these lasting values one has to keep trying again and again. The need for new attempts is permanent. The more the attempts are neglected the more they are needed. Therefore, a practical precept is: "Do whatever you can no matter what the outcome is. Your duty is to try to be useful and not to worry about the effect".

There was an element in my new situation that gave great strength to that attitude. Namely, I was independent of the Yugoslav authorities and I did not need any favor whatsoever. Therefore, there cannot be any interpretation of the steps I took to improve the work at home as being a way for personal gain of any kind. I considered that the lack of any personal interest was a strong trump in my hands and I decided to use it.

Regarding the method of making contributions from the outside, I had doubts as to the suitability of standard approaches, such as writing proposals or talking to responsible persons about the possibilities. I did not belong to a circle of people who could be trusted. Therefore, my proposals would always be rejected just because they came from an outsider.

An efficient method for this purpose was used by a colleague of mine who happened to work in the office of one of the leaders of the YCP. My colleague was an able public relations officer and his minister appreciated the work that he was doing. However, he realized that the minister did not like his initiative. The minister was obviously afraid that he might be taken by his staff in the wrong direction. Therefore, when my friend wanted something to be done in a particular way, he would use his next visit to the minister to tell him: "Comrade minister, some time ago you told me to do this and this in such and such way. I kept thinking about your idea and I now think we have to do it. Are you still of the same opinion?" In this way his proposal was transformed into minister's will.

I used this approach on many occasions. When I received documents about meetings, I would send them to the director of statistics and/or his associates so that they could see by themselves how far they were behind the level of discussions in other countries and how much they needed to work to catch up with the others. When I received some publications showing problems in important areas or a review of steps taken by other countries to promote studies of these problems, I would sent them to responsible people of Yugoslav statistics to give them the facts for an appraisal of their own work. I also asked the organizers of meetings to invite the leading Yugoslav statistical staff to attend these meetings to have a chance to mix with people and develop an appreciation of the willingness of the profession to help each other.

After the hard line was imposed on Yugoslav statistics and almost all contacts were discontinued with world centers, it was particularly important to secure a window to the world for the benefit of the staff who remained convinced of the value of studies and the attempts at keeping in touch with international developments. For the benefit of these people I used to collect new literature and, particularly, the publications of important statistical centers. Whenever I was able to make a convenient stop over in Yugoslavia, I would take off a day or two and talk to these colleagues, give them the publications, and provide them with additional information about new events in the profession, the people playing various roles in statistics, and the possibilities that might be used by Yugoslavs to profit from the achievements of others. I considered it particularly important to contribute my personal share to the success of the UN effort to build cooperation between countries. The UN campaign had of course its political aims. A favorable atmosphere of cooperation was an essential element of stability of the future world. In addition, it was an equally essential element for the promotion of development. For that reason I thought that it was vital for Yugoslavs to appreciate the existing arrangements for cooperation, participate in these arrangements, and make use of them in the efforts to solve problems.

In order to be successful along this line it was very important to pull in the official top representatives of Yugoslav statistics. This is why the arrangements were made to include them in the membership of international statistical associations, make sure that they always get invitations to the international meetings, offer them a chance to take part in discussions, make them agree to visits by outstanding statisticians with a view to contributing to the promotion of respective work in Yugoslavia, ask for their help in the recruitment of Yugoslavs for UN technical assistance etc.

The individual achievements resulting from this effort cannot be presented as it would be embarrassing to refer to names. However, the achievements were many and considerable. The publications that were made available to Yugoslav technicians helped them survive technically during the period of the blackout. They also helped them strengthen their belief that progress in other countries was going on and would be available for us as well, as soon as the conditions permitted. However, among these achievements, primary importance was attached to melting the ice of mistrust. After Morris Hansen from the US visited Yugoslavia and worked there for some time his achievements were admired and details of the visit were discussed for quite some time. One of the party bosses said: "Now I understand the efficiency of American capitalism". Another one added: "This man is proof that Americans are not necessarily spies".

Needless to say, the primary influence on changes of the situation in Yugoslavia came from the UN. After some time, changes were also obvious on the part of hard-core fanatics like Novak. He entirely stopped talking about the Soviet model of socialism and went as far as ridiculing its basic approaches and the work that he was doing before when transferring Soviet views. The category of spies and enemies was broadened and included Russians in addition to Americans. The people willing to help and cooperate were now living everywhere, not only in socialist countries. There was nothing against cooperation with any center known for its achievements.

However, Novak had no time to make use of the new atmosphere. In fact, in 1963 he was removed from the position of Director of Statistics in Yugoslavia and was put in charge of the Institute of Philosophy and Sociology in Ljubljana. It is not known whether the transfer should be considered as a promotion or a demotion. However, many questions arise. If Novak was considered successful, why was it necessary to remove him? On the other hand, if he was not satisfactory in statistics he would be even less so in a new field that was entirely outside of his competence. There was no official answer to any of these questions.

However, if Novak was late in making use of the new orientations, it was certainly not true of his successor Milosh Macura who took over the directorship of Yugoslav statistics. In fact, he was in from 1963 to 1966.

Macura's past record qualified him for this job. It will be remembered that he rushed to sign an appeal to the YCP to protect the future of young generations in Yugoslavia through firm action against the "enemies of socialism" who were marching under the shield of mathematical statistics. He did it without having ever opened a book of modern statistics to see what it was. Nor did he care to quote any paragraph from the accused books to show the type of action that enemies suggest taking against socialism. He did not lose time joining those who were against the establishment of statistics department at Belgrade University as he knew, without any interest in the proposed curricula, that it would become a center of opposition against socialism. He also rushed to join Novak in imposing a hard line in statistics and accusing the subordinate staff for cooperating with the enemy from the US.

Macura was always quick in sensing the taste of power. Therefore, he never failed to offer personal services for the implementation of official politics no matter what it was. His past moves show that he was not very selective in carrying out the will of the power.

Having these experiences, he realized that the time had come for a change of music. Overnight he forgot about his earlier attitude; overnight he erased from his memory the fact that he had invited the action to protect the nation against those who wanted a modernization of statistics. He joined Novak in ridiculing Soviet socialism, as ewll as the Soviet economy. Moreover, in his public statements he frequently pointed out the poor state of Soviet statistics. Here and there he also presented his diagnosis: there can be no statistics without freedom.

Now that he was in charge of Yugoslav statistics he realized that the best thing for him to do would be to go back in history and pick up from the enemies of socialism their idea of establishing a department of statistics at the University of Belgrade. He took it as his favorite project and put a great deal of time in its realization.

Needless to say, the establishment of a department of statistics was a project that required much more than Macura was able to give. This is why the project soon failed irrespective of promises of the Prime Minister to secure finances.

At that time the protagonists of earlier attempt were already all out of Yugoslavia or had withdrawn to a dark corner after the experienced disappointments. The only possible way of renewing the idea was to check with those who were involved in the project before, ask them to support a new attempt, and assure their participation in the realization of the project. Other people for that purpose were not available. There was no alternative to making an appeal to the same people to start again.

Macura failed to do this. He could not imagine asking the people to cooperate whom he had accused before. This is how Macura himself killed his own plans. There was no solution available in his approach.

The next issue was of a moral nature. Macura was very well aware that, as a result of his own action, it was arranged for the players of the earlier version of the project to get a taste of jail. Therefore, the earlier promoters of statistical education were not willing to engage in a new venture of the same type without getting assurance that the evil of the past was silenced forever. Macura had the means to achieve that aim. He only had to ask all the co-authors of the earlier appeal to issue a public statement on the problem, admit the mistake made, apologize for the steps taken and ask to be excused for the sake of future and new cooperation. A step of this kind would have been very effective. It might be that those who were able to carry out this project would have abandoned their new jobs and come home to continue what they started before.

Although simple, a step of this kind required high moral standards. As it was not taken, the necessary favorable atmosphere for the project was not established and the project was thus condemned before it started.

On top of everything was the fact that Macura was not a professional qualifications to guide such a project. At that time (and even today) the statistical work of Yugoslavia consisted primarily of government data collection and related activities, such as data processing and data dissemination. This is just the type of work where the progress of modern statistics has made it possible for countries and governments to greatly expand their statistical work, improve its quality, increase the speed of operations, and secure efficiency beyond the dreams of the preceding generation. Yugoslavia thus faced the task of modernization of its statistical work in order to be in line with the trend in more developed countries. This is why the concept of modernization of statistics was used so frequently during the early stages of our involvement.

Needless to say, our modernization concept was defined in a broad way. One of its components was the statistical department as a source of qualified personnel. The other part of the project was research that was primarily conceived as survey research with all its ramifications. After attaining some success, it was also planned to think of refinements and higher level research. For that purpose it was necessary to strengthen university statistics and facilitate a more systematic involvement in theory. However, all these components had to be implemented as an integrated programme of statistical modernization. The curriculum of the statistical department had to take into account the survey research of statistical offices, the problems that arise therefrom, and the related suggestions for the future.

During his career Macura was director of various statistical offices. However he never gained any experience in methodological work. Therefore, the modernization of Yugoslav statistics was beyond his reach. The country was thus lucky that his project failed before the disbursement of the government budget had started.

It is not easy to say what Macura's purpose was while he was pushing the old project of the statistical department at Belgrade University. If he were interested in the promotion of statistics, he had obviously better opportunities to contribute to this project. His office offered him broader possibilities for the promotion of statistics than any university. We started a programme of systematic courses for statisticians as early as 1949. The leading staff of his office were graduate students of these courses. It was just necessary to strengthen the existing institutions and achieve all the success needed. He also had an excellent opportunity to establish a research programme at his office and involve graduate students in research. That research could have contributed considerably to the modernization of statistics in Yugoslavia. The results achieved in research would unavoidably have an effect on universities. The universities would realize what a modern statistical education was and what benefits it offered. An outcome of the step would be a revision of statistical curricula at universities in all the parts of the country.

This is obviously just a small range of the possibilities that Macura could have been able to use for the promotion of statistics if he were interested. However, he never used the chances he had.

Macura realized quite early that his preferred area was not statistics but general managerial work combined with political and diplomatic activities. It might be that Novak noticed that affinity and arranged for the continuation of Macura's career in what could be called statistical politics. As Deputy Director for international matters, Macura had frequent briefs in Foreign Affairs regarding his attitude in course of international contacts. There he picked up the instructions to provide cooperation to UN agencies, appreciate good will from any direction, support international organizations in their assistance to LDC and, above all, be always cooperative and offer Yugoslav institutions for the realization of that line.

Macura highly appreciated the new line of his work. It made him forget the past. In fact, Macura quickly became a champion of international cooperation. He was everywhere. His name was on many lists of candidates for roles in many international bodies. International cooperation required supporters in many fields and many places of the world. A particular hunger was felt for citizens from communist countries. Macura was an ideal candidate for the international scene. He had no hesitation; he plunged wholeheartedly into his new work.

However, a person's career only partly depends upon the ability to sense the direction of wind. There is also an element of luck.

In order to demonstrate the new mood in international relations, the Yugoslav government invited ISI to hold its 1965 session in Belgrade. It was part of leadership ambitions of the YCP. It was the first ever planned ISI session in a communist country. The YCP was hoping to get credit for pushing far enough in the implementation of constructive politics of international cooperation. As a result, the Government of Yugoslavia granted considerable resources for the session. The leading Yugoslav official statisticians, viz. Vogelnik and Novak were briefed to play the role of good hosts and make sure that the session be a success. For that purpose they were provided with a special hospitality fund.

However, at that time, the YCP adopted the praectice of rotating high government offices by republics so that nobody would hold an office for too long a time. As a result of that, it happened that Petar Stambolich became the Prime Minister of the Federal Government. He was a leading personality of the Serbian Communist Party. When the party had to fill the position of the Prime Minister he was the proposed candidate.

This was a big day for Macura. In fact, Petar Stambolich was the President of the Serbian Government after the last war and Macura served under him as Director of Serbian Statistical Office. Macura has always been particularly careful in cultivating good relations with his superiors. This is how he was noticed by Stambolich and used by him on several occasions for a variety of purposes. Stambolich was happy about that experience and considered Macura as one of his loyal staff.

After Stambolich became the Prime Minister of the Federal Government, a new chance arose for Macura to serve his old boss. Stambolich had to open the ISI session and deliver a speech; he had to give a reception to all ISI members; he had to invite some ISI members for dinner, etc. Macura offered his assistance. He took over the local responsibilities for the ISI session and put aside all those who prepared the session for themselves; he brought the Prime Minister to the opening ceremony and accompanied him out; he was next to the Prime Minister during the reception; he was responsible for the composition of lists of ISI members to be invited for dinner parties by different personalities; he had sufficient Government resources to offer dinner parties each day in his house no matter whether he would have time to attend or not, etc. Briefly, the ISI session was Macura; Macura and Prime Minister were next to each other and they shared the honor, the hospitality, and the duty. Macura was the top star in the skies of international statistics.

The Belgrade meeeting was a good opportunity for statisticians from different countries to settle a number of issues. One of these was the matter of population studies at the UN. Dr. Durand, the former chief of the UN Population Branch, resigned as he did not see good prospects for the satisfactory development of work. The resignation was effective. The UN decided to establish a strong programme of population activities and entrust it to the new Population Division. The selection of the candidate to be proposed for the post of director of the new division had to be made during the session. The obvious candidate was Macura. Future projects of the Population Division would be carried out at a high level of international politics and the selected officer in charge should be able to deal easily with prime ministers and other people of that kind. Macura was the choice suggested under the circumstances of the session.

Needless to say, the position of Director of the UN Population Division was a low level job for a person with the image that Macura helped create about himself. No other person with that image would even consider the idea of taking such a job. However, Macura was aware of his position. He jumped at the chance at once. The UN job was outside the reach of Yugoslav political variations. Macura was aware that it would give him independence from Yugoslav authorities and, at the same time, a chance to court the YCP as an independent citizen who was not obliged to do so. He equally needed a safe refuge from the action of all those who planned the ISI session for their own reputation and had to see Macura collecting for himself all the fruits of the arrangements that they planned in different ways. An advisable attitude was to forget about the level of the job. Macura bent his spine and took the job.

Macura left for New York and never came back to statistics. While he was in charge of Yugoslav statistics, no significant development had taken place. At variance with other directors who introduced new approaches, no matter how wrong they happened to be, Macura's directorship had not left anything that survived the day of his departure from the office. A prerequisite of new ideas and new approaches, that were particularly needed in that period, was a vision of developments and the courage to get involved in difficulties of clearing up new ways. These qualities did not fit Macura's character.

In 1966 Ibrahim Latifich was appointed Director of FIS. He kept that job longer than anybody else. He retired in 1980.

Before he was appointed to that job, Latifich was Deputy director under Macura. He had been Director of Statistical Office of Bosnia and Herzegovina. I also heard it said

170

that the rise in his career started when he was a member of a task force established after the last war which aimed at starting an action against the dispersed enemies of the YCP. This was a highly confidential assignment and the officers entrusted had the power to carry out their duty quickly and without formalities, such as jails, courts, trials, lawyers, etc. This assignment might be an explanation of why Latifich always behaved as a man who was deeply rooted in the power.

Latifich never attended a university. This fact left visible traces in his behavior. In fact, he was a young boy when the war started and he had no time for education. After the war he was involved in the above special assignment. After that his career in statistics started and it was not appropriate for him any more to go to school together with youngsters. So he never got a "diploma". I am sure that he suffered from that. During various ceremonies and public appearances he would never go to a corner and have a chat with other people. He would always go to the center, to be next to the host. His conversations were directed to persons occupying the highest level in the official hierarchy. When he attended meetings of UN statistical bodies in Geneva he would always take a crowd of staff members with him. Some of them would carry his bag and the others would open doors for him in the hotel, in department stores, in UN buildings, etc. In addition, he would never stay in the same hotel with his colleagues. This is the standard practice of communist bureaucrats. The "chief" is always treated as a separate case. Latifich's secretary had to make sure that the hotel booked for him had at least one star more than the hotel for his colleagues, who came together with him. If he had something to ask or tell his colleagues, no matter what their number was, they had to go to his hotel and wait for him in the lobby.

In spite of that, Latifich was the first director of postwar Yugoslav statistics who possessed some standard characteristics of a government employee. Vogelnik was an isolated commander who never asked the staff to search with him for the solutions needed. Krashovec was a man with many sound ideas. However, he would frequently change views and mix up attitudes so that, at the end, it was difficult to identify his line. Novak was an unpredictable dreamer and a fighter who was unable to cooperate with others. Macura conceived of his career as his personal success. Statistics was just his means. At variance with all these predecessors, Latifich was willing to listen. He would recognize the staff in his office as partners in the same business. The staff had to be given a chance to shape the work in their respective fields because of their long experience and specialized knowledge. He institutionalized consultations with the staff and frequently went too far in moving big machinery in case of minor issues. He wanted the staff to feel corresponsible for the work of the office.

The "willingness to listen" was a good aspect of Latifich's character. On that basis I developed sympathy for him, and I expected that he would have a much deeper impact on Yugoslav statistics than he really did. It is also because of my appreciation of this quality of his that I abandoned the position that I had in statistical matters abroad and decided to go back to Yugoslavia, make myself available to Yugoslav statistics and try to contribute my share again.

However, after some years, Latifich eliminated the impact of his good qualities. Namely, he started putting emphasis on politics in any aspect of his work. Gradually he went as far as seeing in statistics nothing but politics. As a result, he brought statistics to an absurd position. In fact, he ruined statistics and himself as well. I also found myself in these ruins.

My contacts with Latifich were established on the understanding that he was willing to listen. I never worked with him or under him before he was appointed director of FIS. Therefore, I had no personal experience about his ability to guide statistical work. However, I noticed in the course of various meetings his interest in getting in touch with people and listen to their ideas for the improvement of work. This is how our contacts developed. I considered myself a lucky person who had a chance to live at a variety of places. It gave me an opportunity to see a lot of matters regarding the development of statistics that could be quite useful to him. I took the initiative to talk to him and he reacted favorably. As a result, I visited him frequently. On a number of occasions I went to Belgrade just for this purpose.

In my contacts with Latifich, I touched on hundreds of useful points for the orientation of a person in charge of statistical development. I told him what other statistical offices were doing and in what way. I gave him publications dealing with important issues. He did not know foreign languages and was not able to understand them. However, he kept these publications as physical proof of the growing tendencies that he appreciated. Needless to say, my main argument was always the same, viz. the one that appeared as early as 1949 when we started pressing for the modernization of Yugoslav statistics. I continued that argument. Our conversations included the need to open all the doors to studies of experiences of other countries, the development of a systematic cooperation, the improvement of statistical education, the establishment of reserach in our statistics to test the applicability of the available methodology and build our own solutions wherever needed and to the extent our abilities permitted us, etc. For each of these points, I brought illustrations of activities in other countries and insisted on both the understanding and the appreciation of advantages that should arise for us. It was thus not abstract talk but an effort to bring to his attention the ongoing work of those who were more advanced.

Our contacts were progressing nicely and we were near to becoming friends. I got a feeling that he was not afraid of any secret intention on my part, such as spying or creating an embarrassment to socialism. He probably realized that there was a genuine desire on my part to be useful to Yugoslav statistics. I was an independent person who did not need either a job or money. Morover, I was spending my own money to meet him and bring him the publications and documents.

In the course of our contacts, I got an impression that he was willing to engage in the implementation of the spirit of our discussions. He asked me if I would agree to participate in the new direction of Yugoslav statistics by coming to Belgrade. I told him that I was willing to quit everything that I had abroad provided he could give me an assurance that a big change in the life of a person who was not young any more would not lead to a waste of time or effort. He promised to talk about these matters to political personalities and his superiors and check on their willingness to support the new course. Fort that purpose I prepared several statements for him so that he had a brief on important points in case the need arose for something in writing.

At the next stage, we entered into the preparation of more specific arrangements. We agreed that an adequate first step would be the establishment of an institute of statistic in FIS with responsibility for research related to government data collection programme, preparation of methodology of projects included in the programme of work, the in-service training and possibly a contribution to improvement of statistical education. At Latifich's request I wrote a few statements on some specific issues and a paper that he needed for discussions of the idea of establishing a special institute for the purpose. The approval of a number of bodies was apparently a prerequisite. In order to strengthen the preparations for the establishment of an Institute of Statistics, Latifich arranged for the publication of that paper.[15]

The establishment of an institute apparently encountered less resistance than expected. The expected resistance was an outcome of an earlier decision of the Federal Government to transfer to republics and their governments the authority for science, research, and education. The establishment of the Institute of Statistics in a federal agency was thus an act against the government's own decision. However, other precedents were available, such as various institutes in the army. In favor of the idea of an institute was the modernization mood of the government in this period. In fact, a decision was taken to modernize the operations of government agencies through more science and more computers. Our institute was in line with other steps included in this design.

There was also another interpretation of the origin of the institute. At that time Latifich had friendly relations with Bijedich, the Prime Minister of the Federal Government. Latifich convinced Bijedich that the planned institute had to serve as an important contribution to the modernization of government statistics and the improvement of its efficiency. Bijedich pushed the project at a meeting of his cabinet and afterwards signed a decree on the establishment of the institute. The institute of statistics thus became a reality.

I accepted the establishment of the Institute of Statistics with great pleasure. At that time I was convinced that statistics in Yugoslavia was moving in the right direction. I was sure that the Institute had to be a success. I thought that the arguments in favor of an institute were extremely strong and I could not imagine that it would encounter anything but support. It seemed to be a realization of similar trends in other countries. To me, our institute was the way for Yugoslavia to catch up with developments in the world.

The establishment of the Institute was a new stage of my life. I promised to engage in this project. Upon receipt of the news, I did not hesitate. I decided to join. It was a far-reaching decision. While abroad my children went to the best schools. Afterwards they married abroad. My income was sufficient to afford from time to time visits to places where they lived. Going to Belgrade would reduce my income to less than twenty per cent of what I had. A danger of separation from the children thus appeared. The future of Yugoslavia was also a big unknown. Some people anticipated difficulties in travelling abroad. I also had a flat in Belgrade that was not convenient any more for the increased size of my family. A host of problems appeared. However, I did not hesitate. I had a sort of feeling that statistics was my duty and my life. It seemed to me beyond

---

15   Zarkovich, S.S.: A proposal for discussions about the establishment of The Institute of Statistics, *Statistical Review*, Vol. 11, 1971.

any personal matter. I told Latifich that I would be available as soon as the formalities and the budgetary matters of the institute were over.

I was not able to imagine our Institute to be less than a reasonable center of promotion of statistical development. Latifich told me that the government had the intention to make it to be such a center. He himself also promised to do his best to achieve that aim. I was equally convinced that nothing would prevent us from building an institute that would be generally respected. I had seen statistical offices in almost all countries in the world and it served as a good background in designing a programme of work that should be suitable for us and interesting enough for the others as well. I also had close contacts with most statistical centers in the world and it gave me the necessary confidence that they would do everything possible to help the efforts of a new sister institution. I had a large number of personal friends all over the world whom I could always ask for any assistance under their authority.

In order to increase further confidence in the success of my new mission, I again visited all the important places of the promotion of statistics with the specific intention to ask for guidance and cooperation. I lectured at a number of places about the aims, organization, programme and methods of work of our institute, and invited comments and suggestions. After I completed these visits, I was ready to assume my duty. I was convinced that statistics of the world was available at any moment for consultations, advice, and assistance in any form.

XVIII The Institute of Statistics

At the end of 1974 I left FAO. On 1st of January 1975 I was in Belgrade.

Many friends of mine laughed at my decision to abandon the possibility to take part in statistical activities all over the world, the freedom of movement, and so many other advantages for promises included in a vaguely defined project. However, to me the Institute was more than a job. It was established after more than 25 years of insisting on modernization of statistics in Yugoslavia. After such a long involvement, one might easily lose the ability to rationally appraise all the related factors. At some point the emotions override. This is how I accepted a project that was not established in an orthodox way. A detailed specification of objectives was missing. Also, commitments were missing from sponsoring institutions to support specified activities.

Had I insisted on clarification of those factors the project would have never started. A detailed project document would go from one agency to the other and there would be no end to comments and reservations. Much more important decisions were taken within equally vague limits as to the way of carrying out the task. A reference was made to planning of the national economy, centralized management of the economy, record keeping, etc. Therefore, it did not seem possible to expect more than the government offered. I was aware of the resulting risk. In order to assess the magnitude of the risk I talked to Latifich on several occasions. I ended by taking him seriously. It was not possible to neglect the fact that the government approved the establishment of an institution employing about forty people. Latifich insisted that, after the steps taken, the future of the Institute and the amount of support it could expect would depend upon its achievements. The challenge seemed to me worth taking.

After I took the intention of the government seriously, it was much easier to overcome other types of risk. One of them was associated with the status of the Institute. In the legislation of that period there was a difference between an institute as an independent scientific institution and an institute associated with some non-scientific activity helping in research work. The institutes falling in the first group have their Workers' Council that is responsible for the establishment and supervision of the programme of work. The advantage of this solution is that the governing body is composed of research workers. Therefore, there is no danger that decisions fall in the hands of people who have nothing to do with science. However, the disadvantage is that the institutes in this category have to be able to earn the necessary income through cooperation with those who have money. There was also another snag. An independent institute cannot be established without a minimum of ten persons on the permanent staff with a doctor degree in some science. The other class of institutes can be established and financed by any type of institutions that provide resources, appoint the personnel and assume the managerial responsibilities.

Our institute of statistics was of the latter type. We were a part of FIS. Also, we were on the government budget and did not need to worry about the difficult task of making money. As a result, I was appointed by the Director of FIS, who became my boss. At the same time, the Institute did not have its governing body. All the current decisions of the Institute were in the hands of government administration which, in practice, meant the Director of FIS.

After I took the intentions of the government seriously, I could not refuse to accept the latter type of arrangements. It seemed to me essential to be free from money raising jobs. Our intention was to put the emphasis on survey research. Possibilities to make money in this field of work were modest if not negligible. Therefore, not much choice was available. As to the governing body I also thought that one should not worry too much about this issue after one takes the government support as granted. Cooperation with independent scientists might be more difficult than work with cooperative common sense people. In other words, I expected smooth cooperation across the board. I thought that the government would not have gone through so much work in connection with the Institute without being firm in the intention to assure its smooth work.

However, my expectations were wrong.

After the events in the period 1949-52, the Institute seemed to be the first serious chance to make another attempt at modernization of statistics. I saw the Institute as part of a newly declared policy of the government to modernize its operations. In that situation my strategy was to emphasize research strongly. I expected that we should be able to arrive relatively fast at some important improvements of the ongoing operations and get credit from the government and public opinion as well. This success would prepare the basis for subsequent expansions of the programme and particularly for the improvement of statistical education. This was the task that universities were unable to carry out successfully. In that period they were free to shape their curricula in a way considered adequate by teachers themselves. The era of "statistics as class science" was over. However, most professors were of the old type. They were not qualified for a new content of education. Even those who, in principle, opted for statistical education as in Western countries, were new to that tendency and did not have a satisfactory insight into recent developments. In that situation the Institute's involvement in education seemed promising. Our research achievements would provide strong arguments as to the profile of graduate students whom we wanted to have. In addition, I had in mind making arrangements for visits to the Institute of top statisticians in the world who created the existing theory. They would bring us modern theory and would tell us how statistical education is organized at the best centers. Their authority should be strong to the extent that no doubts would arise any more as to the direction to follow in statistical education.

In this way the future of the institute was made dependent upon the achievements in research. I thought that it was the strongest possible orientation. We offered the work and requested the evaluation of our involvement on the basis of the work done.

It was so easy to achieve important results in research. The following is an illustration. At that time, the statistical offices of all the republics had on their programme a quarterly livestock survey and a broader annual livestock survey. For that purpose, the field staff would visit a sample of households four times a year and each republic would prepare, for their own territory, the estimates of the number of livestock. FIS would do it for the country as a whole. When the Institute started its operations, the preparation of estimates from these "current" surveys took approximately a year. Some of these estimates were without sampling errors. In addition, reports from the field intimated that these surveys were transformed in course of time into a bureaucratic routine. The enumerators would not visit the households. In a good percentage of cases the enumerators would fill in the questionnaires in the office. However, no study whatsoever was made of what was going on and how accurate were the data. Nor was an attempt made to shorten the field work to a few days and issue the estimates within the same week.

It was thus obvious that we should be able to substantially improve this work and make out of these "current" surveys modern data collection projects the results of which would be in the hands of users of data a couple of days after the date of the survey.

There were so many other fields where the situation was similar. We were thus facing an unprecedented success and a very strong support to the Institute that should follow as a result of our achievements.

Before we would start with our research programme I thought that we should first organize ourselves. For that purpose I convened the senior staff to look into this issue. I learned that there was nothing to discuss. The organizational chart was already discussed, adopted, and approved by the responsible authorities. At the next step all the approved posts were filled. As none of the related decisions could be changed any more, I was advised to adjust my attitude to the facts, viz. accept everything as it was and see what could be done with everything as it was.

This was the first time that I realized my mistake of accepting the directorship of the Institute. After I examined the organization of the Institute and the qualifications of the staff it became obvious that the programme of modernization of Yugoslav statistics could not be carried out under the circumstances. The Institute was shaped by Latifich and his assistants. They simply put in the Institute all the staff who did not fit FIS for various reasons. Other senior staff were sick people, difficult characters, or persons who kept changing jobs and could never find something satisfactory. Some of these people were not bad. However, only a few of them could be used in the programme of the Institute as it was accepted by Latifich beforehand.

The examination of the situation showed that Latifich used the Institute as an opportunity to get rid of some people who were a headache. He also used the Institute to streamline his office and reduce his worries about the inadequate organization of work. He divided the Istitute into four sectors of work. One of them was the office for nomenclatures. The related work was going on in FIS on an *ad hoc* basis. If that work had to be done in the statistical office, the right solution would be to have a permanent unit for the purpose and the staff qualified for that work. As conceived, the Institute was not qualified for that nor could this unit in any way contribute to the main activity of the Institute. Another sector had the title "Statistical system". People from other countries may not know what it is. The statistical system is the ongoing programme of work which is of course affected by hundreds of elements, such as needs for information, available resources, international agreements and recommendations, specific require- ments of the moment, etc. Thus, if the concept of the system had any meaning, it cannot be but an effort to coordinate all these elements into a coherent whole. However, in Yugoslavia "statistical system" became the highest level of technical specialization. In practical terms, this is the specialization created for the staff with political qualifications or, in other words, for the members of the party. The qualification involves knowledge of the government programme of work, the organization of the country and the power, knowledge of the Constitution and basic legislation, a broad view of all statistical activ- ities, etc. Therefore, "experts" in the statistical system are normally the top people of statistical offices who are responsible for the formulation of the programme and a dis- cussion of all the related issues with whatever institution might be interested. It was primarily the Federal Parliament and some ministries. Therefore, persons in charge of the "system" had to be available on call to spend their time in antechambers.

The strongest part of the personnel of the Institute was concerned with the "sys- tem" work. The rest of the Institute was much worse than that.

After I realized the threat of that situation, I wrote a couple of memos on the subject and went to see Latifich on this matter. He was evasive. However, he told me that the Institute, as conceived in the adopted decision, was extremely useful. I referred to our understanding that no binding decisions regarding the future of the Institute would be made prior to my arrival and our joint consideration. He told me that he was obliged to fill all the posts as this was the condition for the approval of the budget for the first year of operations. In other words, there were many excuses for the grim future of the Institute.

The situation thus became tragic. Moreover, the tragedy was much deeper than I was able to admit in the beginning. Several colleagues helped me understand the real causes of the trouble. After the Institute was approved, FIS and the party organization had several discussions of the project. Apparently, they were requested to go ahead with the implementation. In that situation, they could not say that they were not able to do it. In that case, the question of their responsibility would arise for pressing for an ap- proval of a project that they were not able to implement. In order to save face, they behaved as if they had all the necessary know-how. In order to satisfy my requirements they would need to disagree with their own decision and declare themselves incompe- tent. They preferred to ruin the Institute for ever than admit a mistake. The party does not make mistakes.

This experience resulted in far-reaching conclusions regarding the political leader- ship. It showed that the party lost both flexibility and courage. Instead, it settled for a shallow routine. Some time ago, it had the courage to raise the issue of Soviet socialism, the efficiency of a centrally planned economy, the approaches to planning, etc. Some years later it lost courage to say that it was not qualified to build modern statistics let alone carry out statistical research. I was not able to understand the moral and intellec- tual profile of the party membership. What can the party hope for with members who, after heroic acts in war, degenerated, in a few years, into people who prefer to see bankrupcy of an institution and the related budget than agree to an adjustment of their earlier decisions.

No wonder that I was not able to understand the situation. I had come from a world where people have to observe some moral and intellectual standards which make impossible apathy and indifference that I encountered in my experience with FIS. It was for me the first lesson of a morbid psycholgy that was already spread over most layers of the Yugoslav population. Its essence was: keep quiet; let things go as they are; do not raise problems and do not press for changes.

A colleague of mine realized my embarrassment and he asked me to adjust myself to the circumstances. He requested of me to be aware of the mistake that I had made. "You wanted the party to depend upon you and your guidance. The party has made all the decisions considered necessary because this is how it works. This is the principle of the leading role of the party in all the matters. You may not like these decisions. However, they are the reality that you have to accept. In addition, all these decisions were made on purpose to show that the party does not want to depend upon you. They wanted to show you who the boss is and what your role is. If you are not able to digest that you better quit right now. Otherwise you will have many conflicts that will finish you".

I could not accept this explanation. Why should the party treat me that way? I did not come to compete with the party. I came to help without asking for anything. I accepted the existing conditions of work, the monthly salary that I could make in the world in a few days, an entirely inadequate house, etc. and I never opened my mouth. I, therefore, could not accept the treatment reserved for a person doing forced labor.

I decided to observe the conditions and see in what way, if at all, the research programme of the Institute could start under the conditions imposed.

In the meantime we switched our attention to statistical education. The improvement of statistical education was as an important task of the modernization of statistics as research. In that period all the prejudices had already disappeared regarding statistical theory as a tool of imperialism. It was an opportunity to fill the vacuum and orientate statistical education in the right direction. However, other difficulties appeared that had nothing to do with ideology. One of them was the resistance from professors who got their jobs during the domination of "statistics as a class science". The universities did not have the possibility to replace these people. Retirement was the only hope. The other difficulty was related to inter-republics rivalry. Any initiative - in statistics and in other fields was juged by its origin. If backed by the authorities of a particular republic the project would leave the others cool. Each republic had to have its own institutions and its own solutions. If that was not possible the preferred alternative was no solution whatsoever. In other words, the establishment of a center of statistical education at one single place, no matter what it was, no matter how good the programme looked like, would be limited to the territory of that republic and not be used by the others.

This unusual situation was a result of new political developments that were all inspired by the strengthening of the authority of the republics. Use of educational facilities in other republics was against the officially backed trends. It was better to send students abroad no matter how costly it might be. These officially inspired tendencies were also favored by financial difficulties. At centers of their own republics, students could count on some facilities that were not available elsewhere. This is why the existing educational centers counted essentially on students from their own republics.

In this situation, the Institute of statistics considered the improvement of statistical education in a way that was contrary to the trends of the moment. Our line was to build a relatively strong center for statistical studies that would serve the country as a whole. As a result of that we found ourselves immediately encircled by rivalries, opposition, appeals to the recognized rights of republics, personal jealousies, etc. that were all working under the shield of the accepted political arrangements. Fortunately, we had a strong ally. This was common sense. Much larger and economically stronger countries than Yugoslavia could not afford more than one single and strong center for the promotion of statistics. Going beyond that would mean a waste of resources.

Our educational ambitions were supported by the federal government. Yugoslavia had no staff with modern education for involvement in statistical research and the improvement of work efficiency. Therefore, we had to do something about it. However, it had to be done in accordance with the existing political decisions. Namely, the right to provide university education is the exclusive authority of the existing universities irrespective of their inability to carry out that role.

This is how incredible difficulties started. The country was already up to its neck in the mud of formalities and neglect of substance. We were able to build a strong center that would provide quality. That quality would speak for itself. We pointed out that the Indian Statistical Institute in Calcutta developed that way. However, in Yugoslavia this was not a solution. Young people wanted certificates, a piece of paper. The salary and the career depended upon documents rather than knowledge. As a result, we had to make a project in cooperation with universities as the institutions authorized to issue certificates.

What university?

During the initial negotiations for the establishment of the Institute the idea arose to locate the Institute in Dubrovnik. Nice premises at the International Center for Post-Graduate Studies were available. The University of Zagreb would offer all the facilities that were needed from a university in terms of formalities. However, the idea was rejected because of the lack of other educational institutions, lack of computer facilities, separation from data and facilities of federal statistics, etc.

After the establishment of the Institute in Belgrade, a logical way out was cooperation with the University of Belgrade. However, it did not work for reasons of jealousy. At that time, the Department of Economics had the best statistical programme in the country.However, their own ambitions made cooperation impossible. They wanted our project for themselves. We could not accept that solution as the Department of Economics was not equipped for international cooperation nor did they have teachers who were ever involved in the kind of research that we were interested in. Other departments were less ambitious. However, they all wanted a major responsibility in the project. In addition, a special difficulty arose with the Department of Economics. During the domination of the Soviet views of statistics, the Economics Department was the school with basic responsibilities in statistical matters. A related provision was included in the university statutes. As a result, all matters concerning statistics had to go to Economics Department for opinion and/or action. Using this provision, the Economics Department opposed the idea of arrangements between the Institute and other departments that would put our educational programme under the umbrella of the existing rules and regulations.

Other difficulties were not less serious. For illustration, the case of the budget will be pointed out. The Institute was a part of the Federal Government. As such, it was included in the federal budget which consisted of contributions from all republics. The educational programme of the Institute is therefore financed by all the republics. If this programme is carried out in Belgrade in cooperation with the University of Belgrade, it means that the contributions of all republics would be used to strengthen the institutional setup of Serbia for the benefit of young people living in Belgrade. In other words, Serbia would grow at the expense of the other republics.

In the political climate of the moment, it was obvious that the centers of power in the other republics would blow up any educational programme of the Institute in Belgrade. In search for a solution, I went with Latifich to see Vogelnik who, at that time, kept the position of President of the Federal Committee for Culture, which is nearly equivalent to Ministry of Education. Vogelnik told us that he would energetically oppose any move of the Institute in the direction of education. I appealed to his awareness of the related facts. I reminded him of the US Bureau of the Census, Indian Statistical Institute, INSEE in Paris, etc. He not only refused to consider the facts. After we left his office he called the Vice Prime Minister who was responsible for the work of federal agencies and requested him to keep an eye on our Institute and its attempts to use the federal budget for purposes that were against the existing regulations. As a result, we got a reminder to stay within the limits of the rules.

These and other difficulties killed our ambition to operate a four-year programme of undergraduate studies of statistics that would end in a valid university degree and would provide graduate students with equivalent status in the service.

After we failed with the undergraduate studies, we thought that we should modify our approach and carry out a programme of postgraduate studies. The existing regulations were more liberal with respect to postgraduate studies. They also had to be carried out under the umbrella of some university. However, the initiative and the main sponsorship could come from users of future staff. This was a chance for the Institute. It could provide resources, housing, administrative assistance and some teaching staff. The problems to solve were the affiliation with some university and the additional teaching staff to assure a modern education.

As to the first problem, we looked around to find a university that would be willing to accept our programme as part of their own postgraduate studies and provide students with all the related degrees. The first to offer cooperation was the Department of Economics from the University of Zagreb. I talked to Prof. V.Serdar about that problem and the need to build something serious at one place for the country as a whole. He was fully appreciative of our arguments. Being the retired President of the University of Zagreb, he used his connections to influence the people concerned with this matter. The result was that our programme of postgraduate studies of statistics was put in operation as part of the post-graduate studies of the Department of Economics, University of Zagreb, which provided all forms of university backing to the programme. For that purpose, I was elected professor of the University of Zagreb and delegated afterwards to operate the programme of statistical studies in Belgrade, at the premises of the Institute. In this way everything went smoothly. Our students would receive regular university certificates and the authority to continue studies toward a doctorate degree in statistics.

As to the content of studies we had to accept the existing conditions. For our programme of postgraduate studies, we could not get students who finished four years of statistics with a regular undergraduate programme. Therefore, we decided to admit graduate student from any department who passed the entrance examination that was heavily oriented toward mathematics. As a result, most of the admitted students were graduates from the mathematics department. About ten per cent were coming from other schools. Our entrance examination also included English so that we enabled our students to follow lectures by foreign teachers. In this way, we got students who were relatively strong in mathematics and able to concentrate on intensive studies of statistics without losing time on parallel studies of mathematics.

As to the curriculum, we took steps to carry out our programme in cooperation with the known centers of statistical studies. We collected a great deal of information about courses in other countries. We also had the benefit of visits of many distinguished scholars to advise us about the approach to take. We particularly benefited from Prof. C.R.Rao who was at that time Director of Indian Statistical Institute. He came to Yugoslavia on several occasions and helped us to draw plans for the future. He also talked to some top government officers and proposed a programme of systematic help. As a result, Latifich and the author went to India. One of the results of that trip was the subsequent UNDP project that brought to Yugoslavia Dr. T.V. Hanurav from the Indian Statistical Institute. Through cooperation with Indian statisticians we got all the assistance that we needed. Dr. Hanurav was heavily involved in the implementation of the programme of studies, the work with students and the general effort to channel studies toward problems of research.

The success of the postgraduate studies was considerable. Many young staff got a reasonably modern statistical education. Some of them continued their studies. One could say that the present young generation of statisticians consists almost exclusively of graduate students from the educational programme of the Institute. This success shows that much can be achieved if an adequate foundation is established. If the Institute had a longer duration, we would have again reached the position that our statistics had in the period 1949-52.

A great deal of literature is available about this programme. It was the highest level that statistical education ever reached in Yugoslavia. The selection of students made it possible to carry out a very compressed programme of studies. We were also able to secure fellowships for all our students. Later on we also succeeded to obtain employment for almost all of them with the task to do at the beginning their full time studies. This made possible a heavy programme of work that consisted of 400 hours of class work per semester coupled with an obligatory study of three foreign languages (English, French, and Russian) and individual work on seminars, practicals, and preparation of thesis. For each of the topics included in our curriculum we used the well known text-books in the original language.[16]

Our orientation to intensive international cooperation led fast to visible results. We wanted to secure for our country the transfer of the modern know-how from the whole world. Cooperation was the only possible way to secure respect of world standards in our work. For that purpose we established, as a part of the Institute, a Secretariat that was equipped to carry out contacts. We were on the mailing lists of many institutions. The biggest publishers also kept us informed about their activities. As a result, literature started coming in quantities that its commercial value exceeded the salaries of all our staff. When we faced a new project in a field with considerable experience in the world, we would mobilize the machinery of our contacts to get the available documents on the subject. For illustration, one might point out the case of the request that we got from the Federal Government to consider the possibility of taking labor force surveys in Yugoslavia. These surveys are carried out in most countries in the world except the communist countries. Our government wanted to know where we stood in that respect and what could be done. We wrote immediately to our contacts and received, within a couple of months, the respective documents from about twenty of the most experienced countries. As a result, we learned about the past work and the accumulated experience. If we had wanted an independent attempt, as would happen without cooperation, we would have needed several years without probably ever being able to match the know-how received from the others. We also had plans to keep expanding the cooperation quantitatively and qualitatively parallel to the broadening of our programme. Yugoslavia was conveniently located for that purpose. Many statisticians flew over our territory and it was feasible to ask them to stop over for a couple of days and consult with us. These visits frequently led to valuable and costless results. On top of everything, we hoped to become a member of the great family of centers for the promotion of statistics. In that capacity, we had the right to expect that the grown-ups keep an eye on our efforts and give us a hand whenever possible.

Among the achievements of the Institute, I would particularly mention our effort to develop the capability of the Institute to carry out work in certain fields at the level of modern standards. An illustration is the problem of the presentation of data which had a particular importance in a government agency for data collection. In addition to methodology of data collection, the estimation, the processing, etc., the problem also includes the computation and presentation of sampling errors, non-sampling errors, their assessment and presentation, etc. Through our contacts we collected a great deal of documents on these points, involved the staff in a study of the issues, and gradually built something that could be called "collective capability of the Institute". Quite a few staff members were involved in these "joint studies" and quite a number of papers appeared as a result.

However, there is a difference between dreams and reality. On the part of our in-

---

16 Further details about this programme are available in the book *Post-Graduate Course of Statistics* (in Serbo-Croatian), Department of Economics, University of Zagreb, 1978. A summarized version of this book is also available in English under the same title. In this book information can be found about entrance examinations, content of various courses, textbooks used, the examination papers, titles of theses, etc.

stitutions that cherished similar ambitions the Institute created jealousies. Although they never did anything similar to our programme, the work of the Institute was considered competition, damage to their prestige. This is a normal outcome. In a democratic society, it would generate positive developments. The competing institutions would intensify efforts to do better. As a result, the level of the respective work would be improved. In communist countries all sorts of destructive forces are generated in such a situation and they are all unanimous in their aim of ruining the competitor. The protective power of freedom is missing. Freedom imposes an obligation on all competitors to present their aims and seek public support for their programmes. As the support can't be secured without convincing arguments and constructive efforts, the competitors are obliged to work hard and expect that their achievements speak for themselves.

Such a sound competition did not exist in communist countries. The Institute did not grow as a result of the public consideration of the issue and appropriate recommendations by the profession. The origin is unknown. Somebody with sufficient political power decided to build it. The same action intensified the ambitions of the competitors. However, the losing parties could not utilize public discussions as they were unable to offer acceptable arguments, viz. the work. Nor would they be willing to oppose the political power behind the Institute. That would develop into a political fight that the party would hate. Besides, in a political fight the outcome is uncertain. Contenders frequently become losers. As a result, the argument goes below the surface of a public action and becomes a part of underground frictions. Everybody is aware of them and everybody feels their impact. However, nobody speaks out.

This is what happened to the Institute. Our programme of postgraduate studies started nicely. However, after some time, I heard that the authorities of the Republic of Serbia were aware of the illegal character of our programme but did not want to use the police to dismantle the programme as it might be interpreted as a provocation in the already tense relations between Serbs and Croats. It was said, however, that the Serbian authorities kept an eye on the Institute and reserved the right to intervene.

Subsequent investigation has shown that there was a provision in the respective legislation obliging each postgraduate course to be sponsored by some institution of the university to which the territory is assigned where the programme is physically carried out. The conflict was clear. We were a part of the University of Zagreb while our work was done on the territory of the University of Belgrade. The case for public intervention was obvious.

XIX The Institute of Statistics (continued)

In that situation, we decided to take steps to transform our postgraduate programme into a national all-Yugoslavia programme. Rather than doing the work, we concentrated on politics and political maneuvering. We decided to find a university in each republic to cooperate with the Institute in the operation of a joint programme of postgraduate studies. The procedure was very complicated and time consuming. We also encountered a great deal of hesitation on the part of universities because they did not understand why we should all waste our time on formalities rather than real work. However, we succeeded after some time to have formal contracts with several universities. The contracts were made as friendly gestures following our request rather than the result of a belief that such a waste of time was useful.

After we were able to show the all-Yugoslavia character of our project, the voice came again that our operations continued to be illegal. We needed a sponsor from the University of Belgrade as we operated on its territory. To be in line with the regulations, we made a contract with the School of Electric a Engineering of Belgrade. University which had the reputation as the best school in Yugoslavia. This school cooperated with us from the very beginning and their teachers were involved in our programme. This school also considered our contract a waste of time. However, they agreed to sign it to show their cooperative mood.

However, that was not the end of our difficulties. The contract was declared void. It was again a matter of formalities. In the Statutes of the School, there was a list of areas of work which fall under the competence of the school. Statistics was not on it. Therefore, our contract with the School was not any better than a contract with the Department of Theology, notwithstanding the fact that the school of engineering was widely known for its involvement in different branches of mathematics, probability, operational research, construction and uses of computers, etc. In other words, there was no other school in Yugoslavia that could offer more to our programme. However, this fact had no meaning. The only important issue was the missing word of "statistics" in the statutes.

As a result, in spite of several contracts with a variety of universities and so much useless paper work, we continued with the illegal character of our programme. There were only two schools at the University of Belgrade that could have helped us, viz.

185

Department of Economics and Department of Natural Sciences and Mathematics. However, they wanted our programme for themselves without being able to meet our needs and carry out the work with due regard to developments in the profession. On the other hand, we were not able to surrender our resources to an institution of the Republic of Serbia as it would raise the issue of misuse of the federal budget.

This was a war of formalities that discouraged the people who did not appreciate anything but technical work. However, our programme was attacked on other points as well. I was informed that FIS decided to convene a public discussion of statistical education with particular reference to our programme of post-graduate studies. Prior to that meeting I heard that some senior statisticians with long membership in the party were grumbling about our programme. One of them happened to be a mathematician. He told me directly that he was against our programme as we taught "useless matters", such as multivariate analysis and design of experiments. He obviously knew nothing about the topics. I did my best to convince him that these were fundamental areas of statistical theory. As such they are unavoidable in a modern study of statistics. In the end he told me that he would continue to be opposed to our programme.

Another colleague, who happened to occupy a leading position in government statistics, came to tell me that he would do his best to reduce the level of studies to something that could be called reasonable. He qualified our programme as a "useless exaggeration" and announced his opposition.

At a public meeeting, that was probably convened at the party's request because of grumbling within party circles, quite a few younger people spoke against our curriculum. The senior staff kept quiet. They probably wanted to see what the rank and file of the party would do. Most of what was said was based on Soviet views of statistics as "class science". However, there was a new argument that was probably carefully prepared. One of the speakers put it in a clear way. The post-graduate course, he said, wants to teach students the methodology of research. The Communist Party however teaches people dialectical materialism as the methodology of science. After the victory of revolution in our country, we expected that there be no attempt any more at the replacement of dialectical materialism with an alternative methodology. However, we were wrong. Instead of teaching dialectical materialism our postgraduate course of statistics has not mentioned at all the philosophy of the communist movement and is offering a substitute.

Some other speakers followed the same attack. Without having ever seen a book of statistics all these people had a nerve to ask for the floor and speak publicly. Their intervention was obviously agreed upon before by a group of people who had specific purpose in their mind. In other wards, our position in the party ranks was not very strong.

This was only part of our headaches. Many other problems appeared in the current management of the business. I accepted a position as an employee without any power or any independence in the business. My signature could not authorize any staff member to get a pencil. The Institute depended fully on the existing services of FIS that was located in another building. It meant a great deal of running around for our staff. There was no possibility of any control of movements. After a couple of months, the whole situation became lose. The staff were not responsible to me. They were treated as part of FIS. Orders came to them from Latifich and other senior staff. Orders were also coming from the party organization, labor union, and other organizations requesting cooperation and/or involvement of the staff of the Institute. Not more than half of the staff were on the spot at any given time. The others were at unknown places. When I inquired about the whereabouts of one or another, I would get the answer: "I was busy". On one occasion, I inquired further and got answers that closed my mouth forever, such as: "I am getting orders from people who are more senior than you are". I realized that no work was possible under these conditions. I told Latifich that my office had become a mess. He promised to intervene and he did. Nontheless, everything continued as before.

This was still the beginning though. I also have to add my own difficulties with Latifich. Soon after my arrival he asked me to accompany him to various meetings as his interpreter. I did it on a number of occasions hoping that it was a result of chance factors. When I realized that it was part of a system I refused to do it but not without consequences. As I had no authority to make any decision, I had to write memos to him, ring him up, ask for an appointment, etc. I soon realized that the communication was not working. He would not answer my memos. When I called him he would say, through secretaries, that he was busy and unable to take my call. My inefficiency was growing. The staff became aware of the situation and they rushed to add their contribution.

After some time, major problems started. In one of them, Dr. Ivanovich, my younger colleague was involved. He joined the statistical office under Krashovec and had applied for a fellowships to go to France and take his Ph.D. degree in statistics. He was lucky and he got it. However, the police kept investigating him as they were convinced that he would not come back. Krashovec was interrogated about this issue on several occasions. My turn came afterwards. The police asked my guarantee for his return. I kept saying that he would come back. However, I refused to speak about a guarantees. Ivanovich did come back. He developed into one of the best Yugoslav statisticians in pure theory. He was quite active and contributed considerably to the improvement of Yugoslav statistics. However, at a later stage, he left the country. While abroad, we kept in touch. We were both willing to go back at any time should the conditions for work become promising. When I decided to go back I informed him about my decision. We also discussed going back together as part of the same deal. We were both interested in an institute. I asked him to take the post of the director of planned institute in Belgrade as he was younger. He thus had better chances to arrive at useful results. I planned my involvement as chief of research. However, some months later, before my departure, he told me that he had changed his mind. I went alone and did what was presented above.

After a number of months, Ivanovich came to visit me in my office at the Institute to tell me that he came to take over the duty of dean of postgraduate course. I took it as a lack of standards in his behavior toward a senior colleague who had never failed to be friendly to him. I told him that the Institute had no interest in his services unless he presented an application for a job so that we could consider the matter. He told me that he made a deal with Latifich who was the real boss and therefore had nothing to discuss any more. I realized the tragedy of the country. Latifich had forgotten his limits and had gone as far as appointing a dean of studies. I told him that Latifich had no power whatsoever in matters of postgraduate studies as they belonged to the University of Zagreb where I was appointed dean of studies.

The issue of the job for Ivanovich threatened to develop into a major crisis of corruption and abuse of office. After this incident, Ivanovich apparenthy told some of his friends that he had made a deal to get the job, housing, facilities for his personal studies, etc. According to the same voices, Ivanovich imposed on Latifich a contract in writing which provided these favors in exchange for services received by Latifich in Switzerland.

Ivanovich was married to a Swiss. According to gossip, through this marriage he became the owner of a factory or a workshop in Switzerland and used a part of his income to make gifts, "loans", and other services to his superiors in the Yugoslav administration. As a good businessman Ivanovich was doing it in a way that the receipts and written traces remained in his hands. After I refused to give him what he wanted to get from the Institute, Ivanovich went to Latifich and requested strongly the implementation of their contract. He told his friends that this time he decided to use the proof should Latifich hesitate to carry out his requests.

Some days later, Latifich came to me to "settle the Ivanovich case". He was furious to hear that he cannot oblige the University of Zagreb to accept his interference in postgraduate programme. In his rage he threatened to abolish the programme of postgraduate studies altogether, withdraw the resources and facilities, etc. Eventually he accepted limits to his power and told me that Ivanovich would be on the payroll of the Institute without any responsibility to me, without doing any work, and without an obligation to come to the office.

It was a very serious violation of regulations and I did not know what to do. If I reported the case, I was sure in advance that I would be made guilty. Latifich was not alone on the other side. He was the end point of a chain of abuses of power and all other and stronger links would defend him in case I opened my mouth. I decided to proceed with caution. We asked Ivanovich to read a course of probabilities at out postgraduate programme, and in this way, I expected that dust would cover the case. However, it was not so. During a period of heavy involvement in lecturing, he left for Switzerland without informing anybody. He was out for fifty days. Later on he continued doing so. In the first year of his assignment, he was out of the country for about eight months.

It was clear that Ivanovich must have kept in his hands the documents that made Latifich dead afraid. In fact, Latifich continued with reckless abuse of the office. He gave Ivanovich a government house from the supply of houses available to facilitate the recruitment of high level technicians. He was also ready to cover other forms of abuses in Ivanovich's case. Somebody reported at a meeting that Ivanovich was abroad most of the time. All the staff started grumbling about it. However, nothing happened. Somebody came to investigate the issue. It was found that Ivanovich kept another job parallel to the one at the Institute and was receiving another salary. Sometime he would appear at the institute and sometimes at the other place of work. At both places he was present only seldom. However, no action was ever taken.

After some time the abuse of government resources went further. According to his contract with Ivanovich, Latifich was obliged to establish research facilities for Ivanovich. In fact, Ivanovich wanted to have another institute where he could carry out his personal studies at the expense of the government. Thus, a parallel research unit was established and nobody knew what for. The establishment of new posts and a major change in the organization had to be approved. In the absence of such approvals the realization of this part of the "contract" was only possible through a long list of new abuses of power.

The "Ivanovich affair" had many other aspects. This case comes to my mind from time to time and I ask myself if my attitude in this matter was correct. Abuses are partly possible because people are aware of what is going on and they all keep quiet. We thus become accomplices. I was chief of an office where many illegal decisions were made and I never insisted on any investigation. My excuse was the fact that so many people, including party members and director's assistants, were aware of the abuses and they all kept quiet. Had I opened my mouth I would have been kicked out at once while Latifich would certainly find somebody to intervene in his favor and "clear" him. My next problem was the impact of these abuses on Institute and the programme of postgraduate studies. So many years of efforts were needed to build up these studies and it would be too bad to see everything ended because somebody wanted to oppose the wrongdoing.

However, my forecast of the future was wrong. One of my staff came to me with a request for a paid leave of six months. I told him that it was not possible. He referred to Ivanovich, accused me of discrimination, and called me "dishonest". When I requested some people at staff meeting to come to the office on time and stay till the end of office hours, they publicly exposed my behavior as a lack of moral standards. One of them said: "We are in the office each day. How about somebody else"?

Experiences of this type continued. I realized that I was losing authority. I lost the courage to call the staff to order. Discipline disappeared. The office was on the brink of disorder. The staff became aware of my conflict with Latifich. I was hardly able to convene staff meetings let alone impose decisions or a respect of commitments. Without seeing any possibility for the improvement of the situation, I submitted my resignation hoping that it would lead to a reconsideration of the whole situation and to some measures to restore order. However, some colleagues who were on good terms with Latifich asked me to change my mind for the sake of the work and our aims. Apparently, they agreed with Latifich that improvements would be made.

I continued at the same position without being clear as to what the miracle was that I expected to take place and improve the atmosphere. However, I expected somehow that the idea of modernization of our statistics would survive.

In fact, the Institute continued on paper only. Everything was ruined. I became an obstacle to Latifich's ruling style. Through my resistance to his orders and maneuvering, many staff became aware of his moral standing and the abuses that he was pressing for in his capacity as chief of the office. He hated me. He did his best to avoid me wherever possible. We discontinued direct contacts. I had to communicate with him in writing. The staff lost confidence in both the work and the future. They behaved as if they were on a sinking boat.

In this situation, I was anxious to involve the Institute in some major project that would give all of us a chance to concentrate on work and gradually forget past frictions.

However, there was no success. The work that was coming to us was primarily concerned with the "system". The situation was desperate. Our UNDP expert, Dr. Hanurav, who was promised a broad programme of applied work, was losing patience and faith in the assignment.

In that situation, a police officer came to me to inquire about foreigners at the Institute. He was informed about our contacts and visited us to see what we were doing. He requested information about the political views of our visitors. I told him that I had no idea about them nor were we interested in politics. He requested guarantees that none of the foreigners would ever say a word about the regime in Yugoslavia. I refused to control the foreigners. I told him that we were excited about their deep knowledge of statistics. This knowledge was our real aim. In the course of other visits, he told me that we failed to observe the instructions that oblige all the institutions where foreigners are lecturing to send special observers to attend each lecture in order to intervene against any word by foreigners that would not be in line with Yugoslav politics. I refused to do that. I told him that we were pleased with everything that we were getting from foreigners. We saw no reason to control them nor did we have the staff to do that. At that point, he pulled out of his briefcase a bunch of instructions regarding the control of foreigners that I was not aware of. When I realized how dangerous the matter of foreigners might be, I told him that the only safe way out for us was to discontinue any contact with foreigners. This was an obvious threat to our idea of international cooperation and the growth of the Institute with the help of usual assistance from professional community. That was the only concrete proposal that I made. I asked him to take it seriously as the only offer in answer to his requests. He kept quiet and left. I never heard from him any more. However, I realized that we might be obliged to close down our contacts with the international professional community. The visit of this policeman was a clear warning.

The police visit was obviously an integral part of the position of the Institute. I certainly do not know who requested the intervention and what its real purposes were. It might have easily been just a demonstration of interest in our work. The news about these visits spread around rapidly. It contributed substantially to the deterioration of the situation and a growth of disorder. The staff understood that an institution where the police is studying the operations has lost credibility. It contributed greatly to a psychology of carelessness.

In that situation, we were requested to explore the possibility of taking current population surveys (including labor force surveys). It was an ideal job for us. However, it was too late. The staff had already lost faith in our ability to keep a level of serious research. In subsequent discussions, everybody insisted on the own views. Some staff even refused to participate in an effort to reach a compromise. When requested in writing to take part in various working groups, they did it without interest. Many pieces of the resulting work were of little use. An illustration is the processing of data from a pilot survey. Because of mistakes in the programme, data were processed fourteen times. At that point the work was discontinued as nobody was interested any more in that experiment. We offered to prepare a report. However, there was no institution willing to consider it.

This is how I again came to the decision to resign. Latifich was very happy with my resignation. He came immediately to Institute and requested a colleague from the "system" unit to become the new director. In other words, the matter of director was as easy to solve as having a cup of coffee. However, it happened again that a group of colleagues intervened and pressed on Latifich to withdraw his decision. Eventually I continued again. The Institute, nontheless, was going rapidly down hill. Nobody expected good news any more while the bad ones followed one after another.

Some of them will be touched upon as typical of the approaches to work in communist countries.

In connection with the preparations for the Manila session of ISI, Latifich, in the capacity of chief statistician, wrote a report to the federal government about the state of statistics. In these reports, the chief party mandator had an opportunity to disclose confidential information and suggest action. Suggestions are made about the value of certain persons, need for transfers, demotions, promotions, etc. The reports are unpleasant in the sense that the accused persons will never know what information about them was put in circulation and where it comes from. One is thus easily accused without having a chance to defend oneself.

In his report, Latifich accused A.Stokich, the director of the statistical office of Serbia, who had used the opportunity of the 1977 session of ISI to go to India without having ever attended any meeting. Instead, he went to a Yugoslav restaurant in New Delhi and stayed there till the end of the session. He also accused Macura as a person who was using ISI opportunities to build himself up while disregarding the policy of Yugoslavia in favor of LDC. He also offered my name as a potential witness and an additional source of information.

Latifich hated both Stokich and Macura. Stokich opposed Latifich at meetings of directors of statistical offices and dared to insist on views that were quite different than those expressed by Latifich. In the case of Macura Latifich was probably jealous as Macura made many acquaintences all over the world, got university titles, was a member of many bodies, etc.

In the practice of the federal government, the circulation of these reports would be restricted to a couple of persons. The matter was highly confidential. However, at the time when Latifich presented his report, the government decided to broaden the circulation and include prime ministers of republics as well. In this way Latifich's report came to Stokich's friend who was in charge of going through these reports and preparing summaries for the prime minister. He took the matter seriously and told Stokich that action would be taken against him, including removal from the office, unless he was able to lift the accusation. This is how the case gradually became a social event. It was put on the agenda of many meetings and became unpleasant to many people and particularly to Latifich. Later on the whole issue went against Latifich. What he said in his report was not far from the truth. Nobody had anything against that. However, the statistical public opinion was fully against Latifich as people hated the method of stabbing a person in the back without giving the accused a chance to defend himself. In the eyes of many people, Latifich was a man without the courage to be straightforward and speak in the face.

This incident probably speeded up the end of Latifich's career in statistics. However, Latifich blamed me for the slap that he got. In fact, I told Stokich that I had no intention of participating in secret accusations and reporting. I do not know if my attitude had any importance in the case. However, the authorities never made any investigation. They probably did not want a non-party person to be put in a position of judge in a flick between two old party members. In this way the case was removed from the agenda and I had to continue working under Latifich.

The case of Latifich's report was mixed with another story that came from the Department of Economics of Zagreb University. At that time both the dean and the secretary of the department were Serbs. During their office term some frictions arose between different groups of professors on the basis of the old dispute between Serbs and Croats. Apparently the Croats accused the leadership of the department of pro-Serbian favoritism. Our postgraduate course was one of the proofs. The accusation said that the work was done by the university of Zagreb while the beneficiary of the work was Serbia.

Communist regimes are extremely sensitive to any question that might develop into a political friction. In theory, communist society is monolithic. Frictions between Serbs and Croats would show that there were no improvements under communism.

This matter was taken seriously. I was aware that some investigation was going on. However, in this and in so many other situations where problems arose, nobody ever asked me for my opinion or my assessment of the importance of the problem. I pretended that I knew more about our programme of postgraduate studies than any other person. Therefore, I expected that I would at least be consulted. However, nothing happened. The corridor gossip reached to me as if I was not more interested in this case than a messenger.

This event certainly contributed to a deterioration of the situation in the office. Some time later on, I asked the registry for a copy of a letter of mine and it was found that my letter had not yet left. The chief of the registry told my staff that he had an order to bring the mail signed by me to Latifich for inspection. In the same period, a young staff member came to me to tell me that he and his colleagues were approached on several occasions by my assistant director who, among other matters, told them that the director of the Institute was not satisfactory and should be removed. My own Assistant Director went as far as requesting the staff to refuse the work coming from their director. At another occasion, while talking to a group of staff, he said: "At present we have to have modest ambitions. We have no director. After the new director is appointed ..." In other words, quite a few people had already been briefed that I had to go. However, I got the news in corridors and from the staff who came to express to me their sympathy in opposition to such a treatment. On another occasion a staff member talked to my Deputy and said that he would wait to see the reaction to the director's memo on a problem. My Deputy told him: "You do not need to wait for anything. I stop his memos on the way between this building and the registry". Thus, there was somebody in the institute stronger than me who had the authority to stop the mail with my signature.

Although this prelude was quite clear, I did not take steps to resign for good. In matters that are dear to their heart, people are frequently blind. This was the period when discussions started about the 1981 census. I was involved in the promotion of census methodology for many years in various parts of the world and I expected that this moment would be an opportunity for the Institute to contribute to the modernization of the forthcoming census. Development in that direction was called for as earlier census was prepared in a rush and without regard to possibilities offered by recent progress in both theory and its application. We were particularly unable to get out of the confusion about censuses of agriculture. The politicians were talking about agriculture as the way out of the economic crisis and, at the same time, they put a ban on the census of agriculture as the basic source of information about agriculture. There were many issues that required the serious involvement of the Institute. I expected that this project alone would justify the existence of the Institute.

For reasons that I was never able to understand the cooperation of the Institute was not appreciated. We followed the developments in census methodology and we were able to carry out our task in this field with full authority. However, I realized that we were systematically dropped out from the list of individuals and institutions to be invited for consultations. Meetings were held without our presence. Quite a few persons proposed meetings to invite the Institute for consultations. There was no answer. In that situation we organized our own meeting on census methodology and invited many participants. At the meeting we presented alternative solutions to certain problems and proposed systematic studies and experiments in order to get facts for final decisions. Our report was distributed to a number of addresses without any reaction on the part of the official statistical leadership.

Even now I have no explanation of this desire to separate the Institute from the work. The case was particularly grave as we were there, on the spot, an institution created by the federal government to work on the methodological preparation of the ongoing statistical projects. From some people, I learned the interpretation that both the authorities and the party put the emphasis on political aspects and considered the census as a *par excellence* political issue. Accordingly, they wanted to keep it within these limits and avoid any contact (let alone consultations) with non-political circles and even "enemies". The others believed that the top officers of Yugoslav statistics, who were all political appointees and had nothing to do with statistics, wanted a political emphasis on the census as it gave them a chance to play a role in various public discussions. Any association with the technicians would take away part of the credit that they expected to get.

I do not know what is true. However, I do know that we had all the credentials for serious involvement in census work. We also took a variety of steps to get some role. In spite of that, nothing came out. There was somebody who did not want either the work or the achievements.

After the census chance was gone, there was nothing for us to hope for. The methodological studies in censuses were widely recognized but our services were not appreciated. In other fields it would be more difficult to develop interest in research.

The end of the Institute was thus very near. In fact, these days we heard the news that the programme of postgraduate studies was abolished. By that time I had already learned that the most incredible developments have to be accepted with indifference. As a result of my respect for institutions and people with whom I worked, I decided to inquire as to what happened. I called the Secretary of the Department of Economics in Zagreb and I was told that he was not in. After repeated attempts failed, I called a colleague who told me that they had some storm in the department. The Secretary of the Department was transferred to some other job. The new officer in charge told me that he had no idea whatsoever about any programme of postgraduate studies. Afterwards I called the dean. After many calls I learned from others that the dean was removed. Some months later I called the new dean and he also told me that he had no idea of postgraduate studies of statistics. I also asked colleagues in the statistical office, who were members of the party, to tell me what happened. One of them told me: "If I were you I would keep quiet about the programme of postgraduate studies. The best thing is to pretend that you never heard about".

Even today I do not know what happened. I hope, however, that my colleagues in other countries will appreciate my embarrassment. I wonder if it ever happened before that an institution was abolished without saying a word to the man who was in charge of it.

After I survived the funeral of the post-graduate studies, I had no more appearances left in this act of my drama about the modernization of Yugoslav statistics. Everything was dead around me, there was no work, there was no school, there were no plans, there was no future. I told myself: "This time the dream was rather short".

These days my secretary told me that Latifich wanted to talk to me by telephone. Something similar had not happened for quite some time. It must have been an important issue. I called back and got from him the following message: "The government has taken steps to retire the old staff. You are one of them. I did my best to keep you. However, I was not successful. I am very sorry that we shall not be able to cooperate any more".

After that removal from work, I wrote a memo to the chief of the office of personnel of the federal government. I said that my association with the Institute pointed out clearly that neither I nor anybody else would be able to make any significant achievement under the conditions of work in FIS, viz. an absolute dependence of the Institute upon a bureaucratic agency that never had the courage to face any major problem. I also offered my services to continue the work started at some other place and under more promising conditions.

Needless to say, I never got any answer. Who would care about a statistician. Instead, my memo was referred to Latifich for explanation. I was told that he pulled out his old weapon. It was so easy to disregard an "enemy" and a source of opposition to socialism. After some time, the party members started boycotting me and turning their heads in the opposite direction in case I happened to pass by.

I went abroad again. The Institute continued its existence on paper. Most of the staff were idle or busy with something outside its original intentions. Most of the accumulated books disappeared; the archives of documents went into pieces; the registry was destroyed "as nobody will ever need it"; the mailing lists were thrown away; the secretariat for international cooperation was dismantled and the staff transferred, etc., etc. After several years FIS proposed to formally abolish the Institute. However, the government was puzzled about this request that was preceded ten years ago with a request to establish the Institute. The government refused to take action. The Institute continued without having clear purpose. Eventually, in 1986 the Institute of statistics got involved in econometric studies.

A point remains to be added. After the last war, Yugoslav statistics emerged twice from the darkness. It was in the period 1949-53 when we were not far from the leading countries. The second time it was during the Institute. Details of the achievements made in both periods remain to be presented to the Yugoslav public. Very soon that task might not be feasible any more. The people who played various roles in these events are dying out. Very soon there will be nobody who would remember technical issues. Written documents about other issues have already become very rare. Special steps were taken by the official representatives of Yugoslav statistics to erase any trace of the work that brought us to the light of day.

On December 14 of each year, viz. Statistics Day, all sorts of celebrations take place to remember the achievements. It so happened, however, that at none of these occasions a single word was ever said about the hundreds of achievements in the above two periods. The recognition went to those who were suppressing the real achievements.

XX Recent developments

In recent years all the major difficulties that Yugoslavia was experiencing after the breakdown of the Soviet model of socialism continued to bother the country. Some of these difficulties developed further into a real plague. The regional centers of power increased their impact. In economic matters they have become almost independent empires. In their aspirations there was hardly any common denominator. Delegates to federal bodies were accountable to the regional centers of power for their work. Above the authority of the republics nothing is tolerated except powerless bodies, such as federal parliament, the federal government, etc. The decision making process runs below the federal level. For each particular sector of work the republics have their own organizations. The growth of administration went beyond any forecast. The economy had to carry the burden of that growth. Heavy taxes were imposed on the suffocating economy. Taxes killed interest in the productivity of work, technological improvements, and the use of science. The improvement of efficiency had little meaning as compared to the weight of taxes. The whole society was marching toward the darkness of the unknown. Unsolved problems rapidly accumulated. At the end of each year, the federal parliament establishes the levels of prices, production, imports, exports, etc. while the achievements have very little to do with wishes expressed. Hundreds of bodies keep discussing the same issues and recommending the action to follow. However, they are all aware that nothing of the kind will be done. The problems of the country have become permanent items on the agenda of interminable discussions. Various bodies end their decisions in resolutions without impact. Mountains of resolutions have been passed so far regarding Kosovo. The issue is threatening the very existence of the country and in spite of that nobody has moved a finger so far toward a solution. Politics was reduced to endless talking and continued celebrations. There is practically no day without some celebration of events from the history of the YCP. There is no day on television programme without various commemorations. The cost of celebrations is exhorbitant. At the same time, inflation is running at a high level while all the elementary textbooks of economics speak of the drastic reduction of expenditures as the first and absolutely necessary step out of crisis.

Needless to say, in this situation, the maintenance of power becomes a primary concern. A gigantic propaganda machinery is kept to fill newspapers, magazines, television, radio, etc. Equally huge is the army of "security observers" who are responsible

196

for a close follow up of everything printed, shown on television, said over radio, communicated in public discussions, shouted at sporting grounds, etc. As soon as they detect a word that goes out of the prescribed limits they move all the levers of power control to ring the alarm bells. Yugoslavia has become famous for enemy searching sessions in newspapers, on television, radio, in publishing offices, etc. that are held to identify crimes of the enemy and call for vigilance. This is how the country is obliged to keep listening to the same music.

The situation in statistics truly reflected the political situation of the country. As an activity without appeal, statistics could not expect any attention. The highest ranking officers in statistics were recruited from among those who could not get anything more prestigious. Because of their modest intellectual capacity, none of these people had the courage to go beyond the inherited routine. Nor did the political leadership have an ear for problems. The principle was thus imposed: stick to the routine and keep quiet.

The situation in statistics however required an action in depth. At most universities the statistical education was in a state of confusion of ideas and approaches. Qualified teachers were missing everywhere. The universities and research institutions needed a couple of hundred of highly qualified statisticians who could not be made available without a huge project of all concerned. Such a project was impossible under the circumstances. The federal government lost interest. The governments of the republics were equally unable to put on their agenda any project of long-term importance. As a result, apathy developed its rule over the profession.

That situation was obviously ideal for all those who were hungry for recognition and credit without significant contributions. Latifich provided a model for all of them. He realized that he would never get any recognition for achievements in technical matters. Those who distribute the honors of this world never notice the work of that type. He, therefore, produced an useful maxim for his behavior: run after politicians. This implies steps to see them, invite them to office for a talk to staff, talk to them, be seen with them, please them, make them happy, squeeze out of their mouth compliments, etc. In pursuit of this line, he was always busy. He was not available for consultations with the staff. However, he kept the position of director longer than anybody else.

There is probably no other director of statistics in any other country who can beat Latifich in his "politization" of the statistical office. Namely, Latifich found out that no amount of published data is able to give him the prestige that he would get by transforming the statistical office into a kind of party organization. Whenever the party decided to organize a congress or a large-scale meeting Latifich rushed to involve his office and the staff in the preparation of a publication in honor of the respective meetings. In connection with the third congress of self-managers, Federal Statistical Office prepared and issued the book *Thirty Years of Self-management in Yugoslavia, 1950-1980.* (Belgrade, 1980). In connection with the 12th congress of the YCP FIS prepared and published the book *Development of Yugoslavia* (Belgrade 1982). The book was included in the documents of the congress as one of the publications prepared by the party. The work needed to produce these books was done exclusively by the staff of the office who were getting, in the respective period, their regular salary. In the same period they were freed from other duties. At the end of the work, they were all given prizes. This project strongly contributed to promotions and the improved status of the respective employees with respect to others.

This amount of abuses of office has never been seen before in statistics. However, •it gave Latifich a great deal of credit. This is probably why he felt safe while he was committing other abuses of his power.

It should be added, however, that the above two books were listed as illustrations. Latifich did more of that. Quite a few books were published in honor of various party activities. On no occasion did Latifich hesitate to use his own staff for the purpose of his maneuvering for prestige.

The politization of statistical offices was not done exclusively in FIS. As soon as the directors of statistical offices in the republics realized what Latifich was doing and how fast he was getting credit for his work, they also decided to make similar publications, mostly under the same title, for the territory of their own republics and in honor of the same political organizations within the respective republics. In other words, in addition to the above *Development of Yugoslavia*, the books appeared under the same title with the name of republics instead of Yugoslavia. Needless to say, the respective directors got credit for those works.

This was not the end. Other people like credits as well. The design is thus continued. There are more than five hundred communes in the country, a number of cities, many villages, etc. It was difficult to stop the proliferation of abuses.

At the same time no resources were available to build up a research programme that would gradually lead to a methodology of projects that should be suitable to the conditions of the country. No funds were available for supporting research work. Research workers had to pay for writing, typing, photocopying, etc. material from their own pockets. The institution of grants to research workers to meet the cost of their studies was unknown.

In this period, another form of waste of resources appeared that secured for Yugoslavs the world leadership. An institution was established that was called "Statistical encounters". The encounters took place once in two years in places convenient for vacations. The time of the encounters is the month of October, when the main tourist season is already over and a lot of space is available in hotels. The encounters are arranged for the staff of statistical offices of all the republics. During the encounters teams of statistical offices compete in a number of games, such as soccer, basketball, chess, athletics, etc. Several busses carry the staff from each republic to the localities chosen for encounters. The total number of attendants exceeds one thousand. The cost is covered from the budgets of the respective offices. For each staff it includes the cost of the trip, hotel, and food. The duration of the encounters is almost a week. During that time the statisticians play games. There is no work. Those who remain at home relax as all the senior staff are participating at the encounters.

These encounters are taking place at a time when the country is experiencing a deep economic crisis. The country has accumulated debts that many generations in the future will not be able to pay. The inflation makes impossible any long-term orientations in economy. In that situation, the import of books and periodicals from abroad is made impossible. Research is declared a personal hobby. However, the encounters are included in the government budget.

The statistical encounters are also used as an opportunity to dispose of another burden inherited from the past. It was already pointed out that in 1953 the Yugoslav Statistical Society (YSS) was established to serve the usual purposes of a professional association. However, the YSS had no resources and lived all the time with help from FIS. This help covered the printing of *Statistical Review*, reproduction of circular letters, mailing of letters to members, etc. The Society was thus heavily dependent upon government administration. This explains why all the directors of FIS served as Presidents of the YSS. The programme of work of the YSS has also had a heavy bias toward problems and activities of FIS.

One of the main activities of the YSS was the organization of biannual meetings that gave a chance to statisticians to meet each other and participate in discussions of various items included in the programme. Although these programmes were seriously lagging behind the level of submitted papers to meetings of comparable societies, they reflected adequately the state of statistics in Yugoslavia.

As a result of help from government statistics, the YSS has managed to continue as a professional association. However, this dependence had a negative impact on the YSS. Rather than being a forum of academic discussions of all the problems of the statistical profession, the YSS behaved as a branch office of government statistics. The choice of topics to be considered was already mentioned. However, more important was an absolute lack on the part of the YSS of orientation toward an objective appraisal of activities and solutions adopted by government statistics. The government has carried out many serious statistical projects and the YSS has never put on its agenda these problems nor has it ever invited the membership to evaluate the work done. In fact, FIS was using the YSS as an additional channel to promote its programme. However, the creative and fertile component of an objective consideration of work was always missing. Rather than being an independent judge of government statistics, the YSS has become its servant.

Needless to say, the consequences were serious. The government statistical machinery worked without pressure from the awareness that its work would be followed and publicly evaluated. The lack of that evaluation contributed greatly to an understanding that the quality of achievements had nothing to do with career and standing of statistical officers.

The lack of an adequate evaluation was compensated in the earlier years by an attempt at assuring the participation of all members in the main activities. This was particularly true of biannual meetings. In this way the statisticians at least had a chance to get information about ongoing activities and develop for themselves a judgement about success achieved, the main actors of various projects, etc.

In recent years a clear deterioration has taken place. It was due to the pressure of politics on all the professions to adopt a structure of public activities that would correspond to models already adopted in politics. Each activity had to be organized by republics. Therefore, statistical societies had to be established in each republic. These societies make up a union of statistical societies. On the board of the union there is a delegate from each society (in republics). The president of the union of the statistical societies is elected by the board by adopting a rotation scheme by republics with a term of two years for both the president and the board.

This bureaucratic approach to the organization of a professional association contributed to a decline of interest in the association of statisticians. In our situation, Serbia has more statisticians than all the rest of the country. In some republics, there is no single person who can claim to be a statistician except from the point of view of employment. These people are now becoming presidents of the union. They do not know what the profession is nor are they able to develop any involvement of the union in the promotion of statistics. Their office is a matter of chance. As a result, they keep quiet and wait for the end of their term to forget about their presidency.

Through this reorganization, statisticians joined similar trends in other fields. The imposed reorganization was a contribution to the decline of the authority of work and achievements. The involvement of individuals in work, the contributions they make, the level of responsibility at which they carried their past assignments, etc. lost the value as decisive factors for career and recognition. At the same time, prominence was given to non-technical characteristics, such as place of work, nationality, affiliation with republics, the order of a particular republic in the rotation scheme, etc. Many chance factors are also in the game. An association can certainly not claim any authority after quality was abandoned.

Later on the process of deterioration continued. Biannual meetings of statisticians were suspended as an independent event that draws its importance from the contributions that the profession is trying to make. Instead, the meeting of the union was attached to the event of statistical encounters, viz. soccer and basketball games. In such a combination the primary emphasis is put on the sporting activities. The professional part is to be happy with whatever remains of the available time and attention. Sporting activities also influence the choice of items for the programme of meetings. The large majority of participants of encounters are employees of statistics rather than statisticians. Therefore, the programme should consist of items that do not require any knowledge of theory and can thus be discussed by any participant with common sense.

The association of technical work with sporting activities has also had an impact on the choice of participants who will attend meetings at the cost of government. As it is not possible to cripple football teams, the only choice is to forget about those who are not lucky to be on the budget of any government office. This is a large class of statisticians who retired from government work, research workers and teachers at small institutions, etc. They do not attend. They are worthless from the point of view of sporting activities. However, it is a matter of very deep concern if the Union of Statisticians of Yugoslavia has accepted the practice of ignoring the participation of members who might wish to attend discussions as independent technicians. The next stage of deterioration was reached with the practice of dropping the invitations to those who might insist on equality of members and fairness in treatment. For several biannual meetings of the association of statisticians of Serbia, the author received an invitation five days after the meeting. The stamp on the envelope showed that the letter was mailed on the day of the meeting or later. There are also cases of members who never received any invitation or announcement of meetings.

Among the changes in the statistical leadership that took place in this period was

Latifich's retirement. At that time the practice was established to appoint chiefs of the technical agencies for a four year mandate. In cycles of four years all the top officers of the federal government would change. Latifich held three mandates in succession and was eventually retired at the end of 1981. He was thus able to flatter himself that he had to go because he was already an exception with such a long service. The others pretended that he behaved in recent years in a way that made a termination of his mandate unavoidable. Gossip about his abuses of the office were already mentioned. His staff also spoke about other cases of wrongdoing. He also had many conflicts with colleagues, such as directors of statistical offices in the republics. They have used recent developments to strengthen their position of independence. But Latifich wanted to play the role of a strong emperor whose job was to issue orders to his subordinates. On this basis Latifich was almost continuously in conflict with his colleagues who did not fail to report their experiences with him to their respective centers of power. Even worse was Latifich's position in his own office where his primary concern was to rule without any sign of opposition. To achieve that purpose frequent use was made of the available means, such as promotions, demotions, distribution of services and favors to the obedient ones, etc. After he was retired he behaved as a man who was ashamed for so many events in his service. He left the office and never appeared among his former colleagues.

Latifich was succeeded by Komel Franta, director of statistical office of Slovenia, in Ljubljana.

This is how the succession was arranged. The federal government announced the vacancy. In that situation, each republic had the right to present its own candidate. The future of the candidate depended upon the support by the respective republic. For each post in the federal government, the respective republic had to surrender a pre-established number of points. As the job of director of the federal statistical office is not a prestigious job, the number of candidates is normally zero. If in this situation a candidate has strong connections and supporters in the office governing the disposal of points, the business is finished. Franta had strong supporters in Slovenia. He was also interested in the job as it would give him a substantially higher salary and a better pension that depended upon the peak salary.

Franta's directorship in federal statistics was a real catastrophe for Yugoslav statistics. Before coming to statistics, Franta was an army colonel specializing in army intelligence. He had no experience in running a civilian office. He particularly had no experience that was needed for a leading position in a profession that requires contacts, cooperation with many different types of persons, and the ability to listen. He behaved as an army officer who could not distinguish more than two categories of people, superiors and subordinates. As he occupied the position of chief statistician, he was not able to see his colleagues as anything but subordinates. He was not able to cooperate nor was he able to tolerate an interlocutor as his equal. As a result, he isolated himself and never showed an interest in the opinions of people around him. He would see no point in convening a meeting of professionals and seek their advice. His view was that he got his mandate from the government as an act of confidence in his abilities. He thus thought that he had to proceed on the basis of his own understanding of the work. He could not see any source of guidance beyond his own interpretation of his responsibilities.

201

After he was strongly in the saddle I visited him to offer my services in statistics. In so doing, I told him what I started doing under Latifich and what I could do in the future. At the end of my talk he told me: "I did not understand a word of what you were saying. Either you do not know what you are talking about or I am not used to this type of talk. I am used to short military statements". I left and never came back. I had done my duty.

As any other man who did not understand the business that he was supposed to run, he was a great admirer of computers. In his mind computers were able to solve all problems. Searching books and periodicals did not have much sense to him. It was sufficient to introduce to computers the items dealt with in the books and retrieve the information afterwards by all concerned. This will be done that way in the future by the developed countries. We thus have to wait and receive the ready fruits after some time.

He also proposed that the federal government abolish the Institute of statistics. Most solutions needed in a LDC are already available as computer programmes. Other programmes will follow soon. An independent attempt at the development of science is neither promising nor economical. The Institute was such an attempt. Thus, a rational step is to abolish it.

Franta contributed to the feeling of despair among the technicians. I contacted some colleagues on the subject and we all agreed that some action for revitalization of our statistics was urgent. In order to examine a programme of steps that could lead to an appropriate action it was thought adequate to convene a meeting of senior statisticians and circulate afterwards their recommendations as widely as possible with an appeal to all concerned to support the action. For that purpose I wrote an identical letter to Serdar in Zagreb, Blejec and Vogelnik in Ljubljana, Kitaljevich, Balaban, Bogdan Babich in Belgrade, etc. The letter was sent out on October 4, 1983. Its initial part is reproduced here as it is typical of the situation. It reads:

"This letter is an attempt at an examination of the possibilities to launch an action for the revitalization of our statistics and get out of our present unpleasant situation. You probably have your own evidence of where we are. In the recognized and leading periodicals in the world - there is no single author from our country. At symposia and other discussions of important problems - there is nobody with our name. In the sector of data collection or in the main fields of applications where there are so many periodicals and collections of contributions from different countries - there is nobody from our area. The conclusion is clear: in our country there is no interest, there are no serious studies nor have results been attained that could be presented to others.

We have not always been in that situation. Our voice could have been heard in proportion to our place in the culture of the world. However, in recent years a rapid deterioration has taken place. It seems that the alternative of the moment is: either we take the steps to get out of our unpleasant position or we enter the competition for the bottom level of development.

I made an attempt to talk about these matters to a number of colleagues in Belgrade and encountered apathy, lack of interest, and a readiness to abandon our matters to the wind to take them in whatever direction it blows. From the point of view of world developments, this is an unpleasant situation. Other people are struggling for each step ahead while the initiative and drive are the main qualities of the top staff. Instead, we are all talking about difficulties. However, it seems that statisticians have done little to make things better. What bothers me is our own responsibility for the state of our profession. I am convinced that people are able to achieve a great deal under the most difficult circumstances.

It seems that a discussion of all these problems would be appropriate to seeing if we can agree on some programme of work that could eventually lead to useful results. If we do not achieve any progress at least our conscience will be clear".

After that, details followed about arrangements for the meeting. However, the meeting was never held. There were too many difficulties on the way to an unofficial meeting.

In the meantime Kitaljevich, Balaban, and the author had a meeting on this subject with M.Zhivkovich, the new director of the Serbian Statistical Office who succeeded A. Stokich. Zhivkovich was ambitious and anxious to participate in such a project. Therefore, he was happy to do his best to move the issue of Yugoslav statistics from a standstill. He thought that he could impose a discussion of this issue by the meeting of directors of statistical offices. At that time he was serving as Vice President of the Union of Yugoslav Statistical Societies and in that capacity he had a right to include items of his choice on the agenda of meetings of directors. However, in order to prepare the ground for this action it was necessary to have something in writing. As a result of that request, I prepared a paper "Speeding up the statistical development in Yugoslavia". This paper contained an introductory statement (as in the above circular letter) and the following sections: research projects, research institutions and associations, joint projects of science and applications, new developments in statistical education, additional educational programmes (primarily those leading to a Ph.D. degree in statistics) statistical development in other countries, publications, and Committee for the promotion of statistics.

This paper was too long as an annotation to the agenda of a meeting. Zhivkovich requested Babich to make a summary. Babich did a free interpretation of my paper. However, he did it in a way that served as a basis for subsequent incriminations. He said that a group of leading Yugoslav statisticians met recently to prepare a programme of promotion of statistics in Yugoslavia. After that Zhivkovich requested the Union of Statistical Societies to put this item on the agenda, discuss the issues and implement whatever programme comes out. In fact, the item appeared on the agenda of the meeting of directors of statistical offices that was held in 1982 in Neum, on the Adriatic coast, jointly with the occasion of statistical encounters.

The meeting of the directors was chaired by Franta. It concluded that Yugoslav statistics was in good health. Should anything be done, it will be taken care of by the existing bodies. Therefore, there was no need for "distinguished statisticians". In fact, at the meeting it was found out that the whole issue was a "diversion" worked out by agents of anglo-american imperialism to seed confusion in the country and divert attention of the staff from their regular tasks. The meeting condamned this action of the "enemies" of socialism and recommended implicitly a boycott of persons involved in this "project".

After the meeting was over, Zhivkovich realized how dangerous an initiative might be. It might take you straight into the hands of enemies. Of course, the worst enemy was the author. Zhivkovich discontinued contacts with us. The same happened to Serdar and Blejec.

Although it might be instructive to present details of the treatment that was prepared against "enemies" in order to protect the society from the impact of "diversions", I give it up for the sake of my colleagues who might find themselves in an embarrassing situation.

To end this story, let me just add that some colleagues involved in this case were members of the YCP. However, membership in the party does not cover the members against the crime committed here. The crime is terrible. Some party members permitted themselves to think that a piece of work done under the guidance of the communist party could be improved. This goes too far.

Generally speaking, Franta was a courageous man. Any director with a standard respect for his colleagues would convene recognized experts in the fields concerned, get their opinion, and obtain their support for the action planned. Franta did not care for consultations. On his own and without any external advice he undertook to change the system of statistical publications. He introduced a reorganization of material, distributed it differently, and made use of some recent innovations that were already widely used in the more developed countries (such as microfish).

On this basis, public opposition was organized against him. The fact is that the profession was always neglected in policy matters. However, the earlier directors consulted the leading party mandators in statistics and the agencies concerned. The influential people were thus kept quiet. As Franta never consulted anybody, he created many enemies. Among those enemies there were some people who had connections and influences, such as Macura. Neglect of these people was Franta's great mistake and he was obliged to pay for it. For the statistical encounters in 1984 and the parallel meeting of the Union of Statistical Societies, Macura wrote the paper "Problems in publication of statistical data"[17] and secured for its discussion a conspicuous part of the available time. The Vice President of the Federal Government was invited to attend this meeting and hear with his own ears what kind of steps were being taken in one of the agencies under him.

Macura's paper did not offer valid arguments. Some of the innovations used by Franta were already introduced by other countries. There was no point in accusing Franta for changes in an area where the technology is rapidly progressing. All the countries are introducing changes. The real issue was to open the file of publication of data in general, identify problems that we were facing, and recommend steps that could solve some of these problems in the future. The old system of publication of data contained very serious problems and in many aspect was below the level of acceptable standards. Franta's changes were just a small formal case as compared to a broad area of substantial issues.

---

17 In Serbo-Croatian.

In fact, Macura's paper misled the meeting by preventing the discussion from entering into fundamental problems of the publication of data that Franta inherited from his predecessors among whom was Macura himself. The meeting ended in a strong condemnation of Franta's attitude. In order to deepen the accusation and specify Franta's sins, a committee was established including Macura and Krashovec. The author refused to serve on this committee. I did not want to mix with personal rivalries nor did I see any sense in talking about the issue of publication of data with people who had no qualifications in these matters. A prerequisite of these discussions was the familiarity with survey techniques and recent achievements just in the collection and presentation of data.

Macura was probably very happy with the outcome of this meeting. In the beginning of 1985, Franta was transferred to a non-existing job of consultant to the Federal Government. This device makes possible the removal of a person at once yet keeping him on the payroll pending a final solution. Franta paid his mistake of neglecting people who did not like to be neglected. The offended personalities thus obtained full satisfaction. However, there was no satisfaction for the profession. In fact, Franta badly hurt the statistical profession of Yugoslavia. He inherited and further developed the neglect of the rising role of science in the government statistical work. He never showed any interest in getting information about the related developments in the world. Many of those who needed encouragement to keep abreast of events in the world at the expense of their own resources and their leisure time lost hope for the better and gave up. The remaining voices were also silenced. While the people in other countries, who were much behind us, were progressing rapidly by opening their doors to science, Franta's term reflected a total neglect of developments in the world. The real issue remains to be: how long the YCP will tolerate its own practice of appointing to high positions candidates who are without abilities for the job envisioned?

The tragic outcome of Franta's assignment was not taken into account as a lesson. In the beginning of 1984 a search started for a new director. There was no interest in this job among politically strong candidates. The republics were not anxious to surrender their points in exchange for this job. And it so happened that Dr. D. Grupkovich, former Undersecretary of the Ministry of Finances was happy to get that job. According to rumors he did not manage to get along with his minister and was anxious to change the job. He came to statistics in 1985. There was no need for his republic to surrender additional points as it was already done before he took the job in finances.

Before he took over, Grupkovich was briefed by the corresponding government office about the displeasure on the part of the government with Franta and his behavior. As a result, Grupkovich rushed to get easy credit for a cancellation of all the decisions taken by Franta. Franta sold the printing office and Grupkovich got the resources to buy a new one with a difference that the new price was ten times higher. Federal statistics will issue again the statistical publications and not the public publishers as arranged by Franta. Franta's demotions were cancelled and the people were retired who played a prominent role under him. Franta needed four years to put everything upside down. Grupkovich erased his work within a couple of weeks.

After all the memories of the Franta regime were erased, Grupkovich could not avoid the fundamental policy issues in statistics, such as the role of research, statistical education and the supply of young qualified staff, international cooperation aimed at following up the developments, the establishment of institutions to be in charge of research, etc., etc.

In a search for orientation amid these difficult issues, Grupkovich talked to various persons. Among others he saw B.Kitaljevich, whom he had known from his earlier contacts with Montenegrians as they frequently met together. Kitaljevich had a good reputation among the Montenegrians and Grupkovich benefited greatly from Kitaljevich. Among other advise, Kitaljevich requested Grupkovich to see me for all the problems of data collection.

As a result of that recommendation, I had a meeting with Grupkovich. It was a four-hour meeting. At the end Grupkovich told me that he got exactly what he needed. At his request we met again after several days. It was a new three-hour discussion. Finally he asked me to prepare for him a paper about the measures that had to be taken in our statistics should we wish to catch up with developments in the world. He told me that he accepted wholeheartedly the programme that I outlined for him. However, he needed an approval of that line before he could start implementations. For that purpose it had to be a document.

In considering this task my mind went over a very long series of documents that I wrote in the course of my career on the subject of improvement of Yugoslav statistics. Needless to say, they were all discarded. However, I could not refuse participation in a new attempt at modernization of statistics in Yugoslavia after the man who was in charge of statistics told me that he just wanted what I told him to do. I was, therefore, obliged to make a new attempt although I was afraid that my new document would finish very soon in the paper basket.

As to the title of my document I decided to use an unpretentious form, viz. "Improvement of scientific work in Yugoslav statistics". This title did not say that everything done so far by party mandators had to be redone. It suggested some steps in a side activity and left open the bulk of work so that party had plenty of space to develop its activities.

In the document itself I included everything that I was talking about in course of my forty years of involvement in the modernization of statistics in Yugoslavia. I dealt particularly with the role of science, measures to secure the transfer of the know-how, international cooperation, organization of research, statistical education, recruitment policy, etc. I elaborated on the role of the profession and the sense of public consultations. After the tragic practice of earlier directors to disregard the cooperation, I thought that it was essential to achieve a change of past practices as this was the only way to safeguard a complex and expensive social activity from the impact of whims of directors of statistics and their personal maneuverings. I was happy with the outcome of this work. I thought that I presented a succint picture of the programme of modernization.

I left my document with Grupkovich and I never saw him again on this issue. My document did not go to the statisticians. Instead, it finished in the hands of those who were searching for "diversions". Before any reading, my personal file was probably taken out of the store. It was clear that enemies were lifting their heads again. The document finished as many others before.

206

Another attempt at being useful ended.

After this unpleasant experience with me Grupkovich turned to the old practice. Namely, if one does not know what to do, the best thing is to continue the old line. In this case the inherited approaches are continued and nobody will be able to accuse him for what the predecessors had done. Thus, he copied Latifich. He continued with preparation of books for party celebrations. He also started visiting foreign statistical offices one after the other although it was difficult to see what the purpose of these visits was. Being an economist, he could not possibly understand the philosophy of other statistical offices nor could he appreciate their methodological solutions. In addition, some of us spent quite some time in foreign offices and we could have given him an account of their basic approaches.

Grupkovich accepted the government decision to keep the Institute. However, he did not know what to do with it after he dropped my ideas about modernization of statistics. At that moment he was lucky. The World Bank sent some of their staff to Yugoslavia to inquire if an agency would be willing to carry out econometric studies under their guidance. They promised financial assistance, computer facilities, documents, fellowships, and payment of services. Grupkovich jumped at the chance.

In this way the Institute moved again in the wrong direction. Rather than doing statistical research that all the institutes associated with government data collection are doing, it became involved in econometric studies that would never achieve any significant result within an agency with specialization in data collection.

It thus seems that Grupkovich already made all his choices. However, a pursuit of Latifich's trace will not take him for. This conclusion could have been anticipated before he took the job in statistics. Namely, years ago he was put in a concentration camp as a follower of the USSR views of communism. He was released after some time and lived quite long in a dirt, discarded entirely, and boycotted by everybody. He was pulled out of that misery by Veselin Djuranovich, at that time the Prime Minister of the Federal Government under the condition that he declares himself aware of a great mistake that he committed and makes a promise to behave in the future as an enthusiastic member of the YCP. He kept his promise. He has became undersecretary and developed the ability to ask for guidance in whatever issue arises in his office. In this way he would certainly not go to a jail any more. However, building statistics requires courage.

XXI The 1981 Census of Population

Past efforts toward the modernization of Yugoslav statistics left behind some results. There is no question about it. However, there results were small compared to the input. Namely, we did not achieve sufficient progress in the penetration of the modern spirit in government data collection activities. It was, therefore, obvious that further efforts were essential.

However, it did not seems adequate to write a new document for that purpose. Those who would read such a document have already accepted the basic aspects of the modernization programme. Nothing would change if they were given another document. Those who have never accepted a word of the modernization programme are the policy makers or members of the YCP. They rejected past efforts and they would not care for a new document no matter how good it might be. The problem was, therefore, to conceive of a way that will oblige policy makers to take it into account and, without mentioning it, accept for implementation some of its proposals.

However, for that purpose an appropriate opportunity was needed. It had to be a renewal of the modernization issue in connection with an important project that would offer a chance to point out the shortcomings of the existing approaches and the advantages that would follow, with respect to the same project, from modern policy orientations.

A good opportunity to realize this plan appeared in 1984. At that time I was in the US. I had some time available to work on this issue. In addition, I was living near the University of Pennsylvania which had a relatively good library of statistical publications. This was a chance for me to use the available documents and raise the problem of the state of Yugoslav statistics. I kept following the preparations for the 1981 Census of Population in Yugoslavia and I was aware that the adopted census plans included various questionable approaches. The census had quite a few methodological problems. The documents available in this library made it possible to show how far we were from the standards of the related world practice. It was easy to show that this census was far from employing a careful use of resources. I expected that references to specific shortcomings would wake up the authorities and oblige them to take some steps to introduce a new spirit in statistics.

For illustration, the following are some of the raised problems.

1. The official title of that census was: The Census of Population, Households, and Housing of March 31, 1981. The title itself points out some problems of this census. The usual practice in census taking is to combine the census of population and the census of housing. The combination follows from the fact that the enumerators of the census of population, in their attempt at securing a full coverage of individuals, enter each dwelling where people might live. While doing so, they list the housing quarters (or the apartments) in addition to the people living there. In other words, a list of housing units is a byproduct of the census of population. Thus, if the two censuses are combined a relatively small additional effort is needed to get both the census of population and the census of housing. Therefore, the Yugoslav combination of these two projects was justified.

However, difficulties arise with households.

In censuses of population there is normally no separate interest in households in addition to individual persons. There are no separate questions about households. In fact, households are treated as derived products of the census of individuals. Data collected for individuals make it possible to group the persons living in the same household, and present their distribution by size, by composition, etc. *UN Principles and Recommendations for Population and Housing Censuses* (UN, Series M, No. 67, New York, 1980) recommend the tabulation of data for individuals by households without including in the census questionaire separate questions about honseholds.

Household data are thus derived from data about individuals. The same is true of data for enumeration districts, settlements, communes, cities, and other clusters of individuals. Each census of population leads to data by these clusters of individuals without separate questions. Therefore, in order to be consistent, the title of the census could be: the census of population, households, houses, enumeration districts, settlements, communes, districts, cities, republics, etc.

2. The origin of the prominence given to households is in the desire to achieve savings by adding to two censuses (population and housing) the census of agriculture as well and combining all of them into a single field operation. The outcome of the combination should be three censuses obtained in a single expanded project.

The logic followed is this. A farm or an agricultural holding in the private sector of agriculture is in fact a household involved in agricultural work. Each of these households operates and/or owns some land, livestock, agricultural machinery, etc. For that reason the basic data of a census of agriculture could be obtained in a census of population and housing by asking each household the following additional questions: i) cooperation with agricultural cooperatives (Yes on No), ii) area owned by all members of the household, iii) area operated, iv) number of horses owned,v) number of cattle, vi) sheep, vii) pigs, viii) poultry heads, ix) beehives, x) tractors, and xi) combines. In this way - say the organizers - the essential information from a census of agriculture is obtained at a cost that is no more than a small fraction of a separate census of agriculture.

Needless to say, the agricultural characteristics listed here have nothing to do with the characteristics of individuals that are requested in censuses of population. This is why the organizers of the census were obliged to introduce the household as a new unit of the combined census operation and ask data about agricultural characteristics from households. The attractive side of this approach is in the fact that lists of households will need to be established anyway for purposes of the census of population.

The position of households in this census is thus clear. Households appear in this census because of the census of agriculture. The combination used would not be possible without households.

3. It is not difficult to see that agricultural data collected in this census do not replace a separate census of agriculture nor do they have any clear meaning. In fact, it is not easy to say what this census has achieved. In censuses of agriculture the fundamental unit is the farm or an agricultural holding. The farm is a unit of agricultural production in the same way as the establishment is the unit of industrial production. The census of agriculture is the collection of data about characteristics of farms, such as area, land tenure, livestock, employment, agricultural machinery, etc. The interpretation of the resulting data is straightforward. The census shows the number and the distribution of farms over the national territory by their characteristics. The picture obtained shows the structure of agriculture, the available assets, their distribution, the relationships between the characteristics, etc. Such a census is a fundamental source of information about agriculture in any country.

4. The agricultural part of the Yugoslav 1981 census is very far from such a census of agriculture. There is no identity between farms as units of agricultural production and households reporting ownership of agricultural characteristics. Some households residing in cities will report ownership of agricultural characteristics although they may have nothing to do with agricultural production. At the same time real farms will not appear as "agricultural households" in case the respective households do not own the characteristics that the census is interested in. A case was reported of a farm that was split up into two separate parts from the ownership point of view. Both parts belonged to children of the operator. Thus, according to this census the two parts will be included in "agricultural households" in two different cities (where the children live) while the real operational farm with the father of children as the operator will not be included in the census. The list of "agricultural households" that follows from this census will certainly be different from what a census of agriculture would yield.

The outcome of this census will be even worse if the area used by households becomes a criterion for the establishment of a substitute for the population of farms. The concept of use was not specified. In addition to agricultural production, the area might be used for parking purposes, for cultivation of flowers, as a playground for children of parents living in cities and visiting country areas when they are free, etc. Uses of a similar nature will include the respective households in the group of "agricultural households".

The results of such a census do not make possible standard uses of data. The authorities have never published an investigation that would clarify if data obtained in this census can be used, for what purpose, and to what extent.

The procedure used is embarrassing after the government declared agriculture as one of the priority development areas. Agriculture is expected to provide a basis of economic recovery from a long crisis. For the related planning, a census with a clear meaning would be essential.

5 The lack of interest on the part of the Yugoslav authorities in a properly conceived census of agriculture was explained as follows: a) there is no point in taking a census under conditions of continuous changes in agriculture. By the time the data from the census are tabulated the resulting picture of agriculture will belong to the past and there would be no interest in the related information, and b) the country is in a severe crisis and the need arises for savings.

However, none of these arguments is convincing. There were many changes in agriculture in the amount and type of government interventions, such as nationalization, the establishment of a socialist sector, the availability of financing, obligatory deliveries, etc. However, these changes had a limited effect on land use, the number and type of agricultural machinery, the distribution of crops over the national territory, production of different crops, etc. Changes call for more frequent censuses than a stable agriculture.

The argument of cost is not much stronger. For the census of population, the existing segmentation of the country into enumeration districts was up-dated and presented in the form of maps. The preparations for the census of population also left behind the lists of households in each enumeration district. The census field machinery was also there. Not much had to be added to that to have a modern census of agriculture. However, these additional resources were saved while there was no concern about the resources needed to finance an undertaking of a questionable value.

6. Nor were the available achievements in census methodology used to introduce more flexibility in the consideration of savings. Yugoslavia was one of the first countries where sampling methods were used for various purposes in combination with censuses. In preparation of the 1981 census, the developments in the world along that line were disregarded. From a position of leadership, Yugoslavia dropped to the level of a few countries that made no use of sampling in consideration of a way out of difficulties that arose with a broad census programme. With a bit more respect for the progress made in the world, it was not difficult to secure for the country a proper census of agriculture on a sampling basis. With the available infrastructure it was easy to carry out such a project at a price that was quite modest.

7.The general approach to the preparation of this census was not in line with new statistical practices.

In recent years it has become customary to see in statistical work an integrated system. Practical implications of this principle require a combination of activities in the implementation of a statistical programme in the sense that preparations for any given project are used as an opportunity to carry out, within the same effort and cost, some aspects of projects that are on the programme of work in future activities. In this respect, a census of population offers more chances than any other project to save resources. Yugoslavia is a country without important sectors of data about the present society. The neglected sectors are various types of household surveys, such as labor force surveys, expenditures surveys, food consumption surveys, demographic and sociological surveys, etc. The preparations for a census of population offer an ideal opportunity to move this block of issues from standstill and thus secure an essential step ahead in the modern-

211

ization of statistics.

Yugoslavia had many reasons to look into this issue while preparing for the census.

8. After our early work in the period 1949-53, one would expect that Yugoslav censuses would continue the tradition and deal with the issue of the quality of data in a way that corresponded to recent developments. However, there were no appreciable achievements. A sample of enumeration districts was used to check the completeness of enumeration. Good census enumerators were used to take the check. Whenever they found a result different than the check, it was concluded that census enumerators committed an error. The difference between data in the respective series was used to estimate the coverage bias in census results.

Needless to say, this procedure has doubtful value as the experience from many countries provided many indications that check inspectors also make errors. Just at that point, refinements in the techniques are needed to secure the meaning of check data. One of them is a reconciliation of data. The other is a parallel use of different checks. An obvious possibility was in the use of consistency studies. Yugoslavia has many possibilities for external checks. A variety of lists of persons and households were available. The question of objectives of coverage checks also arises. If they are not used to getting information about characteristics of circumstances leading to errors, the census methodology will never have the necessary suggestions for the formulation of programmes of improvements.

It appears that this issue was neglected.

9. Even less valuable was the check of the accuracy of response. For this purpose, a sample of persons was selected from the census and the check data were collected immediately after the census enumeration was over, viz. when the respondents kept fresh in their mind the information given to census enumerators. Discrepancies between the two series of data were again used to measure the response bias and other effects of errors.

This approach has a dubious value. Those who are conversant with the respective theory will understand that this procedure cannot be used for studies of response errors. Fortunately, the results were never published. The whole project was apparently abandoned after the field work was over.

10. Another problem appeared in connection with present statistical practice to provide users of data with some guidance about the quality of census results. This is why response checks and the checks of completeness of enumeration are carried out. This obligation makes it necessary to plan the timing of all the checks in a way that will secure the results of checks prior to the publication of census data. In this case the checks guide the users and help prevent mistaken uses of data.

In the 1981 census, this obligation was disregarded. In census publications there is not a single word about the accuracy of census data. In other words, users of data do not get anything from the project for the measurement of accuracy. Nor did the related field work used to get data for the improvement of census methodology. Why was it then necessary to spend money and waste efforts?

11. Another illustration of inadequate work refers to data processing. In the course of work, certain problems arose and delayed the processing. In addition to other issues, the computer broke down. Negotiations started for alternative arrangements. However, the results were not satisfactory. Four years after the census (middle 1985), the tabulation was far from completed. For some parts of the tabulation programme, it was very questionable if the related work would be done at all.

Here again the planning of work was probably not adequate. The computer did not break down overnight. It was old before the census started and that fact could have been taken into account. On the other hand, after it became obvious that difficulties were appearing, there were possibilities for various emergency solutions. A sample of census data could have been easily tabulated and made available to users within a year after the field work was over. We had a tradition in the use of this procedure.

These are some illustrations of various problems of this census.

I thought that a review of these problems would oblige the decision makers to examine their policies and come to the conclusion that a different approach to work is needed. In order to achieve this effect, I wrote the paper "Comments on the Census of Population, Households, and Housing of March 31, 1981". The paper was deliberately provocative. A review of the world census practices was made in connection with any of the problems included. It became clear to readers that statistical policy makers had disregarded the available know-how.

After the draft of that paper was ready for a restricted circulation, I took it to Dr. Grupkovich, Director of FIS. This was May 1985, at the time when he was happy about prospects of cooperation with me. He looked at the title of the paper and immediately changed the expression on his face. While he was joyful before, his face suddenly became a part of a dead body. He was pale and motionless. He stopped talking. I realized that the best thing that I could do in that situation would be to go. I took my briefcase. My intention was clear to him. He told me: "Please, leave the paper here. I shall read it". I left.

On my way back, I realized the mistake that I had committed. The first word of my paper was "comments". The word implies that the work done in the last census could have been done differently or better. In other words, doubts were expressed regarding the ability of the party to assume the leadership. The author had doubts as to the role of the party. Therefore, the author must be an enemy.

On the basis of past experience, I expected a reaction of this type. However, I did not expect that it would be that fast.

As it normally happenes in that kind of situation, Grupkovich did not try to establish contact with me the day after I left my paper with him. I waited for some weeks to see if reasons of simple politeness, let alone anything else, would induce him to ring me up, thank me for the paper and say some nice words that normally accompany disposing of the paper in the basket. No reaction.

After a month, I realized that I had to forget about FIS. I thought that I should

213

try to have my paper published by some periodical. I went to see a lady who was the editor of "Sociology". My paper pointed out the primary importance of censuses of population for social scientists and proposed intensive cooperation between statistics and various professional associations in the field of social sciences. I also pointed out that some of the problems of censuses of population cannot be solved without cooperation with sociologists. For that reasons joint meetings of the respective professional associations were proposed.

The editor tried to convince me that sociology, for the time being, could not cultivate its overlapping problems with statistics. She advised me to öffer my paper to a periodical called "Population". As an alternative, she also proposed "Economist", that was an official publication of the Union of Societies of Economists of Yugoslavia. She gave me a lecture about the importance of my topic for the association of economists. After she realized that I did not seem convinced of her arguments, she told me: "If you insist on an examination of the suitability of your paper for publication in "Sociology", leave two copies with me and I shall let you know the outcome.

I left the paper. After several months, I got a message from "Sociology". On a piece of paper that was no longer than the area of four boxes of matches combined, it was written: "Such material cannot be published in 'Sociology'".

Needless to say, I had not waited for this reply. I went to see Dr. Breznik, the editor of "Population". If there is any periodical, I thought, that should publish comments on the last Yugoslav census of population it should just be the "Population". However, I did not think of that solution before as I knew well Dr. Breznik. He was a man who was terribly afraid of his shadow. I was aware that he would not have the courage to read a manuscript that starts with the word "comments". I was sure Dr. Breznik would not go beyond that word.

I visited Dr. Breznik and told him about the content of my paper and its intentions. He advised me to go to somebody else. He told me that Macura's green light was absolutely necessary. However, I repeated that there was no other periodical in Yugoslavia that I could consider more suitable for the publication of an analysis of the last census than "Population". I left the paper with him. He promised to read it and let me know his reaction. After that day I never saw him again. He never rang me up. In the meantime, it happened twice that I was about to cross his path in Belgrade streets. In order to avoid talking to me, he made a detour to the other side. I obviously lost a friend because of stupid word "Comments".

I also sent a copy of my paper to "Economist". At that time the editor was in Sarajevo, at the Department of Economics, University of Sarajevo. I never got an acknowledgment nor any reaction. After several months I forgot entirely about it.

In September 1985, I was going to Amsterdam to attend the ISI session. Grupkovich was on the same flight. We were sitting in the same aircraft without talking to each other. As I had to present my paper in Amsterdam, Grupkovich learned about it and he attended my talk. He came to congratulate me. Afterwards we again went in different directions.

Suddenly, in the beginning of October 1985 he called me to say that he would like to talk to me. He told me that he was calling from the lobby of Academy of Sciences where he was talking to Macura.

I went there and I was told the following: "The government wants FIS to organize a symposium about preparations for the 1991 round of censuses. There is a very serious intention to make this census better than the earlier ones. In order to implement the government decision, we have decided to convene a meeting of experts toward the end of November to discuss the important aspects of preparations for the 1991 census. At FIS we have prepared for that purpose a paper called "Proposal of the programme of activities on the preparation and realization of 1991 census". That paper by FIS will be circulated as a part of documents for that meeting. However we would like to start our discussions with your paper. Your paper will be an introductory statement, a kind of evaluation of the last census. Other discussions will refer to census methodology, organizational aspects of censuses, and data processing. We are going to reproduce your paper and circulate it in advance so that all the participants of the meeting get a chance to study it beforehand and prepare their interventions".

This is what I was told by Grupkovich. He was kind. He insisted that I participate at the meeting. Macura joined him. After the earlier experience with this paper, I hesitated to have anything to do with people who were not able to observe the basic requirements of acceptable behavior. However, after some thinking I changed my mind. My attitude was: "Let me do my best to make this meeting successful because of the importance of the subject".

I had a contact in statistics, a friend, who afterwards gave me a full explanation of the new mood. The sequence of events was unusual. I was told the following: Grupkovich sent your paper to the responsible government office. He waited for instructions. In the meantime, he behaved as he never saw you before. This is to be on the safe side. After some time he was summoned to the office responsible for the instructions on these matters. They told him to take your paper seriously. There was no point in neglecting it as it was very likely that it might be published abroad. Therefore, to neutralize the effect of that paper through an appropriate series of steps, the plan was to put the item of the 1991 census on the agenda of the meeting of directors of statistical offices and get from that meeting a decision obliging the Federal statistical office to work out a document about preparations for the 1991 census and convene a meeting for a discussion of that document. In this way, FIS would keep the initiative. It would also demonstrate interest in the future of Yugoslav statistics. Zarkovich's paper will be a part of a big pile of documents that will appear on this subject. It will have little effect. All the credit will go to FIS, the government, and the party!

I got this explanation quite some time after I had already accepted to participate at the meeting of the experts. Therefore, I could not go back on my word. However, I continued my inquiries on the subject. This is how I learned that my paper was given to a colleague at FIS to organize the work on the preparations of FIS's own document with a specific request to incorporate all the ideas and proposals from my paper without ever mentioning my name or making references to my paper. That work was given a very high priority and had to be done in rush. The paper had to go to the meeting of directors of statistical offices for a review, comments and changes.

Colleagues working in population statistics of FIS were puzzled about the rush in this matter. They told me that they never saw before a similar rush. However, the rush was needed because the meeting of directors of statistical offices was convened for July 12 while the paper had to be dispatched to the participants of the meeting beforehand.

The meeting of directors was held as planned. It backed the preparations for the 1991 census and authorized the meeting of experts on 21 and 22 November 1985.

Thus, everything was done as planned. Outside the political leadership of FIS, there was one single colleague who was given specific instructions to carry out the whole project in line with my paper. Other colleagues cooperated in the execution of this project without having ever been given any explanation about the special circumstances of the project. The meeting of directors praised FIS for initiative and leadership. Grupkovich got credit for successful directorship. In the resulting big pile of documents my name was never mentioned. There was no reference to my paper, although it was the only available attempt at an evaluation of the 1981 census. Moreover, it was the only written paper in Yugoslavia about recent statistical orientations in relation to censuses, research, and modernization of statistical services.

For the meeting of experts, FIS invited 350 persons who were either statisticians or persons interested in the census of population. The meeting was convened at FIS's cost. In the name of the government, the meeting was attended by J.Zemljarich, the Vice President of federal government who responsible for the work of government agencies. During the meeting he told me the usual words: "The government is very happy with your paper. One has to talk about mistakes. Otherwise we would never be able to improve our work".

During the meeting any careful observer could have easily come to the conclusion that something was wrong. My paper was reproduced for the meeting in printed form while all other papers were made on a copier. It was clear that my paper had special treatment. Besides, my paper was a review of many census problems picked up in different areas of census work. Therefore, it was outside the structure of the meeting. And yet it was the first item of the meeting. People felt that the declared aims of the meeting did not correspond to the central position reserved for my paper. Whatever remained on the programme of the meeting in addition to my paper was done fast and superficially. And yet, no reference to my paper.

At the meeting of experts, I realized that I was again in the hands of my old co-traveler M.Macura. In the past, I did my best to avoid contact with him. After I left Yugoslavia, in 1955, I was quite successful in that respect. Since that time, the ISI sessions were the only opportunities where I was not able to avoid physical contact with him. On these occasions we were living together in a small area. Besides ISI sessions, I saw him in 1983. At that time I arranged with a publisher in Belgrade to issue in English my booklet *Statistics for Tomorrow*. The booklet dealt with some issues related to the role of ISI in the promotion of statistical development with particular reference to less developed countries. In this case I was again in conflict with Macura. A part of Macura's personality was a strong desire to be in excellent terms with ruling groups. This is how he was highly regarded by the rulers of ISI. He even served as President of ISI. He knew my opposition to some policy orientations of ISI. When he heard about the publication of my booklet he was furious. He told a colleague of mine: "This is incredible. How can it be that somebody wants to issue a statistical publication without reporting to me".

In fact, the procedure followed in case of my booklet was fully legal (according to Yugoslav publishing standards). I had two review of my manuscript by two senior and respected statisticians. However, Macura did not accept that arrangement. He threatened to make a public case out of my booklet. He called the publisher and threatened him with serious consequences and an impact of this issue on his subsequent career. Later on the publisher destroyed everything. I was requested to understand that the publisher had a good intention to be useful. However, he did not expect that this issue would go as far as threatening his future and his career. The poor man must have been dead afraid as he had no courage to call me personally and tell me what happened. Afterwards, he was also one of these who preferred to cross the street and thus avoid talking to me.

When I saw Macura attending the meeting on the 1991 census, my question was: "In what way does he plan to use this meeting"? Although he was never involved in technical issues of census methodology, several censuses were taken in statistical offices headed by him. This was sufficient to him to participate in any discussion involving census generalities. As a result, he presided over a part of the meeting, although many people were there who were qualified for that role. In addition, he also contributed a paper to this meeting. The paper was entitled: "Preliminary reflexions about the content of the 1991 census of population". The title implies that there will be some other reflexions. There is another interpretation of "preliminary" character of reflexions. If somebody is disappointed by the lack of content in the "preliminary" reflexions, the excuse is in the "preliminary" character of the paper.

During the meeting itself, Grupkovich was very happy. Many participants praised the initiative taken by FIS and Grupkovic's demonstrated interest in the development of statistics in Yugoslavia. I thought I should add my share to his happiness. I found an excuse for his earlier behavior. He waited for instructions as any good government officer. After he got them in the form of a request to move the matter of the census he probably had a serious intention to make use of the government green light. At that time I expected that he might need a document that would specify the action programme leading to better census work in the future. I offered to draft such a document for consideration of the meeting at the end of work. The document had a title "Recommendations of the Symposium on preparations and realization of the 1991 census of population". Needless to say, I included in it the essential ideas of my old programme of modernization of Yugoslav statistics. The document was discussed at the meeting and accepted after various modifications. However, it included all the elements of the modernization programme. I insisted on this part of meeting's work because the accepted document provides a mandate of the statistical profession for the modernization of statistics in Yugoslavia. The steps that might be taken to implement the modernization can easily be referred to as a response to specific requests.

However, my interpretation of the situation proved to be wrong. There was no serious intention to use either my paper or the meeting to take any major step for the improvement of statistics. In the beginning of 1987 there was nothing that would promise a better census in the future let alone better statistics. At this point the important decisions regarding the 1991 census should have already been taken on the basis of an appropriate research programme. However, no such programme was formulated so far nor any step was taken that would feed the expectation of a better future.

Before this strange chain of events, I was not ready to accept that the meeting of experts, together with everything else that was associated with it, was a simple show, a maneuver on the part of the power to neutralize any criticism. Unfortunately, I was obliged to change my views.

The basic contributions to the meeting of experts are available in printed form in *Statistical Review*, Vol. XXXV, 1985. My "Comments " and my "Recommendations" are in as well.

I also point out that FIS requested me by phone to give them the name of my bank and the number of my account. At a meeting of some group it was apparently decided to pay me an honorarium for my paper. It was an exceptional amount of 40 (forty) dollars in that period. I took it as a joke. I worked seven months on this paper. At that time, a simple manual and unqualified worker would ask for twenty dollars a day. I requested FIS to send my honorarium to the Red Cross. However, my interlocutor told me that it would be an offense for all those who those who insisted on such a high honorarium for me. He said that usual payments are much less. In order to avoid misinterpretations, I accepted my honorarium.

However, I cheated the government finances. Some months later, I learned from an employee of "Economist" that they also decided to publish my paper. I was told that "comrade" Macura gave them a green light for the publication of my paper. However, the paper was published as a second class contribution. This seems to be a category of papers that cannot pretend to be more than news, reports, reviews of meetings, etc. For that second class material I got another forty dollars.

XXII Lessons for the future

At the end of my cycle, when I look at the past without emotion, I shall permit myself to say a couple of words that follow from our past as lessons for the future.

I shall start this discourse with the statement: "Relatively good statistics can be built even in small countries with modest resources. However, the condition for success is respect for lessons from the available experiences. If these lessons are disregarded, no amount of resources and efforts will help".

Some statisticians are aware that Yugoslavia, or at least some of her parts, have had a relatively long tradition in statistics. Our statistics had its great periods. However, it also had its downs. Our statistics shows the characteristics of circumstances that facilitate the growth of good statistics. It is thus a rich mine for reflexions about rises and falls of statistics of a country.

The beginning of our statistics goes back to the second half of 18th century. At that time, interest widely arose in the German speaking countries of Europe in the new science of statistics. In the last quarter of that century, the students of law of the Academy of Zagreb had to study from the textbook *Die Grundsaetze der Polizey, Handlung und Finanz*[18] by Sonnenfels. The author of the book speaks about duties of the state toward citizens. In order to be able to carry out its commitments the state has to gather data about population and thus fulfill its duty on the basis of facts. The collection of facts and the cultivation of the know-how needed for the purpose is an essential task of the state. In order to help get the facts needed, the textbook presents the procedures for the estimation of the number of inhabitants.

The subject of statistics was thus rather popular at that time. At the end of the century and in the first years of 19th century, statistics was an obligatory part of law studies.[19]

---

[18] Fifth edition, Vienna, 1787.

[19] Herkov, Z.: *From the History of Public Finances, Revenue Law and Development of Financial Science in Croatia*, Zagreb, 1985.

Interest in studies of statistics continued growing rapidly. In this climate J.Jurjevich published in Zagreb, in 1825, his book *Theoria Statisticae* that was an early compendium of the theory of statistics. The book provides a review of the origin of statistics and references to early literature as well. The book earned the reputation as an excellent source of information about statistics. It circulated all over the German language area.

At this stage, statistics is a part of politics. Jurjevich has divided "Doctrina civilis" into "Jurisprudentia" and "Politica". The latter has two parts, viz. "Politica philosophica" and "Politica historica". "Statistica" belongs to "Politica historica". Statistics is a presentation of a coherent system of facts needed by the state.

This early expansion of interest in statistics resulted from circumstances of the epoch. Our scientists kept close contacts with their colleagues at various universities of the German speaking area. They followed the scientific production. Search for information was a feature of the epoch. A familiarity on the part of the scientists with the state of the know-how was a "must". The scientists were open to ideas. The policy of an open door was an accepted orientation of both the authorities and the individuals.

Later on some unpredictable events took place and had a negative impact on our development. Continental statistics exhausted its potentialities relatively fast. Parallel to that, a new current of thought started developing, viz. analysis of the numerical material and the mathematically oriented theory of statistics. The craddle of the new orientation was in the Anglo-Saxon countries.

In the course of these developments, we lost our privileged position. The Anglo-Saxon countries were far from us. The circulation of ideas, personal contacts, and a close follow-up of developments by our scientists was not easy any more. The language barrier must have also had its influence. As a result, a rapid decline of our statistics followed. We continued the tradition and disappeared from the scene of new ideas. Statistical education was limited to schools of law just as we used to do at the end of 18th century. The curriculum was not much different. When the mathematically oriented statistics spread over the world on the eve of the last war we were unprepared for the change.

More developed countries do not fall in a vacuum of this type. They cultivate communication channels in all directions. Their institutions support and even impose maintenance of contacts with any current of thought. They provide study grants and facilities for participation of the own people at international gatherings. They make resources available for periodicals that show scientific production in other parts of the world. They also impose standards of work that guarantee awareness of international developments. Research papers start with a review of the state of knowledge. The periodicals do not publish papers that are defective from that point of view. In addition, special papers are invited from time to time to provide readers with a review of achievements. These papers are intended for those who cannot afford to follow progress in several areas. In other words, society is taking a variety of steps to make sure that important developments leave behind adequate traces and help build on the part of local institutions the use of the progress made by others.

Lack of adequate support for the development of science is usually followed by the theory that poor countries cannot afford much in the promotion of science. This argument is only partly acceptable. No amount of resources will buy development if a favorable atmosphere is missing. It does not cost any money to impose standards in the publication of scientific papers. Nor does respect for adequate policies in university appointments cost money. A single paper in a recognized periodical should be preferred as a qualification to a pile of words without any new ideas. Similarly, it does not cost much to establish prizes and/or public recognition for serious achievements.

The best proof of a relative meaning of resources is the golden period of our statistics, viz. 1949-53. After a long war, the country was in the beginning of reconstruction. A large part of the infrastructure was destroyed, extremely difficult transportation was everywhere, and harsh conditions of life were imposed on the population. And yet, the essential features of statistics in developed countries were closely followed.

The circumstances of that development were already pointed out on several occasions. The work was done by young statisticians who completed their education on the eve of war. They went for specialization to different European countries and absorbed their scientific standards, familiarized themselves with literature, developed contacts with institutions, learned several languages, etc. When they got involved in statistics, they renewed the contacts they had, established new ones, and started cooperating with research centers. Foreign centers responded quickly. They started sending to Yugoslavia their technical publications, reports, internal documents, etc. Literature was coming from many parts of the world. We were fully informed about the scientific production in the field of methodology of data collection. We kept mailing lists and used to send abroad our publications. We also started publishing in foreign languages. We kept intensive correspondence about problems that were arising in our work. We also got an impression that our partners understood our limitations and appreciated our efforts. We got an amount of help that exceeded what we had ever expected. Also, we got frequent encouragement to continue. We were convinced that the authorities were happy with our involvement and we felt responsible for moving further.

When our work was in full swing a sudden change took place. Namely, statistics became a part of ideology. According to the new view statistics goes hand in hand with politics. Theory was squeezed out of university curricula. Statistical education was abolished. There was no transfer of the know-how. The qualities needed on the part of statisticians included clear handwriting, understandable dictation, copying figures without mistakes, reasonably good ability to carry out arithmetic operations, etc. Everybody is good enough to get involved in politics. Everybody is equally good enough to work in statistics. Statistics is a political weapon. Therefore, the role of statisticians is to follow politics, participate in it, and get from politics suggestions for the content of work.

The communist ideology says: data collection in communism is high above the level of the corresponding work in non-communist countries where people hate the state and deliberately provide inaccurate data. In communism people love the state and everything sponsored by the state. In communism errors do not appear, nor is there any need for studies of errors.

A corollary says that those who do not follow politics will never be good statisticians. This is why the positions of the chiefs in the statistical service of communist countries are restricted to members of the party. Nonparty people are confused; they are

221

hardly ever able to understand statistics. This is particularly true of "scientists" and "intellectuals" in general, who tend to complicate the work by introducing to it problems from books. "Scientists" from capitalist countries are trying to blurr the reality with the help of complicated mathematical theories. They are always searching for problems and improvements. In this way they tend to undermine the authority of the socialist state. By insisting on open issues, need for studies, follow up of experiences from other countries, etc. they are creating an impression that government agencies are not doing a good job. They generate criticism of socialist institutions and join the front of the enemy. This is why the best thing to do is to have no contacts with foreign statisticians. A communist statistician will stay away from international professional associations.[20]

Fortunately, this philosphy of statistics changed as a result of the evolution of relationships between Yugoslavia and the USSR. Suddenly the USSR became an enemy of the YCP. A negative attitude appeared toward everything that was going on there. Everything has become bad including the Soviet statistical system and the Soviet literature that had previously invaded the country as a model of thinking. Everything was discarded and forgotten as if it never existed. Soviet books in our libraries were covered by a thick layer of dust.

As a result of these changes statistics as "class science" first disappeared at universities. There was no such thing any more as a prescribed statistical curriculum. Nor were there attempts at imposing a model no matter what it might be. The universities did what they were able to do under their staffing conditions. Some of them took steps toward modernization of education while others are still at the stage of statistics mixed with politics. However, politics is mixed with statistics only by those teachers who did not manage to absorb modern theory. Uses of politics have thus become a pretext for failure to do better.

The same is true of periodicals. None of them would turn down a paper because it includes mathematics. For some of them just the contrary is true. Mathematics gives prestige resulting from the appearance of being in line with international practices.

In statistics under the government control, the situation is very much the same. The party lost interest in statistics. Statistics is not any more a part of ideology. Members of the party make their choices on any ground deemed appropriate. In fact, some members are enthusiastic supporters of mathematical statistics. The party does not care any more for what kind of statistician a member might be.

In spite of that the party has destroyed hopes for the improvements of statistics in the foreseeable future. In fact, the YCP continues with its discrimination. The party continues to consist of "the best sons of our peoples". The party members know everything as before. They are able to tackle any issue; they continue to occupy the leading positions in any kind of work. A good party member is an enthusiastic supporter of the power. Whatever the power is doing is the right thing to do. Doubts are a sin as before. A mistrust of commoners continues. Together with this continue discrimination, favoritism, flattery, and other vices from the totalitarian sack.

---

[20] Only recently the communist governments approved the participation of their top officers in the membership of international associations. However, the change has not yet affected the rank and file.

This is how Yugoslavia gradually became an apathetic society. People lost the hope that something useful could be done about their problems. They learned from experience that their future does not depend upon their ability, their initiative, and their work. They abandoned their ambitions and ideals.

A new attempt at revitalization cannot be taken under the present circumstances of broken hopes. A new start can only be successful if the society wakes up and the hopes in the future begin to flourish. These hopes include a faith in the value of their own work. This is the basis that generates a readiness on the part of the people to get involved in a pursuit of goals that require ones's life.

To those who will have an opportunity to get involved in a new effort to bring our statistics to the level that it deserves it might be useful to keep in mind that the above sketch of the history of our statistics offers many useful suggestions regarding the approaches to use. Some of these lessons are the following:

Social role of statistics. Concern about national aspects of statistical development is rooted in the role of statistics in a modern society. Statistics provides a contribution to the maturation process of a nation. Through its dissemination of data statistics orientates the nation toward facts and a search for facts in any appropriate situation. Developed countries have a highly developed statistics.

Statistics has also improved the general education of people. At present people know many facts about their own country and other countries as well, that a generation ago - were not available. Statistical yearbooks and other statistical publications have become the language of international communications. At present people are better prepared for efficient work than before. Besides, statistical methodology has become an essential part of national research capabilities. Without statistics there is no experimentation in medicine, agriculture, industry, chemistry, etc. In addition, statistics worked out a number of specific applications. An illustration is the industrial quality control.

Any discourse about statistical development refers to all these and many other matters. The stakes are considerable. In addition, the ramifications of statistics are interconnected. Therefore, those who are responsible for the profession have to keep in mind this broad spectrum of issues. There is no adequate ability in data collection or in medical experimentation without an adequate statistical education. There is no application without theory and research. Only through one's own research grows the ability to identify the relevant facts and adjust the available methodology to specific conditions.

For these reasons the responsibility for the promotion of statistics requires an elaborate action programme. If some of the related sectors are disregarded statistics as a whole will suffer. Equally needed is a division of responsibilities and the establishment of control of the achievements in each sector.

Ethics of statistical development. In the promotion of national development of statistics some ethical principles have to be observed as a condition for long lasting achievements.

The development of a nation is a goal that should stay high above particular interests, such as the popularity of political parties and their position in the power, views

223

of different currents of thought, and rivalries between various social, economic, religious and other groups. Particular interests are selective. They emphasize some aspects of the development process and disregard the needs to secure for the nation the benefits that follow from a broad programme. Nobody knows in advance what line of thought will develop strength in the future. It is, therefore, essential that no alternative is rejected in advance.

In this respect, a particular danger comes from politics that frequently concentrates on its own programme and requires a heavy involvement of statistics and its resources in that particular programme. In this way broad aims of statistics are disregarded and the national needs are put aside. It is, therefore, essential that governments take a broad view of their responsibilities. Statisticians have to have the courage to remind them of this issue. Ethical principles require an opposition to the attempts at imposing programmes of particular groups above the national aims.

In this respect the responsibilities of leading statisticians are considerable. If a danger arises of the neglect of national development aims, they have to call the attention of the public to the consequences. Within their possibilities, they have to make arrangements to safeguard broad aims. When the Yugoslav authorities decided to take over the Soviet model in all the fields of work and the statistical services accepted to carry out blindly Soviet approaches, negative consequences appeared immediately. Our national research capability was diverted from the developments in the world. In this situation the leading staff of statistical services had a responsibility to create, under various names, some arrangements that would keep the country informed about the progress in the world and thus secure its awareness of the progress of science. Instead of this attitude the leading staff have eradicated all the contacts with anything different than a blind execution of the orientations imposed.

A courageous attitude is particularly needed in personnel matters. The leading positions in statistics should ideally be in the hands of professionally mature persons with a demonstrated ability to take a broad view of the profession and its role in the society. Instead of that the real life is frequently inclined toward favoritism of different types and the selection of candidates for high posts from among political supporters of the power, viz. people who will be obedient servants of some line of thought. As these people normally do not come from the profession they have no vision of the course of profession nor do they have experience with problems arising in the execution of statistical programmes. These people normally emphasize non-statistical aims in course of their assignment and thus reduce the achievements of the profession.

In the appointment of staff at the lower levels, cases frequently arise of personal contacts, political favoritism, and priorities to religious, social, and other affiliations. This is how conflicts with moral standards arise. Instead of leading to a recognition of work these appointments neglect the achievements and thus kill the hope of young people in the value of work. As a result, the staff will tend to look for better chances elsewhere and the national development will suffer.

Here again ethical principles of the senior staff are at test. Here again a considerable courage is needed to defend the ethical standards of the profession. Insistance on these standards might lead to unpleasant consequences. However, this is the only way to serve the nation in a generally appreciated manner.

Democratic principles. A successful development of statistics requires full respect of democratic principles, viz. the right on the part of the staff to present their own views, to get access to professional community, influence the public opinion, etc. Democracy offers a possibility for new ideas to come up; democracy is the way for the staff to believe in the value of work and effort. A democratic environment stimulates the staff for creative contributions. Democracy is the safest way to secure a coordinated development in a variety of fields of work which all have the right to attention and participation in the use of national facilities and resources.

Impartiality. In the course of its history, our statistics has gone through periods of discrimination, preconceived ideas, deliberate neglect of developments, and attempts at imposing views and approaches of questionable value. All the attempts of this type have had a very negative impact. Therefore, statistics should be able to impose and maintain an unbiased attitude toward all types of developments in the world and all types of people involved in various activities. It is never known in advance where the fertile ideas might come up and what difficulties might appear in the continuation of views and approaches widely accepted at a particular moment. Impartiality is thus an essential condition of development.

Studying its own society. Statistics is unable to accomplish its task of being a satisfactory source of information for the nation and a tool in solving the problems of social and economic life unless it keeps permanent contacts with its own society. The purpose of these contacts is to inquire what users of data are interested in, how well they understand the meaning of data, how adequate their uses of data are, what their proposals for modifications of data collection programmes are, what are the difficulties to meet their wishes, etc. On the basis of information collected, statistics will be in a position to formulate the improvements of its services to the society.

Effective arrangements for these purposes include a large variety of activities, such as reporting about statistical problems in communication media, follow up of uses of data and interventions wherever appropriate, discussion of statistical issues at meetings of professional associations, etc.

These contacts facilitate the work of statistics. Through such contacts, mutual understanding is improved, appreciation of statistical work on the part of the public at large grows, and statistics becomes able to render a better service to the society.

Learning from others. The largest part of achievements in statistics is a result of an international effort in which the majority of contributions come from a small number of highly developed countries. However, their work is taken over by others, broadened, and modified to fit specific circumstances. In this way, the present statistical know-how is established. This is why keeping an eye on developments in other countries is the most important means of the statistical profession to carry out its responsibilities in an adequate way. A follow up of developments in the world is a richest possible source of suggestions for the improvement of one's own work.

The follow up of developments is oriented toward all types of statistical work, such as methodology of data collection, research, improvements of education, tabulation, presentations of data, etc. It provides information about problems encountered, methods used to solve them, results achieved, plans for new activities, etc. The awareness of world developments is the way to assure for one's own country transfer of the know-how developed by others. Statistics of all the countries is more influenced by international developments than by one's own achievements. The transfer of know-how achieved by others is the most important individual source of suggestions for the improvement of one's development.

The transfer of the know-how is the permanent task of each country. Much effort is needed to carry out the task satisfactorily. The programme of steps needed for the purpose involves sending documents to others, making sure that others reciprocate, organization of an exchange of publications, contacts with particularly important centers to get an insight into internal documents and plans for future research, exchange of contacts between technicians in important areas of work, grants to foreign students, seminars, symposia, etc.

A prerequisite of this work is the knowledge of foreign languages. Therefore, it might be useful to impose knowledge of several languages as an obligatory qualification for all the higher posts. This has been our strong point in the past and we should be able to continue.

Association of statisticians. The association aims at the promotion of statistical development in all its aspects. For that purpose it initiates promotional projects in all the fields where needs arise, it supports the promotional steps taken by others, and is available for consultations in statistical matters with all the institutions and other associations that might be interested in such consultations. The association will be concerned with maintenance of high professional standards. It will be particularly concerned about ethical standards. It should endeavor to safeguard the principle of fairness in all aspects of statistical matters. It will insist on the respect of rights of its members. It will take steps to secure equal chances and opportunities for all members to participate in statistical activities and make use of the available facilities and resources. In order to carry out this role it will act as an independent group of persons interested in statistics on any basis. Its membership is open to any person who accepts the aims of the association.

If requested, the association will advise governments and other authorities on steps to take in statistical matters. It will carry out an independent and unbiased assessment of the state of statistics in various fields and of individual statistical projects of major importance. For that purpose it might establish standing or *ad hoc* working groups and/or other bodies.

The association has its President and its Board. They are all elected by secret ballot. The biographies of candidates should be circulated to all the members. The President is elected from among the senior members with a long and outstanding service to statistical profession. In addition to the elected members the Board should include representatives of Sections. The responsibility for the selection of candidates for the offices is with the Nominations Committee. All the members of this Committee are elected by the General Assembly by secret ballot.

The association will involve as many members as possible in its work. The involvement of members is a condition for good care of interests of the profession. It is also an important educational arrangement as several members will develop experience in the leadership of the activities. It is a condition for the successful insertion of statistics in the society. Good statistics implies a penetration of statisticians in all layers of the society.

The association should equally assume the responsiblity for a programme of publications. This programme is established in cooperation with the members and carried out by the requisite number of working groups and other bodies. Contributions to periodicals are refereed. The names of editorial collaborators are acknowledged. Services to the association are included in the professional achievements of the members. For that reason, participation of individual members in the association is always acknowledged. Objective traces are thus left about the extent of contributions made to the profession and the country as well. No office in the association should be kept more than a couple of years. The association has to be able to benefit from persons with different backgrounds.

All the important projects should be presented to the membership for approval. The General Assembly of the association is the organ for that purpose. The President and the Board are mandators of the membership.

Statistical education. Care for statistical education is one of the primary activities of the association. The association's involvement in statistical education is an efficient way of strengthening the efforts of individual teachers in their attempts at making use of international standards and developments. The involvement of the association is a collective effort of the profession to assure its future by means of an approved education of young generations. Therefore, the advisory role of the association should be widely appreciated by universities and all types of schools where statistical education is carried out. The association's concern will particularly be related to specification of curricula, methods of teaching, teaching aids, uses of computers, organization of research, organization of practical work in schools, evaluation of projects, meetings of teachers, organization of visiting professorship, cooperation with foreign teachers and their institutions, etc. For the promotion of this work the association might have a special section.

Education of users. The education of users is an important activity of the association. Many uses of data are inadequate. It is not easy to know all the limitations that should be observed in the use of data. Cases are not rare that data are used in an entirely wrong way. A possibility follows that the resulting decisions are also inadequate.

Use of data is an aspect of the maturity of the society and an indicator of its ability to benefit from statistics as a product of modern society. The use of data is thus a matter of the nation as a whole and a matter of the degree of its development. This is why the use of data is to be cultivated with the help of a particularly prepared programme.

The association is the most competent body for this task. The related work is a standing task. Therefore, a programme of action is needed that should include the collection of illustrations of inadequate uses of data, preparation of articles, papers, and lectures based on these illustrations, preparation of special books or series of articles that clarify some of the basic statistical concepts and facilitate a better understanding of the meaning of data, maintenance of special services for users asking for assistance, preparation of special courses dealing with uses of data, etc.

227

Dissemination of statistical information. Physical aspects of dissemination of data are of course a part of competences of government statistical services. They collect data, prepare publications, and circulate them. This is their assigned task. However, dissemination of statistical information is a broader issue that is related to the social role of statistics. Dissemination of statistics influences the general development of countries and awareness of population of the importance of factual information. Persons unaware of statistics will tend to depend upon guesses, intuition, feelings, etc.

In the discharge of the responsibility for dissemination of data, the association might wish to follow where the publications go, what their number is, in what way data are presented, what difficulties arise in the use of data, what children should know about statistics at different ages, what is the access of the population to statistical data, what possibilities are available to improve the access to data, etc.

Stimulation of creative work. Stimulation of creative work is an important component of the state of statistics. For that purpose there should be a system of prizes classified by type of work. If no resources are available, diplomas and documents of recognition would do. If distributed for valuable achievements these prizes will carry great weight in the society. However, their social and human impact will depend upon the value of criteria used.

It is no less important to operate a system of grants for research activities. For that purpose it might be useful to operate a fund raising programme and obtain donors.

Consultations. All the agencies, universities, schools, and research organizations that are responsible for the operation of more important statistical programmes are invited to consult with the association prior to the appointment of their senior staff. The recommendation to consult equally holds while preparing important decisions for significant projects.

Needless to say, this is an appeal to institutions rather than an attempt at interference with their autonomy. The aim is to make sure that the expertise of the association in technical matters and its knowledge of staff are used to assist in important decisions. At peak periods of our statistics, the top technicians kept the leading offices and the basic responsibilities for policy matters. At periods of crisis the top offices were reserved for political appointees.

No secrets. In a democratic society, statistical work is open to all eyes. Everybody has the right to get information about the activities of the profession. In order to be able to facilitate the implementation of this requirement, statistics has to organize its activities in a way that traces of the past work remain physically available to those interested.

In this way, the publics at large will be able to make an independent evaluation of achievements. In addition, the office holders will be stimulated to carry out the work in agreement with acceptable standards. Deviations from sound principles of work are recorded. They remain a part of history.

XXIII The fanatics

The postwar development of statistics in Yugoslavia was in conflict with lessons learned from the experiences of the more developed countries. One could also say that it was in conflict with Western civilization as well. This is why the question arises: how was it possible to introduce and maintain such a course of events?

For an explanation one has to go back to "dreamers" in Chapter I.

The excitement of the dreamers concentrated on the future society of justice and equality. On the way to that ideal one has to abolish capitalism as a society based on exploitation of millions of workers by a small number of owners of the means of production. Although the workers produce the wealth, only a part of that wealth goes to them while a large part goes to capitalists as their profit. Therefore, capitalists are able to enjoy any luxury in this world. They live in nice houses; their children get a good education; they do not worry about tomorrow. Unemployment and misery are reserved for workers. Profit as a motive leads to recklessness. Powerful capitalists take over the property of less powerful ones. The number of the owners of the means of production is thus declining while the number of proletarians is increasing. This is how the end of capitalism is approaching. The masses become aware of the exploitation. They realize that the means of production are sufficiently developed to secure a decent level of living for everybody. The way to achieve this aim is to eliminate private property of the means of production and distribute wealth according to the contribution of individuals to production. On the ruins of capitalism a society of justice and equality will thus arise.

Although in this dream the end of capitalism is conceived as an historic necessity the fight for the new society is called for. That fight will be long and cruel. The capitalist class will not give up its privileges without being obliged to do so. That will be done by the proletariat and its avant-garde, the communist party whose members are the people who have become aware of the historic process and are willing to sacrifice themselves to contribute to the defeat of capitalism and the appearance of justice, equality, and honesty. In this fight, the capitalists will use the police, jails, and the army. They will not hesitate to permit large-scale bloodshed if needed. However, the final defeat of capitalism in unavoidable.

This is obviously a magnificent effort of the human mind to outline a way out of injustice. The human mind has been active in this direction since the early stages of history. People were shocked by injustice and suffering and they have made many attempts in the course of history at designing a "theory" that could help take the "road of salvation". It is sufficient to think of the number of "Utopias" written so far under a variety of titles. They all talk about a "better" society; they all point out a set of principles to follow on the way to the "kingdom of God", recognition of righteousness, love, justice, equality, elimination of misery, etc.

However, most of these theories, as beautiful and wonderful as they are, have died together with their respective authors. Only some of them have had an impact on the respective societies; only some of them have become "trends of history", "streams of life".

The element that adds life to theories is fanatism.

Theories are not life. A theory is beautiful, nicely written, logical, based on the erudition of its author, etc. Theory is enjoyed over a cup of coffee or while we sit in our chairs. Theory is a construction of the human mind that we admire in the same way as the Egyptian pyramides. On the contrary, life is the emotional charge that provides people with the drive and determination to put theory into practice, to impose theory as a model of behavior, as a pattern of daily activities. Life is fighting, strikes, barricades, political and labor organizations, the conflicts in the streets, the police, jails, concentration camps, and so many other matters that take place under the banner of various theories.

Fanatism is an extreme form of determination to implement a theory. Fanatism means an excitement, a transformation of one's own personality into a means for the realization of theories, an offer of one's own life, and readiness to participate in the promotion of ideals with the help of resources available. Being a deep emotional involvement, fanatism does not tolerate limitations. Fanatism is a maximalistic orientation. It wants to impose itself on the world. It does not care for how many people agree or disagree with its aims. Nor does it care for the destiny of members of the "brotherhood". It preaches a need for jails, bombs, explosives, and innocent victims.

It would be difficult to say how emotions get combined with theories. It seems that there is no explanation in the content of the related theories. In Geneva, in 16th century, Calvinism was associated with considerable fanatism while the reading of Calvin's *Instruction in Faith* leaves a man of our epoch indifferent. Similarly, many people lost their lives in the French Revolution under the slogan "Liberté, Egalité, Fraternité", wheras no excitement arises under other conditions. It thus appears that it is not the content of the theory itself that generates fanatism but the conditions of the society, social crisis, the vacuum created in the society for one reason or the other, excessive sufferings, disease, misery and the like. Under these conditions many people fall in a kind of dispair and get excited about the way out of crisis. For that purpose they pick up a suitable theory, either concocted on the spot or taken over from other situations, and transfer their excitement to the promotion of that theory and realization of its messages. Fanatism implies a group, a specific community of persons who accept and follow the same theory, the same ideology, faith, creed, etc. The members of the community are all missionaries. Their mission is the promotion of their creed. Their involvement in the mission is passionate. They are obsessed by their ideals. They live with these ideals all the time. The fellow fanatics constitute the community of "brothers", "sons of God", "children of God", etc. They consider their opponents as a disgusting breed of beings. Any crime is authorized in the fight with opponents. One might wish to remember the zealots and ther daggers in Jerusalem at the time of Herod or the modern terrorists who do not hesitate to kill innocent people to create publicity for their cause.

An essential element of fanatism is emotional involvement. Only those theories are combined with fanatism which are able to generate emotion. This is achieved through a recourse to ideals, such as justice, equality, honesty, elimination of misery, etc. Another requirement is eschatology. The theory has to include a sketch of history and outline a road to salvation in a way that followers can consider their dream within reach. It also appears that the road to realization of ideals is to be a thorny one. This is a condition for the development of the awareness of a mission. There is no mission without self-sacrificing, hardship, sufferings and even an offer of one's own life.

Communism contains the elements of a theory that can easily be coupled with fanatism. There are many candidates in the capitalist society to become fanatic fighters for communism. It is sufficient to look around and see the excessive privileges based on money and the road blocked to many people because of poverty. While people in many parts of the world are hungry, in other areas subsidies are granted to reduce the production. Adding to that the tragedies of wars and capitalist fights for colonies and markets, it will not be difficult to understand that many people enthusiastically accept the idea of being tools in an action to end the unjust society for ever.

As a rule, communist fanatics accept to militate for "scientific socialism" while young. Young people are particularly sensitive to an idealistic interpretation of life. They easily get excited about justice, honesty, classless society, equality, etc. They also appreciate the idea of life as a sacrifice. Many of them are ready to carry out the burden of the fight for ideals and thus contribute their share to the triumph of the good. They are also ready to accept the hardship and sufferings on the way to the "final" victory. They join in anxious to start their bloody fight. They accept to get killed for their theory while, in most cases, they do not know what the theory is. If asked to write down something about it they would not be able to fill half a page. In some exceptional cases, however, they study *post hoc,* after they have adopted the zealotry. These studies can be compared to painting. They will not modify the orientations adopted. They can only contribute to make the theory nicer. The reading is thus of a cosmetic nature. Choices were made beforehand.

A feature of zealotry is dogmanism. Nobody has ever convinced a fanatic that his theory includes some points of a dubious value. Emotional attitudes are closed to logic. Nor are they established on the basis of facts or logical analysis. In fact, everything is false that is not in agreement with the theory. A fanatic is blind for arguments. No amount of books or reading will change a comma in his views. Fanatism is self-sufficient. It does not tolerate questions or doubts; it does not need further studies or clarifications.

A fanatic is aggressive and reckless in the pursuit of the fight for victory of his own theory. The fight for the "society of justice" is difficult and cruel. A new page of history has to be turned; the old world is to go into pieces; eternal happiness for mankind is to be established. The outcome of the fight depends upon the determination of a small number of "conscious" elements of the society to overcome the carelessness of the common people. For the sake of happiness of future generations, fanatics will not hesitate to use any means to lead the fight to a successful end. The greatness of their ideals requires firmness. The degree of their determination is a measure of their devotion to the cause of history.

Fanatics are nervous and extremely dynamic. Their minds are obsessed by big issues, such as changes of history, classless society, justice, and equality. They do not care for the small events of daily life. Their minds are blocked by the idea of revolution and the establishment of the groundwork for a new society. When they take power, they want fruits of their ideal to grow in front of their eyes. They want the great victory today, immediately. They do not appreciate small contributions and gradual changes. In countries where the communist party took over after the last war, an extreme instability and temporariness of everything followed. Government organizations kept changing their activities from one day to the other. Methods of work and approaches in all the sectors of work changed before people had a chance to know what was to be changed. There was nothing that one was not supposed to touch nor was there any limit to how far one was allowed to go. Everything was reduced to the quality of a tool. Taxes were imposed that could be anything depending upon the aims to achieve; court sentences were shaped freely; one does not know today what will be the shape of things tomorrow.

A fanatic is intolerant. He sticks to his theory whatever it is in his mind. Outside of that he does not need anything else nor is he able to see anything else. Everything else is a "superseded" past that is equivalent to dust on old books. Different views than his own excite him and represent an offense to him. In the presence of such views he will react violently. In his reactions he will be sharp. The vocabularies that fanatics use in their disputes can frequently not be found in standard dictionaries. Communist jargon contains a very high frequency of terms, such as "traitor", "enemy", "police agent", etc. The fanatics are particularly unable to tolerate competitive approaches to social problems. Their theory has a divine character; it is to be taken as a unique revelation. There is no alternative to their theory nor there is anything debatable in it. There is nothing to be amended or improved upon. Their theory is beyond human reach. There are no shadows for fanatics; there is nothing "in between". Their mind is receptive for extremes only, "Yes" or "No", black or white, good or bad.

It will now be clear why the communist parties are against intellectuals. In fact, they tolerate them and use them. However, they do not trust them. Whenever it becomes possible they will give preference to non-intellectuals. In the course of their education, the intellectuals develop a familiarity with the idea of ups and downs in the history of different nations, different views of science, different approaches in philosophy, the ups and downs in moral matters, in politics, and in social action. "Plurality" is thus a natural outcome, it corresponds to the essential experience in human matters. If communist, an intellectual will keep his own ideology and make efforts to promote it. However, he will tend to understand the existence of different views and will admit that in course of time his own views might change. As a result, differences of views are treated as facts of life. One has to live with them and be ready to accept new changes that will arise in course of a universal dynamics. An intellectual has an ear for democratic approaches. This attitude makes fanatics mad. An intellectual is not more than "half-communist". Whenever possible, the best thing is to get rid of them or make sure that an eye is kept on what they do.

A fanatic is also "enemy obsessed". His senses feel the enemy everywhere. The enemy is the culprit for all the calamities of the society. Without enemies the whole world would accept communism as the only correct politics. The enemy is the obstacle to universal happiness. The enemy is a evil. The enemy's fingers interfere with everything. In addition to arms, wars, and other brutal methods of repression, the enemy has created refined means for the continuation of his domination, such as art, education, theaters, sports, and other forms of an illusion of happiness. The enemy knows all the witchcrafts of the world and is ready to use them to hurt socialism. The enemy has unlimited resources available to create difficulties for socialist countries. His preferred method is to find allies within the brotherhood. Therefore, an extreme vigilance is needed to watch on everything and everybody. This is why in all communist countries the topic of enemy is a permanent item on the agenda. From time to time it creates excitement. Top politicians speak about it, request sharp methods of control, and proclaim vigilance as a supreme virtue.

The brotherhood has all the qualities at their best. "Brothers" know everything and are able to do any work. They are honest, devoted to socialism and reliable. A non-party person is unable to compete with "brothers". This is why "brothers" keep in a communist country all the higher posts.

However, within the brotherhood there is a very strict stratification of membership. The stratification criteria consist of party seniority and the past record in party activities, such as participation in strikes, civil wars, party propaganda, obedience, and a demonstrated enthusiasm about the role of the party and its achievements. The members of each stratum have their respective code of behavior. Their aspirations are arranged according to strata. Young party members have to participate in party activities, show an interest in these activities by asking questions and proposing improvements. A particularly appreciated quality is obedience. As a compensation, their employment is safe. They also get faster promotions. Those who have a good record are entitled, after some years, to expect more, such as chiefs of various offices, junior posts in privileged areas of work, such a diplomacy or foreign trade. Transition to higher strata is accompanied by a climb in hierarchy.

The stratification involves a degree of honor, respect, obedience, and submissivness on the part of lower strata. Admiration of the higher strata is part of the expected behavior within brotherhood. At the top all human qualities are at their maximum. The top is thus entitled to receive absolute respect and obedience. Everything coming from "above", viz. party instructions and decisions, is received as a expression of top wisdom. Any form of critical attitude toward the "above" matters is a lack of behavior, a sin, a sign of poor quality on the part of members concerned. Such members are normally demoted to lower strata, isolated or dropped out.

This is the basis of instrumentalization of the party membership. A member is a tool in the hands of the leadership. A fundamental duty of the membership is obedience no matter what the orders are. As in chess, party members are moved on any assignment designated by the top. A person is in the police for some years. Then he is appointed director of statistics and moved afterwards to an ambassadorial post. Everything is accepted with equal devotion to the service of socialism. Stalin, Khrushtchev, Brezhnev,

233

and Gorbatchov used the same machinery with equal enthusiastic devotion to the top. No matter how different these rulers were, the membership always rushed to demonstrate enthusiasm and an aversion against any deviation from the official party line. Doing something against that line is a disgusting crime. Readiness to render the requested services is a high virtue. Any deviation from pure obedience reduces the party's striking force and offers help to the enemy.

For reasons of their behavior, fanatics are isolated. Fanatics find it difficult to get along with people from common walks of life. They find it boring to participate in talks about problems of children, health issues, education, prices, etc. They are disgusted by seeing people excited about love stories, beauty contests, meteoric career of some people, political intrigues, etc. It works in the opposite direction as well. Common people find it boring to talk about preferred topics of fanatic circles, such as strikes, riots, revolutions or art oriented toward social problems, misery, injustice in capitalism, etc. The fanatics are thus separated into a segment of people who do not find easy contacts with the rest of the population.

The interest of fanatics is far from money or business. It would be difficult to imagine a communist fanatic who was involved in a successful business. They work for a salary as they have to live. However, they do not accumulate money beyond the level of current needs. They do not participate in corruption, briberies or any other maneuvering based on money. The Italian communist party claimed "clean hands" for its membership. This is true. Fanatics consider themselves to be the best part of the society.

Fanatics live in a state of collective narcissism.

An aspect of this narcissism is the fanatics' assumption that they are able to do any work above the standards of other people. Their theory is the best. It contains an answer to all problems. Their moral standards are of the highest type. Nobody can match their determination in the pursuit of common goals. They do not recognize any limit to their abilities. They suffer from a complete lack of critical evaluation of their own forces. It frequently happens in communist countries that a high ranking officer, who made his career within the army or the civilian police, gives a talk to congresses of scientists or writers to provide them with instructions about the topics to deal with in their writings, attitudes to assume in their public activities, and the goals to strive for. Although such interventions are scandalous for non-party people, they are alright within the brotherhood. Higher party position - more brain.

Another aspect of narcissism is the theory of the leading role of the party in all the activities including the economy, the military matters, the organization of social life, and art and science as well. The party is responsible for the initiative, the consideration of issues and proposals, and the related decisions. No issue can become a subject of public concern before it receives the party stamp. Nor discussions are allowed to proceed with a view to formulating the shape of the related action before the party has approved the line to follow.

Admiration of the own achievements is a part of narcissism. Nobody else is able to do what the communist parties are doing. Nor has anybody else ever been involved in earlier history in a task of comparable historic importance. Earlier pieces of history had local dimensions. In the communist action the human race as a whole is at stake.

Their political events are the events of the universal history. Their involvement has a lasting value. This is why the party calender is the calender of the history of the world. Party events have to be celebrated. New generations have to be aware of the heroic achievements of their predecessors. Party meetings, discussions, dates of various decisions, and many other insignificant matters become events to commemorate. One has to celebrate them, write about them, deliver speeches, organize manifestations, etc. In communist countries there is hardly a single day without celebration.

These characteristics determine the social position of fanatics. They are parts of society and they do not belong to that society. They are not able to participate in the usual forms of social life. Their interest is in a different society, viz. the society of their dreams. Somebody called them "no return people". They have destroyed the bridges with the society. They are not able to go back and become ordinary citizens. This is why "no return people" keep adding strength to their fanatism. They have no alternative to an intensification of their fanatic involvement. Some success of their fight is the only hope for them to have a future.

Taking into account that the leadership of the YCP consisted of fanatics, it will be easy to understand the exceptional achievements of the YCP during the last war. A handful of YCP secured a success that no other political group could match under comparable conditions. They not only found themselves overnight in the saddle of power. They were equally fast in the organization of power. The government institutions were established at record speed and the whole machinery of the "new society" was set in motion. The policy making positions in any kind of activity were headed by fanatics. Many of them were extremely hard working persons. They did their work enthusiastically, without saving time and energy. They were convinced that they started filling pages of the history of a new world. They sincerely believed in the high mark of their achievements. However, they did their work in accordance with the presented characteristics of their psychology. Fanatism is an accumulated energy, a kind of explosive. This is efficient for destructive purposes. However, in constructive work, a different type of person is needed. This book has provided ample evidence of the price that a society has to pay for damages caused by fanatics.

Abbreviations

DC	-	Developed Countries
FAO	-	Food and Agriculture Organization of United Nations
FIS	-	Federal Institute of Statistics
LDC	-	Less Developed Countries
SSO	-	State Statistical Office
TA	-	Technical Assistance
UN	-	United Nations
UNDP	-	United Nations Development Programme
UNRRA	-	United Nations Relief and Rehabilitation Administration
YCP	-	Yugoslav Communist Party
YSS	-	Yugoslav Statistical Society
USSR	-	Union of Soviet Socialist Republics

Index of names

Babich, B. 93, 202-3
Balaban, V. 202-3
Ban, M. 115
Bayet, A. 12
Bedenich 93
Begovich, V. 61
Bijedich 173
Blejec, M. 84, 90, 93, 97
      118, 202
Brezhnev, L. 233
Breznik, D. 214

Calvin 230
Campbell, A.A. 117
Cholakovich, R. 109
Cochran, W.G. 52

Debevec, B. 59, 60, 70-2, 81,
      84, 118
Deming, W.E. 52, 90
Djuranovich, V. 207
Djuretich, V. 144-5
Dostoyevsky 1
Durand 170
Durkheim, E. 12, 30

Echimovich, J. 70, 84-5, 87, 90,
      92-3, 112-3

Franta, K. 201-5
Frechet, M. 12

Gebelein, H. 52
Gogol 1
Gorbatchov 234
Grdjich, G. 86-7
Grubatchich, K. 26

Grupkovich, D. 205-7, 213-17,
Guzina, V. 113-14

Halbwachs, M. 12-3
Han, S. 94-5
Hendricks, W. 52
Hansen, M. 38-9, 52, 93, 166
Hanurav, T.V. 182, 190
Hebrang, A. 63
Herkov, Z. 219
Hitler 26
Hurwitz, W. 52

Ivanovich, B. 187-9

Jurjevich, J. 220

Kardelj, E. 58-9, 79, 81
Khrushtchev 233
Kidrich, B. 58-9, 79, 81-2
Kitaljevich, B. 202-3, 206
Krashovec, S. 81-4, 86-8, 109-10,
      113-15, 123-4, 205
Kreynin, R.S. 35-6

Lah, I. 32
Latifich, I. 170-74, 177-8, 181, 187,
      189-92, 197-8, 201, 207
Lavrich, J. 32
Lenin, V. 34, 79
Lilich, J. 93

Macura, M. 86-7, 114-19, 123-8,
      166-70, 191, 204-5, 214-8
Madow, M. 52
Mahalanobis, P.C. 92
Meyrs, P.F. 117

237